CW00401380

GRAPHIC DESIGN TECHNIQUES FOR
ARCHITECTURAL
DRAWING

GRAPHIC DESIGN TECHNIQUES FOR
ARCHITECTURAL
D R A W I N G

T O M   P O R T E R

HAMLYN · AMAZON

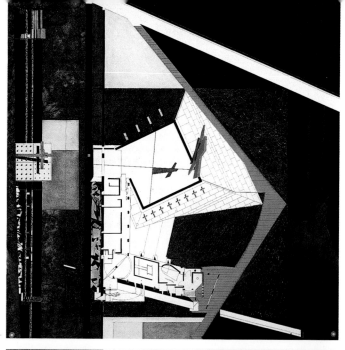

For Andrée and Holly

First published in Great Britain in 1990 by
The Hamlyn Publishing Group Ltd/Amazon Publishing Ltd

Text © Tom Porter 1990
© The Hamlyn Publishing Group Ltd/
  Amazon Publishing Ltd 1990

All rights reserved

A CIP record for this book is available
from The British Library

ISBN 0–600–56957–8

Typesetting by Litho Link Ltd, Welshpool
Colour separations by Fotographics Ltd
Produced by Mandarin Offset
Printed and bound in Hong Kong

Senior Commissioning Editor: Judith More
Project Manager/Text Editor: John Wainwright
Designed by: The Image
Picture Researcher: Cathy Lockley

Title page: Ampliamento del Palazzo del Parliamento à
Roma. Franco Purini and Laura Thermes.
This page: Alternative design solutions for a Church in
Rosythe, Scotland. Kevin Rhowbotham and Robin Serjeant.

CONTENTS

INTRODUCTION

The act of drawing in one form or another appears to attend the entire process of architectural design. Indeed, when describing this process, the architect Michael Graves outlined three primary categories of architectural drawing — each addressing three quite different avenues of communication. First comes the generative sketch, through which design concepts are transmitted; next, the preparatory study which refines and consolidates the evolving idea and, finally, the definitive drawing which, in attempting to accurately represent the resolved design, communicates the design intention to others.

Whenever the designer is confronted by a design problem the initial solving process involves a visualization of potential solutions. His or her creative imagination triggers a concept that is imagined ('seen') as a flashing and dimensionless image within the mind's eye. But these ideas may soon become so complex that they can no longer be contained within the mind and, therefore have to be externalized. Representation in some tangible form is needed so that the ideas can be clarified, assessed and articulated. Through the use of drawings the architect has learned, traditionally, to transfer the shifting images in his or her mind's eye onto the drawing-board. This kind of visualization technique has long been commonly accepted as an invaluable design tool. Indeed, when addressing students in the 1930s, Le Corbusier explained that, for him, architectural form and space was first a concept of the brain, being conceived with the eyes shut; while paper was the only means of transmitting ideas back to the designer and to others. However, if we take a look over the architect's shoulder at the private and initial conversion of design concepts into graphic marks we find, more often than not, a use of embryonic ideograms — that is, flow- and bubble-diagrams and doodled plans. By being drawn quickly, in receptive line mediums, these diagrams emerge to explore early concepts as patterns of spatial relationship. They concentrate not on how a building might appear, but rather on its organizational aspects as a series of abstract 'footprints'. Later, the initial scribbles and doodles give way to other graphic methods of representing the volumetric implications of the design intention. For example, the embryonic bubbles may metamorphosise into finite shapes with a geometry that is then dimensioned and given openings, before being extruded graphically for a re-examination in other drawing forms.

At this point flow diagrams may be enlisted to identify problems and possibilities when circulation and movement is considered between one point and another. Furthermore, schematic drawings may be used to examine the relationship and orientation of physical components, and also to articulate the evolving form in

Tomb of Rameses IV. Soprintendenta
Egyptian Museum, Turin.
Very little ancient Egyptian architectural
drawing survives. However, this ink on papyrus
example reveals structures planned against the
use of preliminary graphics.

High-rise studies. Frank Gehry.

response to external forces, such as air and sun patterns. In addition, the developing design may be rotated, transmuted and surgically sliced into sections, before the form reappears to be scrutinized in the three-dimensional space of a thumbnail sketch. This first and brief encounter with the physical appearance of a building design is an important point in the life of an idea because, at that moment, it passes from abstraction into the simulation of its future and perceived reality. There is no one set pattern for this sequence of events and it will vary from designer to designer. Different types of drawings, together with their hybrid combinations, will be enlisted as a response to the unique demands of successive problems in the design process. However, by acting as the trigger for further development, the resulting drawings are part of a two-way design language that provides a continuous dialogue between concept and mode of expression. That is, it facilitates the development of an idea as it travels through the time and space between mind and paper, and back again — this alternating cycle only being complete when the creative process is exhausted. At this stage another form of drawing takes over. This is the definitive presentation drawing that, in transferring the concept into a form which can be imagined as habitable and fixed in space, will allow the design proposal to be shared with others. Moreover, just as the presentation drawing concludes one process, so it begins another. That is, a phase in which adjustments and refinements take place. The finished drawing thus begins an ensuing process of criticism that, if not superficial, will question the conception of the design itself. This probing of the concept in presentation is interesting because, until recently, the architect has rarely exposed the initial design stages to criticism. However, this is now much more common and, especially in design schools, the public display of projects is almost a requirement. This is because the 'process' drawings, in conjunction with definitive architectural graphics, provide a valuable insight into the mental territory covered by what is known as the 'design route'.

Historical Background

A shroud of mystery seems to have surrounded the drawing techniques of architects prior to the 15th century. There are two main reasons for this. The first is probably a form of professional protectionism — for instance, apart from their sketchbooks containing catalogues of drawn fragments of buildings, little is known about the graphic techniques of medieval designers. This may be due to the fact that, with the secrecy surrounding building methods used in the construction of Gothic cathedrals, knowledge of the state-of-the-art remained firmly locked within the confines of a medieval guild membership. In fact, one medieval architect is known to have assassinated his bishop client in order to protect those secrets from inquisitive eyes! The later invention of linear perspective during the Italian Renaissance was also steeped in mystery. Apart from the more recent debate concerning the methods used by Filippo Brunelleschi to devise his system of accurately depicting spatial depth on a flat surface, those who attended the 1417 public demonstration of his invention did not receive direct answers to their questions. Indeed, Brunelleschi is reported to have remarked: 'Do not share your inventions with many.' Therefore, it comes as no surprise that when, at the end of the eighteenth century, the military engineer and physicist Gaspard Monge devised a means of graphically showing a standardized and precise viewing relationship between the upper, side and front views of a complex object, his development of orthographic projection became immediately classified as 'top secret' French government information. The second reason for an inadequate knowledge of earlier architects' drawing techniques is because few examples have survived. However, the links between drawing and the communication of architectural ideas can be traced back, albeit via a somewhat threadbare chain of evidence, to ancient Egypt, where simply drawn and roughly scaled plans, worked in red and black ink line on papyrus and flakes of limestone, have been found (see page 6).

Whether or not the ancient Greeks produced architectural drawings as an overture to building is an open question. However, speculation has it that the subtlety of curves used in all the main elements of Greek temples — known as 'entasis' — derives from the possible existence of a 'spherical perspective'. This is thought to have been a drawing system that, by being borrowed from a system used in stage-set design and being based on the curvature of the eye, could compensate for the perceptual warping of straight lines when seen in space. However, a more convincing theory suggests that the Greeks did not possess a calibration fine enough to allow small-scale drawings. Rather, they constructed their temples by direct reference to a portable kit of full-sized templates and mock-ups. From the scraps of evidence that have survived, it seems that some basic methods of planning and elevating buildings were well-established in the Middle Ages. When a designer made a drawing it was drafted to full-size on tracing boards, or on a specially prepared plaster screed floor alongside the building operation. Smaller drawings and details were recorded in sketchbooks, or guild log books, or drawn in ink on vellum placed over a trestle-board — the precursor of the modern drawing-board. However, drawings of complete buildings were not produced. Instead, crude plans and fragmented elevations seem to have been the systems in use. The scarcity of evidence of medieval drawings is primarily due to the fact that the plaster screed drawing was 'erased' for re-use after transmitting its intention to the master masons. Also, being a valuable commodity, parchment drawings were recycled for other uses, such as bookbinding — many examples of architectural drawings only recently coming to light on the insides of medieval book jackets.

Perspective

The most significant contribution to the architect's ability to visualize a design concept came with the invention of perspective in a Renaissance Florence. It was Brunelleschi who, in the wake of Alberti's experiments with a perspective geometry, first verified the point projection nature of linear perspective. While Alberti had confounded Florentines with his public demonstration of painted three-dimensional illusions assembled inside a box and viewed through a peephole, Brunelleschi had transferred this geometry — albeit as a reflected image viewed through a hole — to the two-dimensional plane.

Initially, and passionately, adopted by the painters of the Quattrocento, linear perspective was first applied to the delineation of building designs by Donato Bramante and Baldassari Perruzzi (see opposite). This knowledge of perspective meant that architects could now make accurate graphic previews of an as–yet–unbuilt 'architecture of the mind', and show them within the illusions of the space of their settings. This newfound skill was developed and improved until three hundred years later

Above: Clock house from the sketchbook of Wilars de Honecort (c.1250).
A medieval ink on vellum drawing that falls somewhere between perspective drawing and paraline projection.
Right: Cutaway drawing of St. Peters, Rome. Baldassare Peruzzi (1481-1536). This remarkable synthesis of graphic conventions – plan, section, perspective and horizontal section – combines, for the first time, the abstract nature of orthographics with the subjective character of perspective.
Below: Imaginary Composition. Giovanni Piranesi (1720-1778). Pencil, pen and ink drawings intended to invoke the spirit of ancient Rome – a major influence on the depiction of all Classical buildings thereafter.

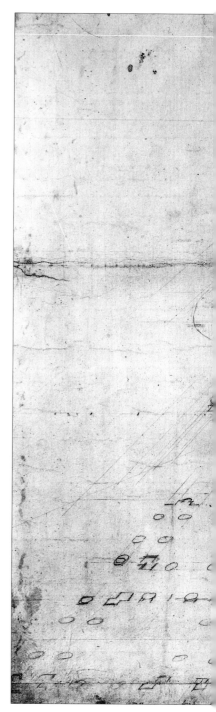

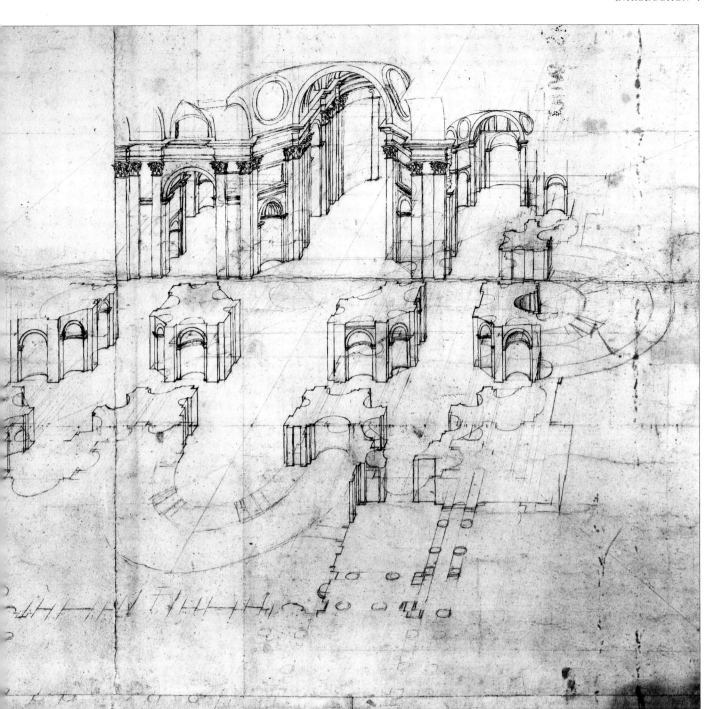

it achieved a high point in the fantastic compositions of master draftsman, Piranesi (see below left).

However, the development of drawing as a prelude to building caused the designer to withdraw gradually from direct involvement in the building operation, and to operate instead from a drafting studio. As a result, architectural design evolved as a drawing-board process which enlisted scaled drawings and models to communicate form and space to both patron and builder.

The Increasing Importance of Architectural Drawings

While ensuing Renaissance artists and designers exported their expertise abroad, the first architectural tourists returned home from Italy with news of a novel type of architectural delineation that employed line and wash. One of these early tourists was Inigo Jones who, in 1613, acquired a collection of Palladio's drawings, which were to have such a profound effect on English architecture. The line and wash technique came to be much exploited by a neo-Palladian following and, by the onset of the eighteenth century, was used to create an almost photographic realism in the hands of delineators such as Colen Campbell, Henry Flitcroft and John Sanderson (see page 53). The emphasis on drawing was to remain at the centre of architectural design. Furthermore, by the end of the eighteenth century its role was reinforced by a new drawing system: orthographic projection (see page 52). Despite its initial censorship, Monge's development of a scaled projection system, which co-

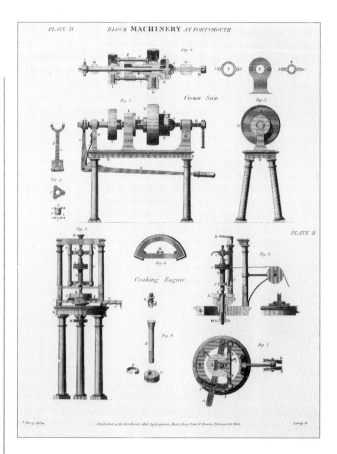

ordinated the plan and the elevation with a section, quickly became common currency in both architectural and engineering design. Indeed, it had been devised in time to serve the accurate delineation of new inventions, such as Stephenson's steam-powered Rocket and Brunel's complex machinery (see above right), both of which were to emerge during the following century of Industrial Revolution.

The Formalizing of Architectural Education

Another significant landmark was also to occur at the turn of the nineteenth century. This was the institutionalizing of the architectural profession and the formalizing of architectural education. The foundation of design schools, such as the *Ecole des Beaux Arts* in Paris, saw a focusing, almost exclusively, on the teaching of fine-line drafting and rendering techniques. This approach was based on the belief that virtuoso draftsmanship was the key to architectural excellence. Techniques taught included a mastery of pencil and pen drawing, together with the rendering of large and sometimes brilliantly coloured elevations and perspectives, worked with meticulously applied washes of Chinese ink and watercolour.

This obsession with graphics and the depiction of the pictorial nature of buildings meant that architectural drawing was now tantamount to an art form. Furthermore, the growth of the print medium and the attendant proliferation of ideas through journals meant that drawing had become the universal language of architecture. Even the invention of photography around 1830 came only to reinforce this drive toward pictorialism, as many drawings of the time reflect painstaking attempts to simulate its realism.

The Modern Movement

The birth of the Modern Movement in the 1920s, however, went on to sweep away the *Beaux Arts'* academism between the two World Wars. Under the influence of Cubism, and in favour of a more clinical and analytical drawing technique, a new breed of designer

Above left: Scene two: a Horrid Hell. Inigo Jones (1573-1652). A brown ink and distemper-splashed sketch for a stage set that organizes a theatrical architectural mass around Brunelleschi's single, central vanishing point.

Above: An engraving showing orthographic views of a crown saw and coaking engine (designed by I. K. Brunel) by J. Farey from Ree's Naval Architecture. Right: Study for the Grand Stair Hall of the Nouvel Opera, Paris, Charles Garnier (1861). This sumptuous watercolouring of a sectional slice through the entrance area to the auditorium epitomises the high level of graphic skills developed in the Ecole des Beaux Arts.

rejected the perspective drawing as '. . . limited, finite and closed'. Instead, designers such as Herbert Beyer, Theo van Doesburg, and Le Corbusier turned to the plan projections created by the isometric and the axonometric, finding the cubic nature of these drawings to be more appropriate for a new architecture stripped of all decoration (see page 12).

Post Modernism

Meanwhile, in its hankering after an earlier heritage of spatial richness and diversity of decoration, a post-Modern generation of designers began, in the 1970s, to restore the roles of a wide range of drawing techniques. This revival began in America — being triggered by an exhibition of rendered drawings that were selected by Arthur Drexler from the archives of the *Ecole des Beaux Arts* and mounted in New York's Museum of Modern Art in 1975.

This resurgence of interest in architectural drawing

techniques is still in vogue today. Although the Chinese ink and watercolour renderings of the past have been replaced by the instant washes of markers, coloured pencils and pressure-transfer materials, etc. Moreover, it has witnessed the return of the presentation perspective, emblematic plans and elevations, and colourful plan projections. And, it has also seen their status elevated to that of a work of art.

Today, the *Beaux Arts'* attitude to architecture as drawing and, in turn, to architectural drawing as *objet d'art*, again recycles in the artwork of Michael Graves, Charles Moore and Arata Isozaki, whose drawings change hands on an international art market. The restoration of architectural drawing as a means to design is also seen in the revival of the artistic impression — notably in the skills of freelance perspectivists who, when hired by architects, specialize in highly-polished renderings for use in prestigious presentations. Despite this development, however, it is important to realize that internationally renowned architects, such as Le Corbusier, Frank Lloyd Wright and Louis Kahn, have always matched a design prowess with a masterly drawing skill. In other words, the act of drawing and design seems synonymous. Without this skill architects are forced to design only what they can draw, rather than being able to draw whatever they wish to design.

Above: Stansted airport terminal building. Design by Foster Associates. Perspective by Helmut Jacoby. Left: Axonometric Drawing of the Maison Cook. Le Corbusier. The cubic nature of the axonometric was particularly appropriate to the rationalist forms of the Modern Movement.

1

MATERIALS

The Drawing Surface

It is known that Joseph Paxton initially sketched his ideas for the design of the Crystal Palace on a blotting pad; that Oscar Neimeyer drafted architectural forms for Brazilia on the back of a cigarette packet, and that Charles Moore doodled design ideas on a table napkin. However, although design concepts can surface at unpredictable moments and be hurriedly recorded on the nearest scrap of paper, architectural concepts and their communication to others usually find expression on more receptive drawing surfaces.

In architectural drawing the selection of the drafting surface is critical because of the various effects produced by the interaction between drawing instrument and drawing surface, and how these relate to the intended function of the drawing: will it be used in presentation as an original, or will it be reproduced using one of the many forms of reprography? Generally speaking, drawings destined for dyeline reproduction require an original produced on transparent materials; while drawings produced on opaque materials are reproduced using the photocopying or photographic print processes.

Tracing Paper and Plastic Film

There are many translucent and transparent drawing surfaces used throughout the design sequence. For example, many architects both originate and communicate their ideas on transparent materials. During the initial stages the 'see-through' qualities of such surfaces allow an evolving design to be quickly extracted, transformed or transferred by tracing from one surface to another. Similarly, transparent overlays are commonly employed for refining rough drafts — the original drawing and its construction lines being used as an underlay from which the ultimate image is selectively traced. Furthermore, transparency of drawing surface finds an important role in presentation, where source images and lettering can be directly trace-transferred into a finished drawing, or when a complex design solution is preserved using a progressive build-up of transparent overlays.

Yellow Tracing Paper is virtually unknown in the United Kingdom, but it is the stock-in-trade of American designers. It is an inexpensive tissue marketed in rolls, has good transparency and can be used in dyeline reproduction. Known disparagingly as 'bumwad', it is highly receptive to graphite and coloured pencils and is used across the design process for origination, layout drawing and sketching. More recently, it appeared in British studios and is now on sale in the Architectural Association shop. Meanwhile, in America, it has achieved a degree of popularity as a presentation medium — especially in the Prismacolor drawings of Michael Graves and Charles Moore.

Detail Paper is the European, white equivalent of yellow tracing paper. It is a cheap form of smooth greaseproof paper available in different thicknesses that are sufficiently translucent for copying and tracing. Marketed in sheets, pads and rolls, its semi-opaque background provides a pleasant drawing surface, particularly for pencil work. Therefore, it is extremely popular for developing ideas, layout work, and the preparation of drafts for subsequent tracing into final drawings. However, its slight opacity means that it is not an ideal medium for dyeline reproduction, and like 'bumwad' its flimsier versions are vulnerable to tearing.

Layout Paper is a similar but whiter version of detail paper and, as its name suggests, is transparent enough for visualizing, composing and tracing new ideas. It is available in roll and pad form, in a range of different thicknesses and surface qualities, including a version coated on its underside to prevent ink bleeding through to the next sheet — this is especially designed for use with markers.

White Tracing Paper is by far the most common medium used in European design offices for overlay work, tracing and, especially, the preparation of drawings for dyeline printing. It is also preferred by many for the production of drawn originals which, to aid a clearer presentation, are mounted over white backing sheets. There are two basic types: natural and vellum, the latter being more expensive, whiter and more durable, but less transparent, than its natural counterpart.

Right: Sketch design for the Crystal Palace. Joseph Paxton (1850). This evocative drawing represents Paxton's prophetic sketch (on blotting paper) of his initial concept for the Crystal Palace.

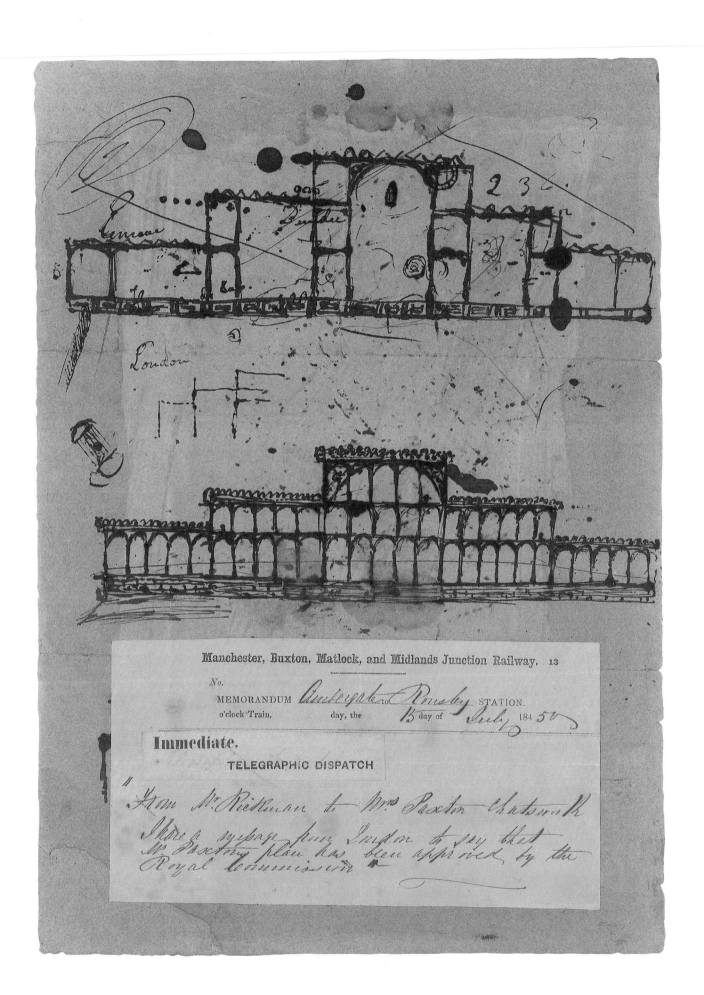

Tracing papers range from clear/transparent, through to semi-opaque versions that offer a variety of tooth (roughness of surface texture) and weight (thickness — varying from 50-112 g/m^2). The thinner papers are more widely used for design origination, while inter-mediate and thicker grades with smooth surfaces are excellent for finished linework in graphite and ink. The more abrasive, matt surfaces tend to abrade pencil leads and are more susceptible to unscheduled smudging. As tracing paper will distort and become dimensionally unstable in climates of fluctuating humidity, it is less widely used in areas such as the southern parts of the United States.

Clear Plastic Film has several advantages over tracing paper. Being formulated from polyester or acetate it is more durable, less brittle with age and more dimen-sionally stable. Although a less receptive and less satisfying surface than tracing paper, it is ideal for high contrast reproductive drafting and easily erasable drawing, in both pencil and technical pen.

One version of film has one side gelatin-coated for a gloss finish; another is matt-frosted acetate film that has one or both sides roughened — a surface on which special pencil leads, toughened pen tips and compatible inks and erasers should be used. If the acetate presents a smooth side, this permits the use of nylon-tipped markers. One drawback of the non-absorbent surface is that, being reliant upon evaporation, the ink dries slowly.

Papers

There is an extensive range of opaque drawing papers which are graded according to their weight and tooth. When selecting a drawing surface it should be established whether the drawing is a rough draft, or a presentation drawing; whether the paper is receptive to the intended medium and, of course, what is the desired graphic effect. Beyond that, the final selection is purely one of personal preference.

Drawing Paper is available in a wide range of qualities, weights and tooth, colours and neutrals. However, as almost all design work tends to be developed on the thinner and transparent papers, special purpose and presentation drawings not meant for dyeline printing are usually worked on opaque, better quality, and more expensive supports. Yet, a good quality paper does not necessarily connotate with a good quality drawing. As a general rule, pens and markers respond well to the heavier, harder and smoother grades, while graphite, coloured pencils and body colour work best on the more textured, medium-weight surfaces. Crayons, pastels and charcoal are often worked on tinted papers, such as Fabriano and Ingres, which, in presenting a more pronounced 'drag', are especially designed for use with these mediums. Heavy-weight watercolour papers have a 100% rag content, and can range in weight from 150-638 g/m^2. They provide supports for liquid washes, and range from fairly smooth — for pen and pencil work — to those with deeply textured surfaces. The smoother, harder papers have a Hot Pressed surface created by the application of pressure between heated steel surfaces.

The 'Not' surface presents a medium-textured support which is also known as Cold Pressed (CP), and is suited to a wide range of drawing styles and wash techniques, while the Rough (R) surfaced version attracts only accomplished watercolourists. Indeed, many specialist papers carry names such as watercolour paper, calli-graphic paper and charcoal paper. However, these labels should not inhibit their use with other drawing mediums. For beginners and professionals alike, the general-purpose support is the ubiquitous cartridge paper. However, for drawings in graphite, ink and coloured pencil, it is important to select a paper with a

A selection of tracing and drawing papers of varying opacity.

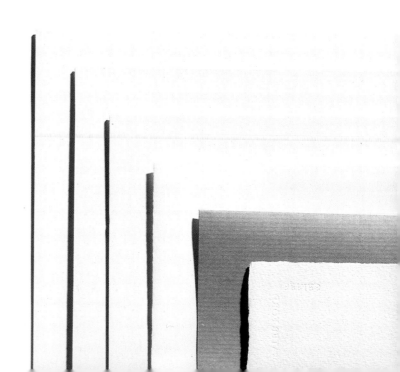

PAPER STRETCHING

Paper stretching is a traditional technique employed to avoid an excessive surface cockling of lighter-weight papers, such as cartridge and even watercolour papers, resulting from the moisture of washes. To avoid this problem a sheet of paper is stabilized by being pre-stretched over an old drawing board, or a sheet of hardboard or plywood. Although paper stretching is usually used on cartridge papers, all kinds of support, including the heavy-duty tracing papers can be successfully stretched.

1. Immerse the drawing paper under running cold water (or in a sink). Remove excess water by blotting lightly with a soft cotton rag, making sure not to over-dry.

2. After smoothing the wet paper over the board, soak two-inch wide strips of gum tape and use them to fix the edges of the paper – taping the opposite ends first.

3. Apply half the tape to the paper and half to the board, making sure it overlaps securely at the corners. Run the heel of the hand over the strips to disperse any visible air pockets.

4. Keep the board flat, and let the paper dry naturally – away from direct sunlight.

suitable surface. A fairly heavy cartridge paper of around 128 g/m² is best for most presentation work. This allows for erasure and correction without damage, and the weight will also receive wash and watercolour. But before using pencil, pen or wash on drawing paper, carefully check each side as many sheets offer a smooth, clay-coated support and a rough uncoated obverse. The sight of a watermark the right-way-around will indicate the correct side.

Boards

Illustration board has a high quality rag surface laminated to a card backing. Strathmore produce a range from one- to six-ply in weight; while Bristol board is offered in a range up to 5-ply with a white face, and comes in two finishes: smooth and slightly textured. Although one-ply board is virtually a heavy paper, such supports are used almost exclusively for finished presentation work.

Display and mounting boards are produced in extensive colour ranges, sizes, weights and finishes. They come into play at the presentation stage, when prestigious drawings can be framed in a sympathetic, symbolic or contrasting colour for exhibition to clients. Specialized mounting boards are chemically treated to remain lightfast and neutral against atmospheric pollution and watercolours and photographic prints can be framed on them without the long-term risk of acid migration from the mount, hence they are used mainly for precious work and archival purposes.

Art boards embody a lightweight, foam core slab trapped between facings of high quality craft paper. Thicknesses vary from 3-10mm. Although used for colour work, they are primarily for framing and flush-backing artwork and photographic materials, and model-making.

Experimental Materials

New students can be daunted when confronted with the newness, blankness and whiteness of a high quality paper. For this reason, I often ask them to draw on toilet paper as an overture to working on the thinner and cheaper custom drawing surfaces — drawing skills developing more quickly in the resulting tension-free climate. Another ploy is to transform drawings on the thinner papers into an 'illustration board' format. The wrinkle-free bonding of flimsier papers to a card backing-sheet can add 'substance' to even the loosest of sketches. Moreover, cheaper papers — including news-print, lining paper — offer unusual drawing surfaces for graphite, coloured pencils and ink. Rolls of paper also offer the experience of taking an idea from concept to conclusion on one sheet — the resulting linear/scroll-like method of design is enjoying a recurrence of popularity in design schools. Finally, there is the potential of mixing different papers in one drawing; the combination of line-work and collage in architectural graphics is not uncommon. So, all forms of paper — from Paxton's pink blotting paper to Moore's white serviette — play a role in the paper trail of architectural design!

Drafting Equipment

In combining the drafting equipment used by the engineer with the drawing instruments and mediums of the artist-illustrator, the architect is faced with the acquisition of a vast range of materials. However, apart from the essential drawing aids, many of the more specialized instruments need only be purchased as and when needed.

When purchasing a basic set of architectural design equipment you are literally setting up a personal work-station. At its centre is the A1 size drawing board. Its function as a drawing support is extended with attachments and additional drawing aids that allow a geometry of straight lines, angles, circles and curves to be accurately plotted and scaled. As accuracy will depend upon precision-made equipment, it is a false economy — even when faced with a low budget — to purchase second-rate products. Therefore, beginners are recommended to buy once and buy the best, and also to learn how to look after their materials. The following is a personal appraisal of the basic items of drafting equipment, how they work, and what to look out for.

Drawing Boards

An essential item of equipment is the A1 size drawing-board, and the serious beginner should plan on purchasing one of high quality. These are constructed from battened slats of pine and fitted with a true working edge of ebony. In order to enhance and protect the surface of wooden boards, many architects will insert an intermediate layer of smooth, heavy-weight paper to act as a resilient base-sheet which will provide a slight cushioning sensation when drawing, and also keep boards free from the grain-deforming effects of accidental spillage. However, should any moisture make contact with the wooden surface, first soak it up with a cloth before allowing the board to dry naturally, and then gently sanding it over with a fine-grade sandpaper block. It is important to note that drawing papers should never be pinned to the board, as this method of attachment can both impede the movement of sliding instruments and irreparably damage areas of the working surface. To avoid these problems, use the traditional method of attaching paper with diagonal corner strips of masking tape, or use the new circular

Below and opposite: essential drafting equipment.

French Curve

Beam Compass

Masking Tape

Double-sided Tape

Magic Tape

Compass

Craft Knife

DRAFT DOTS

Draft Dots

Lead Snake

Spatula

Scalpels

Frisk Film

Cow Gum

tabs of brown adhesive paper.

T-Squares

When engaged with the working edge of the drawing board, T-squares provide an accurate right-angle. Available in both left- and right-handed formats, the best T-squares are made from mahogany and fitted with ebony drawing edges. However, some designers prefer the visibility allowed by plastic versions; while others stick with metal T-squares comprising aluminium stocks and stainless-steel blades. Before investing in a drawing-board and T-square, check that the equipment is matched accurately. To do this, engage the T-square stock on the true edge of the board and, on a sheet of paper, draw a line to the width of the board. Then invert the T-square and, engage its edge on the opposite side of the board. If the blade's true edge coincides with the line, the two instruments are true and compatible.

Parallel-Motion Units

The real alternative to the drawing-board and T-square set-up is the parallel-motion ruling unit, which comprises a drawing support with an integrated sliding straight edge. By using a system of cables, pulleys and, some-

Above: Designed by Steelcase Strafor, this hi-tech seat offers continuous back and lumbar support throughout the range of body movements associated with drawing.

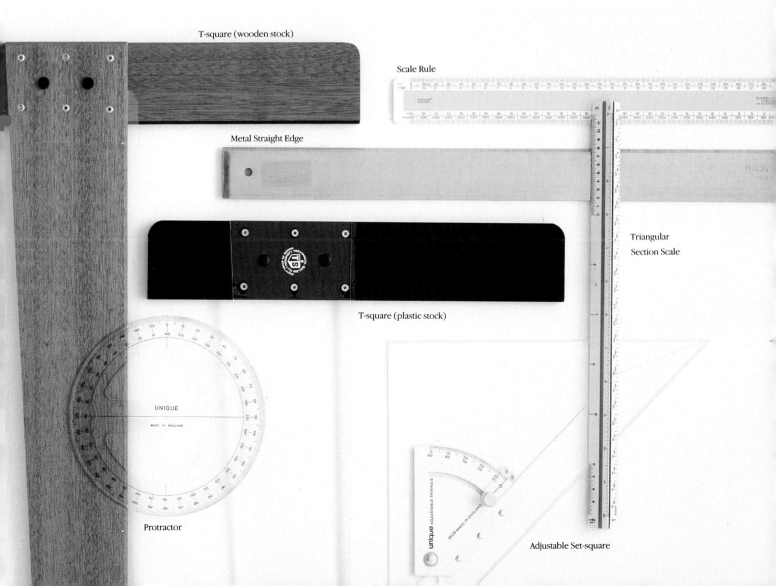

T-square (wooden stock)

Scale Rule

Metal Straight Edge

Triangular
Section Scale

T-square (plastic stock)

UNIQUE
MADE IN ENGLAND

Protractor

Adjustable Set-square

times, counter-weights, the true edge is manually slid up and down the board.

Drawing Stands

Drawing stands are freestanding drawing stations made from wood or metal. They support adjustable worktops, or integral boards fitted with parallel-motion units, or drafting machines.

Alternative Drawing Stands

As drawing stands are expensive, a ready-made alternative is often assembled by my students who, while maintaining a drawing-board in the design studio, will also provide themselves with a home work-station. This do-it-yourself drawing stand is cheaply made using a hollow-core flush door supported on a pair of carpenter's donkeys — a worktop reminiscent of the medieval trestle board. Often, this supports one of the cheaper student-grade boards made from machined softwood and incorporating a metal working edge.

An alternative is the self-made board which is a machine-cut sheet of plywood or blockboard that is either lipped with U-section aluminium or employs a detachable metal true edge (which is made especially for clamping to the sides of plain boards or tabletops). Drafting on a raked or flat surface is a matter of personal preference. For those who prefer the former, a metal-hinged and adjustable bracket is marketed that clamps the board to the worktop and then locks into the desired drawing inclination.

Other types of board rests include a pair of tapered timber blocks, or the more commonly used stack of house bricks.

Drafting Machines

Parallelogram drafting machines represent the ultimate in high-tech drafting. Needless to say, they are extremely expensive and more commonly seen in the large design offices. They consist of a working head that accepts T-squares, set squares, protractors and scales. A clamping mechanism anchors the counter-balanced arm to the top of the board, allowing horizontal and vertical movement.

Seating

As back problems can account for a high proportion of lost working hours, and as architects spend long hours in awkward drawing postures, it makes sense to consider investing in an ergonomically designed drafting chair. Although expensive, several fully adjustable drafting chairs are on the market, but the most technically advanced seems to be the Sensor. Its flexible shell construction and push button controls enable variable height and tension, with the back and seat pan responding to every twist and turn of the body. During these movements, back, spine and feet remain fully supported and, most important of all, the eyes retain a constant viewing level with the drawing board.

Lighting

Although daylight is the best type of illumination for drafting, this is not always available. Therefore, when light levels recede or when 'midnight oil' has to be burned, a form of task lighting should be used. The ubiquitous Anglepoise lamp, with its flexible arm positioned over the left shoulder, is the popular solution. However, when colour rendering is critical, beginners quickly discover that, by emitting an orange-tinted light, incandescent lamps cause distorted chromatic impressions. As a result, it is important to insert colour-corrected lamps that, although offering a shorter life, emit a balanced form of light.

Set Squares

Set squares are used in conjunction with the T-square for drawing vertical and inclined lines. The best type to buy are the clear or tinted plastic versions, as they allow a clear view through to the work beneath. The large 250mm adjustable type, made from clear acrylic, is the most versatile for architectural drafting but, like all plastic equipment, it should not be used with drawing instruments containing spirit-based ink.

Scale Rules

Architectural design ideas are always drafted to a scale that regulates their graphic size so that they fit within the confines of the drawing-board. Therefore, in order to read, transfer or convert these scale dimensions from or between drawings, a scale rule is required.

Scales are made from stable materials, such as kiln-dried wood or unbreakable plastic — or a combination of the two. The two types of scale in common use are open-divided and fully-divided scales. Those with engraved calibrations are best because their figured divisions cannot wear away. Also, being colour-coded, they are easy to read.

Scales are obtainable in three different profiles: a two-bevel section; a four-bevel section, and a triangular section. Although the latter can carry up to twelve different scales on its six faces, it is awkward to use. The best scale for the beginner is the four-bevel version — its slim profile allowing the rule to be tilted for maximum accuracy when transferring dimensions. Scale rules should never be used to draw against, as this will eventually wear away the engraved calibration. Therefore, to avoid any temptation, a small, general purpose ruler should be used as a back-up.

Protractors

Protractors are basic instruments that are used to determined unknown angles in a drawing. Made from clear acrylic, they are obtainable in circular and semi-circular formats and can deal with angles other than those of the fixed set squares. On the large 360-degree protractor, angles can be plotted to an accuracy of a quarter of a degree.

Templates

There are a myriad of plastic and metal templates that come in many shapes and sizes, and allow the designer to accurately draw smaller ranges of geometric shapes, including circles and ellipses. Templates also include versions that enable the rapid outlining of architectural

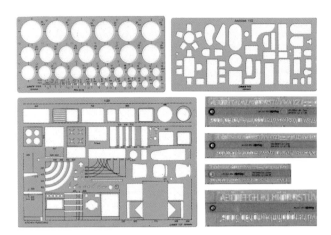

symbols. Many students simply can't afford to invest in a good quality template set, and therefore buy cheap substitutes that are more difficult to use. However, it is far better to buy good ones individually, and build gradually to a full set.

Compass
The compass extends the ability to draw accurate arcs and circles beyond the radii offered by the templates. It is wise to buy a reasonably large version, making sure that it is compatible with your drawing instruments. The best types have precision screw adjustment and adaptors for incorporating technical pen heads and leads. However, whether used with graphite or ink, care should be taken to match the line weight of circles to the rest of the drawing. Springbow dividers with a ruling pen attachment and an extension bar extend the ability to draft even larger circles. They tend to be a luxury item in student studios and, when needed, are borrowed rather than bought.

French Curves and Sweeps
Curves and sweeps are best purchased in the clear plastic form (a 'radius curve' is an edge used to draw curves of constant radius, whereas a 'sweep' is an edge used to draw curves of changing radius). Sets of French curves and sweeps are often referred to as 'ship's curves', but there is another linear and adjustable version known as a 'lead snake'. This flexible spline provides a quick and easy method of connecting plotted points together. It presents two tracing edges — one for leads and one for ink — and can be flexed into most curved shapes.

Scalpels and Blades
Apart from a large pair of general-purpose scissors, a traditional surgical scalpel should be reserved for precision cutting of paper and film. The metal holders are better than the cheaper plastic version and allow greater control over delicate cutting operations, such as mask-cutting and pressure-transfer work. However, they are less suitable for trimming out thick card, which is best cut with the ubiquitous craft knife, with its heavy-duty holder containing sets of alternative and replacement blades. Always useful is the common razor blade

or, better still, the safer version, which incorporates a hard shoulder. This blade finds a particular role in the removal of ink errors from tracing paper.

Straight-edges
A precision cutting-edge is essential in order to avoid the temptation of using the T-square, set-square or ruler, as these will inevitably become nicked and ruined. Also, avoid the lighter metal cutting rules, as these can prove difficult to work with and, in careless hands, cause unnecessary wounds.

A good straight-edge for scoring and trimming is one bought from a builder's merchants — it being simply a 915mm (3ft) length of machine-finished steel. For obvious reasons, cuts should never be made on the drawing-board nor directly on a worktop, but rather on stacked sheets of old card or a sheet of plywood.

Adhesives
Rubber cement, such as Cow Gum, is a petroleum-based, milky, semi-liquid adhesive used for general-purpose gluing. It spreads smoothly when applied with a spatula, without pulling or shrinking and, therefore, is ideal for use in collage work and mounting lightweight papers to stouter boards. Surplus cement is easily rubbed away with the fingers, without causing damage to most artwork. But I have found that it can stain the absorbent coloured papers and flesh-toned pigments. More efficient, and less messy, are the aerosol spray-mount and the stronger photo-mount adhesives. These are good for mounting thinner papers as they facilitate a bubble- and stretch-free bond. The photo-mount type can mount slightly heavier and larger sheets, especially when both surfaces are sprayed before contact. And, when necessary, both versions allow newly mounted papers to be retrieved and repositioned.

However, the current concern with the appearance of a polar hole in the ozone layer has placed some of the blame on the atmospheric erosion effect of aerosol emissions — and some design institutions have banned their use. Quite apart from the fact that, when used in confined and unventilated areas, they can present a personal health hazard, the question whether or not to use these products is now also an ecological one with global implications.

If a bond between a large sheet of paper or artwork and a base-board is required, then the best means of producing a wrinkle-free adhesion is to use a dry-mount press. Found in most offices and design schools, this process involves a sheet of vegetable glue — in tissue paper form — that is trimmed to the size of the artwork and inserted between the original and the base-board. This assembly is then introduced into the press which, when heated, dissolves the intermediate layer of glue to form a clean and consistently bonded laminate.

Stencil and Letter Guides
As architectural drawings involve annotation, such as titles, scales and labels, it is wise to include a set of lettering stencils in a basic set of equipment. Several sets of lettering stencils, that provide letter guides at

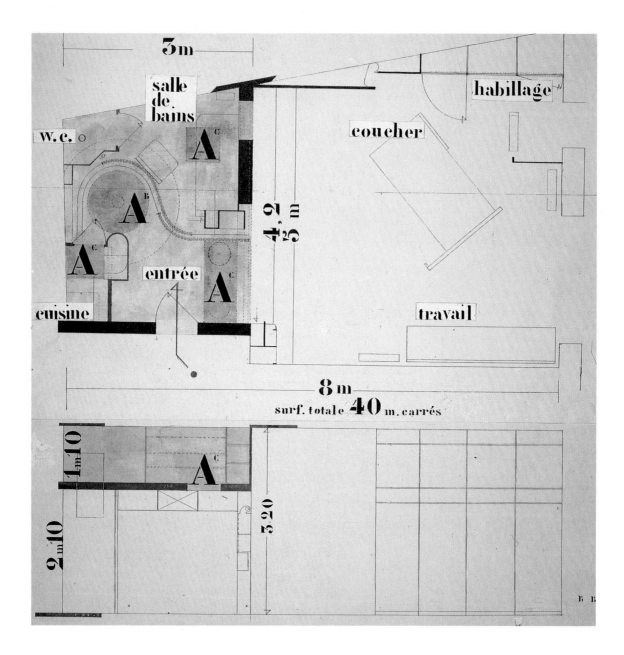

different sizes and styles, are manufactured, as well as ones that are co-ordinated with technical pen stylo sizes, and others intended for use with fine-lead clutch pencils.

When buying a set, make sure to choose the clear or tinted types with a transparency allowing a visible letter spacing to be calculated. Also, to avoid ink blotches, make sure that their profiles suspend the stencil apertures slightly above the drawing surface. The larger, individually packed metal stencils, in sets of numbers and letters, are extremely popular with architects. In fact, one distinctive version — prominent in the orthographic drawings of Le Corbusier and his protégé Eileen Grey — enjoy a cult following, and is still on sale in the hardware section of the *Bazaar Hotel d'Ville* store in Paris, France.

Tapes
Masking tape, in its low- and high-tack form, is widely used in the drawing process. Its functions include fixing

Plan of the Badovici Apartment, Paris. Eileen Gray.
Designed between 1930-31, Gray's annotation of the plan employed four sizes of the metal stencils popularised by her mentor, Le Corbusier.

paper to board, plucking mislaid pressure transfer letters from artwork and, as its name implies, masking areas and edges of drawings.

Other useful tapes include: double-sided tape; a role of two-inch gumstrip paper tape, for paper stretching; and the 'invisible' or 'frosted' clear tapes for repairs, effects and attaching auxillary papers to tracing paper drawings before dyeline printing.

Masking Film
Masking film, such as Frisk film, is an essential for precision spray work, but always check first that it won't pull away the surface that it is protecting.

USING MASKING FILM

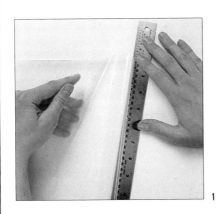
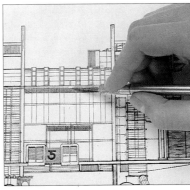
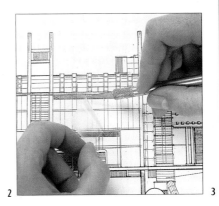
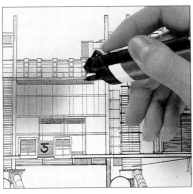
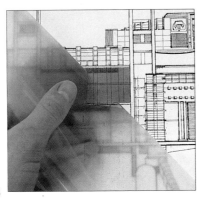
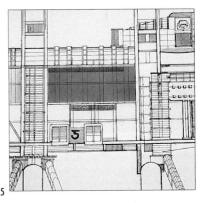

1. Lay the low-tack masking film over the drawing paper – pushing it down smoothly with a ruler whilst, at the same time, pulling away its backing sheet.

2. Using a scalpel blade, gently cut out the shape of the mask. Take great care to cut only through the film – **not** the drawing paper underneath!

3. Now carefully peel the masking film away from the shape to be rendered. Lift it at one corner and pull gently – making sure that the drawing surface is not inadvertently damaged during this process.

4. Having removed the film to reveal the cut-out shape, you can now briskly and freely apply the selected medium to achieve a perfectly flat finish.

5. Once the application of medium is completely dry, carefully peel back the film mask to reveal the finished effect.

6. nb. Naturally, additional shapes may be cut out of the film so that other areas of the drawing surface can be safely rendered without 'damage' to surrounding sections. Simply repeat steps 2-5 as above.

Maintaining Equipment

The adage which suggests that the 'workman is only as good as his tools' is particularly relevant to the architect. Drafting relies upon clean equipment, and therefore those instruments that use a sliding action on the drawing surface, and which are thus likely to get dirty, should be occasionally wiped clean with a clean cloth moistened with a little methylated spirit (denatured alcohol) or lighter fuel. (This accounts for the common sight of a designer who, using the action of a snooker player wiping the cue between visits to the table, will occasionally wipe down the T-square blade with a cloth.) The drawing aids made from acrylic are susceptible to attack from the solvents used in spirit-based inks, some markers and technical pens. Therefore, they should be used with care and kept immaculately clean.

Also, to avoid the risk of ink, particularly from technical pens, flooding under their edges, many architects will affix strips of masking tape to the backs of set-squares and curves. Apart from making sure that their faces are kept free from the drawing surfaces, this trick helps to maintain a cleaner drawing. At the outset of drafting it is important to work with clean hands and to maintain an impeccable drawing surface free from dust and eraser particles. In Europe, boards are usually swept clean with a cloth but in American studios designers are armed with a broad, soft board brush, employed for the same purpose. Furthermore, pounce powder is sometimes used — especially in America — to tone-up drawing paper. The powder is sprinkled over the surface before being gently rubbed down with a felt bag or pad — usually incorporated in the container — and then brushed away. Apart from 'lubricating' the paper, this process leaves behind minute granules of absorbent powder that not only aid the gliding action of drawing aids, but also 'soak up' stray dust from pencils.

The Line Makers

Delineation lies at the heart of architectural representation, but the use of lines to record spatial relationships could not be more unrelated to the way that we perceive the world around us. Indeed, our visual experience is one of patterns of shape, and one of the ways that we read objects in space is to scan the profiles of their edges. By graphically substituting 'edge' for 'line', we employ an abstraction with its own set of rules and its own potential for simulating space — a potential that is magnified by the mark-making abilities of the various line-making mediums.

Two aspects of line in architectural drawing should be considered: line weight (thickness and intensity), and line type. For instance, the exploitation of a hierarchy of line weight — that is, using a descending scale of line thickness that corresponds to a descending scale of depth in a drawing, can bring an implied spatial existence to even the most minimal of diagrams. Types of line can be classified into three basic categories: lines of consistent thickness along their length; lines that fluctuate in thickness along their length, and intermittent lines that break or fragment along their length.

As we shall later see, each weight and type of line plays the triple function of discriminating solid and void, creating visual interest and performing specific roles in the conventional depiction of architectural information. Variation of line quality is determined both by the nature of the line-maker and the drawing surface and, in many cases, is also affected by the speed of application and varying pressure of the hand. In this context, the terms 'hand' and 'fist' have come to be associated with line quality — a highly skilled and sensitive line drawing often described as emanating from a 'good fist'. However, in functioning as an extension of the clenched hand, drawing instruments — apart from their line-giving abilities — should also be chosen on the basis of how good they feel when held in the hand.

Traditional Pencils
Little changed since their first factory production by the Faber company in Germany, in 1761, traditional pencils

A selection of mechanical and traditional pencils plus a charcoal stick and Conte Crayon.

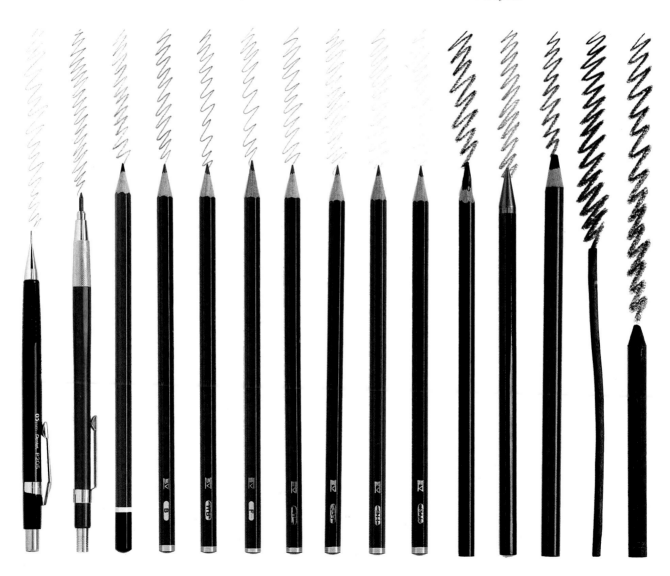

USING A NON-REPRODUCABLE PENCIL.

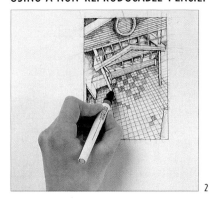

1

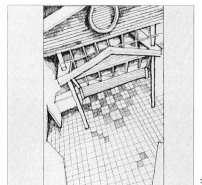

2

3

The non-reproducable pencil offers an alternative to developing drawings using the overlap method, and a complete sequence from origination to finished delineation can be worked on a single sheet of paper.

1. Begin by using the pencil to sketch out a rough version of the image.

2. When you have worked the rough to an appropriate degree of accuracy, it can be used as a guide and directly receive a black-line version of the drawing.

3. When the drawing is reproduced using the dyeline or photocopy process (see pages 132-7) the blue line vanishes leaving only printed evidence of the black-line drawing.

represent the most familiar and versatile of drawing instruments. Their lightness of feel in the hand, the aroma of their wood, and their sensitivity to pressure and to the grain of different supports, has given them a prominence that makes it possible for some architects to work exclusively in this medium. Indeed, the stereotyped image of the architect portrays him pencil at the ready, tucked behind one ear.

Wooden pencils are commonly referred to as 'lead' pencils — a misnomer that derives from when, in 1564, deposits of raw graphite discovered in the Lake District were mistaken for lead. Pencil cores are in fact made from a mixture of graphite and clay, and are manufactured in ranges of up to 19 grades of hardness (containing proportionately more clay) and softness (containing proportionately more graphite).

Pencil barrels are coded with the numerical and letter designations, using 'H' for hard and 'B' for black. At the centre of the scale lies 'F' which, together with H and HB, represents a range of medium-softness that, for general-purpose drawing, constitutes a beginner's starter set.

Apart from H and H2, which are ideal for hard-line drafting, the majority of the hard graphites are specialized leads that enjoy few roles in design. While the versatile HB is the first in a range of increasing graphite softness, with a corresponding increase in vulnerability to breakage and therefore the need for constant resharpening. Consequently, the softer grades — from B to 8B — are usually reserved for sketching and for drawings requiring bold, dark lines. Note: to avoid accidental lead breakage, a good tip is to buy pencils with hexagonal barrels, such as those in the Venus, Rexel Cumberland and Staedtler ranges.

Specialist pencils, such as ebony, carbon, china wax and the wood-encased charcoal and Conté pencils, extend the graphite range of line weight out into the richness of thick black, crayon-like cores. These are ideal for large sketches — their boldness of line relating more to freedom of expression than to precision. Most of these pencils make lines that will smudge — a factor that can be used to good effect in drawing. However, to avoid further, unwanted smudging a finished drawing should be treated with a fixative.

Drawing sticks, including charcoal in its compressed stick and natural twig form, the French Conté crayon with its three degrees of hardness, together with black waxy crayons and sticks of graphite, represent the earliest form of pencil. They also complete a spectrum of line width and quality that begins with the almost invisible, silvery fine line of the 9H grade pencil and terminates in the richness of thick, juicy black strokes.

Drop-out pencils are a specialist drawing instrument worthy of note. In providing a fine, blue, non-reproducible line, they are much used in the setting out of finished drawings, which are later worked up in graphite or ink. When subjected to dyeline or photocopy printing, the blue under-drawing vanishes, leaving evidence only of the over-worked black-line mediums.

Pencil Maintainence

As crisp lines tend to work better than coarse lines, the first essential when using traditional pencils is to maintain their sharpness. This is especially so for the softer grades, but also for the thicker carbon and charcoal pencils. Apart from the ease and convenience of desk-mounted and battery-powered pencil sharpeners that automatically point pencils on insertion, many architects still prefer to hand-sharpen leads. This method gives control over the type of point required for particular tasks. For example, some designers prefer a needlepoint for drafting and a wedge-shaped point for drawing and sketching.

Furthermore, when using the softer pencils, points can be kept reasonably sharp during the act of drawing and drafting by gently rocking and rolling the pencil barrel between the finger and thumb.

Mechanical Pencils

Two modern versions of the traditional pencil have evolved: clutch pencils and propelling pencils.

Clutch pencils embody a push-button on the end of their plastic or metal barrels that allows a high-polymer or graphite lead to be drawn out when required, or withdrawn when not in use. Supplies of replacement leads are available in a full range of hardness, weight and colour, but the standard 2mm leads are recommended for all types of drawing. Points are maintained by a special sharpener, or by pointing on a sandpaper block.

Propelling pencils automatically propel and retract high-polymer leads produced in seven degrees of hardness. Available in four line weights, ranging from 0.3mm-0.9mm, they are designed to resist abrasion during precision drawing on plastic film. The leads are fine enough to obviate the need for sharpening but, as they easily snap when placed under pressure, they are rarely used for sketching.

Erasers

Most pencil marks can be erased to some extent, but it may not be possible to remove mistakes completely — especially if one of the harder leads has been ingrained into the surface of drawing paper. Very soft pencil lines and smudges can be lifted with a putty eraser, while the medium-soft graphites are fairly easily erased with one of the soft plastic erasers, which can be cut to obtain a clean crisp edge. A vinyl compound eraser is useful for removing mistakes made on matt plastic film when using plastic or graphite leads.

Traditional Pens

If the advent of the pencil first came when a lump of light-coloured stone was scratched against the surface of

A selection of ballpoint, felt-tip and technical pens.

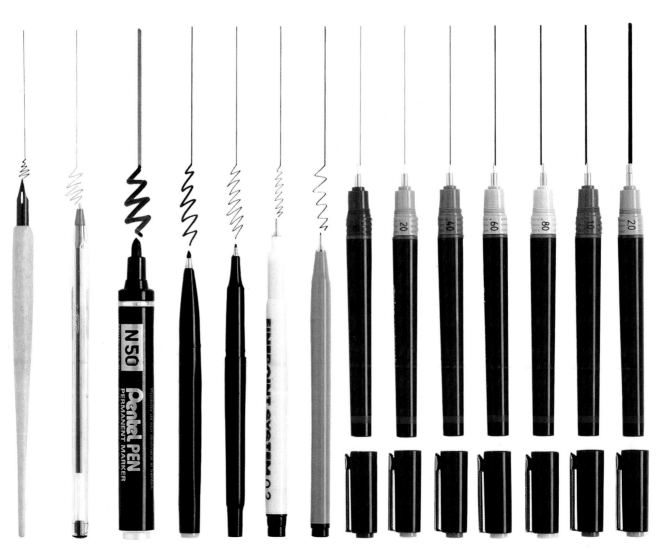

a darker-coloured rock, then the birth of the pen began when someone dipped a stick into liquid pigment in order to make his mark. The pen nib has a geneaology stretching back over two millennium, to when a reed or a quill was sharpened in order to carry and deposit a line of ink onto the surface of papyrus or parchment. The touch of a pen nib on paper is quite different from the feel of a pencil, and the resulting line of ink carries a stamp of permanency and power. The great variety of potential line quality stems from a wide range of specialist nibs, with successful lines depending upon getting the ink to flow smoothly across the drawing support with a minimum of pressure.

Conventional pens with interchangeable steel nibs that are dipped into a supply of ink, have lost ground in architectural drawing — especially in the face of the new generation of instant and disposable line-makers. However, they do provide varying degrees of line width (as a result of altering the pressure on their nibs), and they do have the advantage of portability.

Graphos pens have nibs with a built-in reservoir and offer a range of nib types designed for six specific functions — including lettering, ruling, stencilling, drafting, general purpose drawing and sketching.

Ballpoint and Felt-tip Pens

A new generation of instant pens provides an excellent, inexpensive, and extremely versatile instrument for drawing, sketching, and for various tasks in drafting. There is a huge variety of drawing tips to choose from: felt-tips, fibre-tips, roller tips, brushpens, and ballpoints.

There are a number of different versions of the ballpoint — from the standard ballpoint, in which indelible ink is dispensed via a rolling steel ball, to pens with nylon and tungsten carbide rollers which contain water-based inks. The regular ballpoint is available in medium, fine-line and razor-point line widths.

The fine- and extra-fine liners have gained in respectability as a drawing medium, and have begun to compete with the precision-engineered technical pen. This is because they feel good in the hand, make thin and bold lines, and are especially useful both for the rapid delineation of new ideas and for working lines and hatching into finished drawings. In contrast to the crisp lines of a razor-point fine-liner, the bold and beefy strokes of a felt-tip art or studio marker provide black line weights of up to 40mm.

Technical Pens

Technical pens use tubular points, or stylos, made from steel, nylon or ceramic, to produce lines of precise and constant weight. When a line of a different width is required, the drawing tip has to be changed — a system which tends to dictate a programmed drawing procedure. Although the technical pen is engineered specifically for precision technical drafting, once acclimatized to their regimen of tip adaptation, recharging, and cleaning many architects adopt them for reference sketching, orthographic drafting, pictorial drawing and even as a surrogate fountain pen. A traditional range of point sizes comprises nine line widths, running from 0.1mm-1.2mm. Three tips are recommended for the beginner: 0.2mm, 0.4mm, and 0.6mm. There is also an alternative range of stylo points, produced in nine internationally recognized line widths, specifically designed for the requirements of reduction. However, the finer tips tend to clog without notice — a seizure that can be frustrating when drafting to deadlines. If these finer tips are preferred, it is worth noting that the nylon and ceramic versions tend to clog less than their steel counterparts. Sooner or later, every budding architect will need to purchase a technical pen, and it is wise to test different brands before making any major investment. It is also wise to plump for a well-known range, such as Rotring, Rapidograph or Faber Castell and, rather than buy the complete set, purchase additional drawing tips in tandem with a developing drafting skill.

Inks

Specially formulated, non-clogging inks are made for tubular-tipped technical pens, and work reasonably well on most drawing surfaces. They are available in various colours — most (except blue) being suitable for dyeline reproduction. They are waterproof and do not smear when dry. However, always check to see if your pen requires a special ink.

Non-etching ink is suitable for drafting on tracing paper and coated and non-coated plastic film. It can be used in technical pens, and is waterproof and smudgeproof when dry.

Etching ink is specially designed for coated film, and can be applied to all plastic surfaces. Compared with non-etching ink, it is fast-drying, lightfast and custom-designed for reproduction purposes. However, as its function is to eat into the surface of film, it should only be used in acetate-resistant pens. And for this reason it should not be used in conjunction with plastic accessories, such as stencils.

India ink is a shellac-free medium that, like permanent writing ink, can be used in fountain pens for drawing and sketching. It is almost waterproof when dry, and suitable for drawing and lettering on most surfaces.

Ink Erasers

Hard plastic erasers that are compatible with different types of drafting ink are manufactured by many of the technical pen makers. But errors in ink work on tracing paper or film can also be carefully scraped away with a keen razor blade, before burnishing over with a soft eraser. Alternatively, the best results are achieved using a plastic eraser which literally dissolves ink errors into removeable strands, which can be brushed or blown from the surface.

More common in American studios are electric erasers. These are excellent for larger areas of error but, if not used with care, can warp the drawing surface. Therefore, smaller mistakes should be removed using the electric eraser in conjunction with an eraser shield.

Lines of Action

Any close inspection of the freehand and hard-line drawings of architects will find a wide variety of distinctive line qualities, which stem from a developed and intensely personal drawing style. In one sense, this variety of line functions is rather like a graphological study of handwriting, primarily because it has evolved from a unison between hand, drawing instrument and, of course, the personality and motivation of the user. As such, line drawings exist as a kind of instantly recognizable 'signature' of their authors. For instance, compare the calligraphic dash of the emotionally-charged lines in an Erich Mendelsohn and a Hans Scharoun sketch, with the cool, deadpan lines of a James Stirling perspective. Also, compare the nervous tension of a Leon Krier delineation, or the boldness of a Le Corbusier freehand outline, with the brittle lines of an Antonio Sant'Elia, or the spidery trails of an Adlo Rossi. Not only do all these lines reflect the line-making marks of the different instruments and the drawing hands which made them, but they also appear as an expression in microcosm of the various architectural philosophies from which they were fashioned. Obviously, these sets of lines exemplify different points along the design sequence. As a new building concept struggles for its graphic existence, its birth in the rapidity of flourishes and scribbles of an emergent sketch becomes gradually subject to the increasing crispness of more searching lines, enlisted to test its proportion and, ultimately, its three-dimensional appearance. Finally, in its distilled form, the design is fixed to paper with a conviction of line that, even in its stark precision, allows the different styles of architects to shine through.

Above right, right and opposite right:
If we scrutinise at close quarters some details from the design drawings of early twentieth century master draftsmen, we discover quite different qualities of line that betray a corresponding variation in their production time. For example, Erich Mendelsohn's organic flourish (above right) results from a Zen-like, instantaneous brushstroke, while Vladimir Tatlin's deliberate and mechanical hardline drafting (right) reflects a slow and painstaking delineation. Meanwhile, the stabbing ink lines of a design sketch by Antonio Sant'Elia (opposite right) describe a furious drawing process in which the pen nib attempts to keep pace with a quickly developing idea. (The three drawings are reproduced in full on pages 146 and 147.)

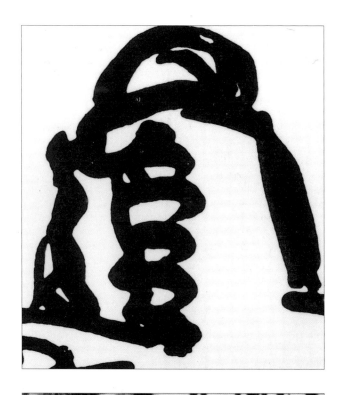

The Tone Makers

When tonal shading is added to a line drawing, a new dimension of meaning is added — one that brings an abstract delineation a little closer to the way that we perceive the real world. As a response to the direction and intensity of light, the structuring of shade and shadow provides visual clues that describe the nature of an architectural space — primarily by emphasizing the solidity of form, indicating surface quality and suggesting distance and depth.

The decision to render a drawing in tone, therefore, is one that accompanies the need to enhance its spatial meaning. To do so, we can enlist the same medium that was used to produce the line or, as is common in architectural drawing, so as not to disrupt the readability of the line, turn to another medium. For example, it is not unusual to find orthographic line drawings rendered with a combination of different tonal mediums, such as the 'washes' of graphite, aerosol spray, marker ink and pressure-transfer materials. When making a rendering in tone the drawing surface must also be considered, because the particular tonal mediums are more receptive to particular papers. For example, a pencil-drawn photographic realism will be best achieved on a smooth paper, because to work on a textured paper would negate its illusion. Conversely, a watercolour or ink wash will perform best on a surface with a degree of tooth; and a marker tone will bleed on ordinary paper, but retain crisp edges and produce accurately defined marks on the special bleed-proof or non-bleed papers.

Pencil Shading

The traditional means of achieving graphic tonal effects was orginated in the fifteenth century by artists who worked in silverpoint. They drew tightly-packed lines that became progressively lighter and finer as they moved from darker areas of tone towards the light. But tones can also be simulated using dots, short stabs of line, or by hatching and cross-hatching (see page 34) — and by mixing the grades of pencil within one drawing. Varying the type and combination of mark is also effective, especially when long, trailing lines are contrasted with hatching in a thicker lead, or when applying dotted textures in a hard silvery tone.

Graphite Washes

The most basic graphite shading effect is the flat and grainless wash that requires little skill in its application. This is best achieved when working on the smoother cartridge papers with a medium-soft pencil, such as HB. A graduated pencil tone that moves from light-to-dark, or vice-versa, is produced in exactly the same fashion as the flat wash, except that, as you move down the paper, the pressure on the pencil barrel is gradually released.

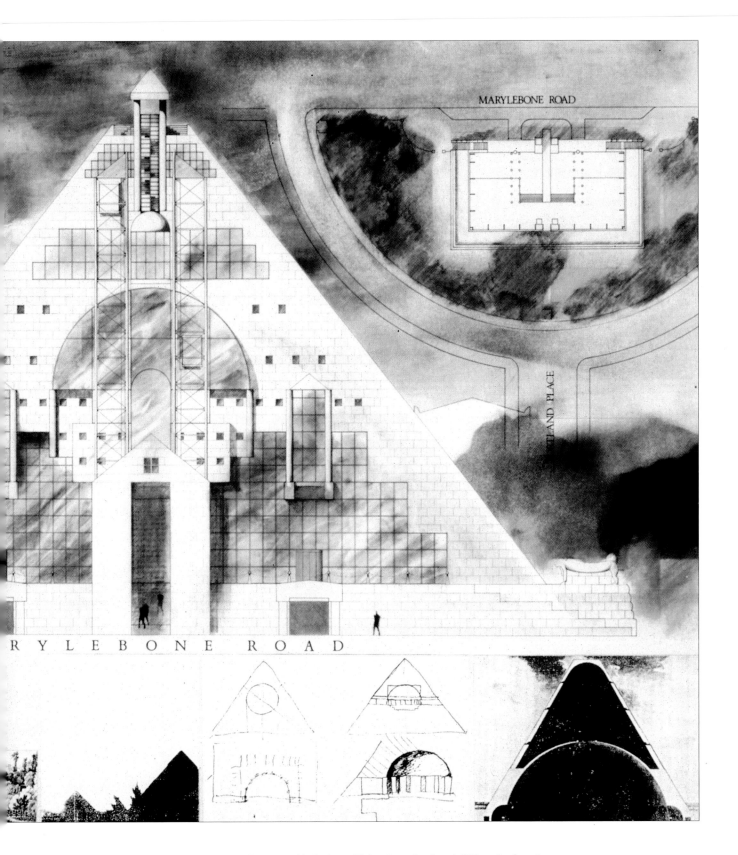

MARYLEBONE ROAD

RYLEBONE ROAD

Graphite Dust Technique. *This prize-winning, 1:100 scale elevation drawing was produced in five hours by Leslie Hooper, Roger Mann and Brian Beardsmore. It was first drawn in pen and pencil and rendered in coloured pencils, graphite and car spray paint, before being masked to allow the finger-rubbed application of graphite dust to the sky.*

PASTEL DUST SHADING

The graphite dust technique offers an alternative to the usual method of drawing with a pastel, and involves using a stick of Conté Crayon to produce a soft area of tone with one hard edge.

1. Begin by using the edge of a craft or scalpel blade to scrape a small deposit of dust from the side of the pastel crayon onto a clean sheet of paper. Obviously the quantity of dust that you scrape off will be approximately determined by the size of the area that you intend to cover and the density of application required.

2. With the sheet of paper carefully placed on top of the drawing surface (it is intended to act as a mask), use either a piece of cotton wool or tissue to push the dust sideways onto the drawing.

3. Still using a sideways motion, work the dust into the drawing surface, spreading it out over the area to be shaded.

4. Carefully pull back the paper to reveal misty shading with a sharp edge.

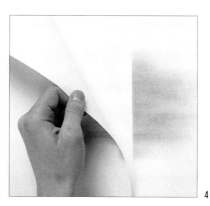

Diagonal Shading

Pencil line shading in architectural drawings is commonly worked using diagonal strokes from left-to-right (right-to-left, if you are left-handed. See opposite page). Apart from its ease, the main reasons for this structured approach is that it avoids a meaningless scribble and thus brings a strong sense of order to the drawing, and reduces any confusion between line and tone. The potential range of effects that can be produced from this technique is enormous, and they are determined by the degree of discipline with which the diagonal stroke is maintained. For instance, it can range from the more deliberate and formal application, as in the work of Giuseppe Zambonini, to one that is fast and furious, in which the pencil rarely leaves the paper, as in the work of Cesar Pelli. You will find that a decreasing tonal scale results from gradually increased pressure on the pencil and the superimposing of one layer of graphite on top of another in order to both build up and regulate its density in specific areas of the drawing.

Graphite Dust Shading

Another tonal medium, graphite dust, is a by-product of the pencil sharpener and, rather than be thrown away, can be employed to achieve delightfully delicate and atmospheric effects in ink line drawings. Also, by producing a soft, even and translucent wash, it can be used on tracing paper originals intended for dyeline reproduction, and can be combined with pencil point

Right: Freehand Cross-Hatching. This design for a Viking Museum by Jacqueline Yahn uses various pencil shading techniques to elaborate the line drawing. For example, above the section beautifully structured cross-hatching both darkens the sky area and emphasises the silhouette of the building.

shading, to create cloudy sky effects over elevations and perspectives, and for rendering shadows in plans, sections and elevations.

As this is a potentially messy medium, care should be taken to screen or mask surrounding areas and as the wash is susceptible to accidental smudging, working with the arm over newly rendered areas should be avoided. However, a means of reducing these problems when working on tracing paper line drawings is to apply the tone to the back of the sheet.

Cross-hatching can be applied freehand or against a straight-edge. However, the latter technique can produce the 'wooden' appearance of insensitively ruled, cross-hatched drawings that is associated with the uncreative hack! But when used skilfully, cross-hatching can produce dazzling paraline drawings and perspectives, as in the work of Peter Cook and Paul Rudolph. Indeed, the freehand version gives access to a wide vocabulary of marks, including clusters of lines, dots and stipples — the endless tone-making potential of which acts as highly personal hallmarks of the drawing style of many contemporary architects.

DIAGONAL PENCIL SHADING

1. Try producing a single layer of tone using diagonal strokes with an HB grade pencil. The 45 degree wrist action required will feel natural – as well as a method of producing tone it is used extensively throughout architectural drawing and is quite easy to master.

2. By employing different pressures on the pencil, and clustering together slightly different lengths and directions of stroke, a whole sequence and range of tonal structure can be achieved.

3. Overworking with secondary and tertiary layers of graphite will both decrease the tone and intensify the textural effect of this shading technique.

Ink Washes

In the twenties, the pioneer Modernists' sweeping away of the *Ecole des Beaux Arts'* emphasis on rendering architectural drawings tended also to dispel the ink wash technique. However, the craft survives and today enjoys something of a comeback. The traditional method of applying a liquid tone to a pencil or ink line drawing employs diluted washes mixed by rubbing sticks of Chinese ink into a container of clean water. Diluted India ink can also be used.

Marker Tones

The advent of the marker in the sixties introduced a non-messy medium that in many ways resembles watercolour. It also provided extensive and subtle gradations of gray — the Magic Marker range includes 18 different halftones subdivided into a series of warm and cool grays — and thus makes an excellent tonal medium for all kinds of architectural drawings, especially those worked on tracing paper. However, different types of marker do dictate their own particular technique of application.

Flat Marker Washes

Markers are designed for speed, and part of their attraction is their rapid drying time. However, this makes it difficult to blend tones and to achieve subtle gradations of tone. Working quickly and boldly, controlling the marker at a constant speed and pressure, is the only way of overcoming this restriction.

Marker Tone Control

Tone is the powerhouse of any graphic, and to control its structure in a drawing depends on the harnessing of degrees of tone to the degrees of distance (either observed or implied) from the eye. Furthermore, the structure of tone in the finished drawing regulates the degree of unity and balance in the overall composition. In other words, the control of tonal contrast is the key to creating drawings with or without visual punch.

Aerosol Spray Tones

Another tonal scale is created by the dispersion of tiny droplets of pigment emitted from aerosol spray cannisters — either those especially designed for artwork, or those sold as auto paints. Three or four tones, including black, white and two degrees of gray, can be used in their own right for tonal drawings, as in the work of Mark Mack. Or they can be used as an atmospheric adjunct to hard-line drawing, as in the orthographic drawings of Derek Walker. When building up a tonal spray rendering, the principle is the same as that for the marker. Namely, work from light to dark, and use a line drawing as a guide. This systematic approach allows control over the developing tonal structure, and the insertion of the all-important dark tones.

Textured spray tones rely on an inventive attitude. For example, delightfully subtle surface patterns can be achieved by spraying a soft gray through different types of screens — made from, for example, wire mesh, extruded aluminium sheeting, open-weave fabrics and even thin layers of gravel — placed directly on the

Waterfront House in Rotherhythe, Kent (detail). Timpson Manley Dean Design Group. Mick Timpson's distinctive drawing employs four different line weights of hardline and freehand hatching, plus s spray wash created by dragging a blade over an ink-loaded toothbrush, to create a range of subtle textural effects.

CROSS HATCHING

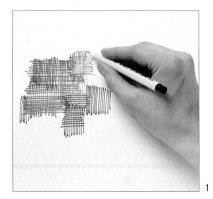  

Cross-hatching is another method of creating a whole range of tonal characters using superimposed lines.

1. Draw a series of lines in one direction and parallel to each other. Then draw another series of parallel lines at right angles over the top of the first batch.

2. To darken the tone of an area of cross-hatching, draw a further series of parallel lines diagonally over the top of the existing cross-hatching.

3. To darken the tone of the cross-hatching still further, superimpose a fourth layer of parallel lines diagonally opposite to those applied in step 2, and continue until the required depth of tone has been achieved.

*Right: Competition Layout
Plan, Business Park, Milton
Keynes. Bruce Gilbreth
Architects.*
*After being outlined in ink
on Mylar film this drawing
was rendered from behind
using coloured pencils.*

*Below: Master Plan Study
for Aztec West, Bristol.
Bruce Gilbreth Architects.*
*A photographic contact print
was made from an original
1:1250 scale outline
drawing in preparation for
a rendering sequence using
markers for trees overlaid
with coloured areas of trace-
cut Letrafilm.*

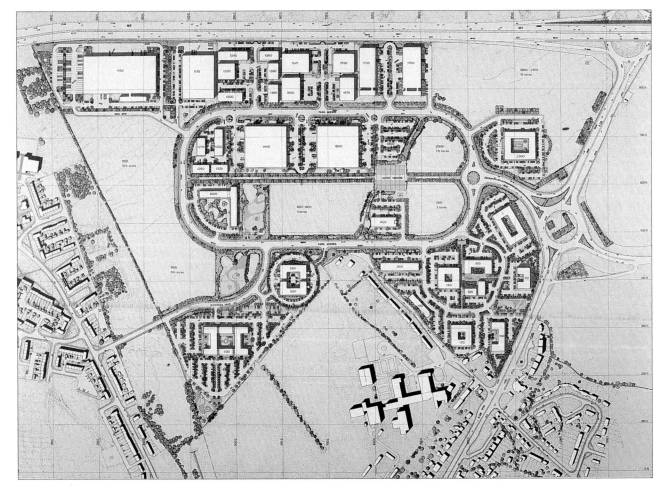

PRESSURE TRANSFER TONE

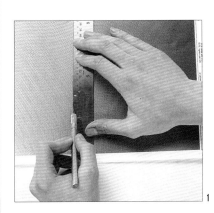

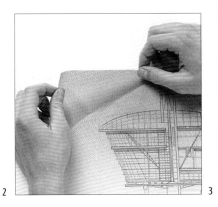

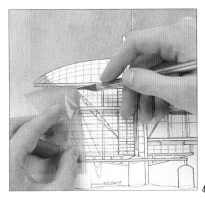

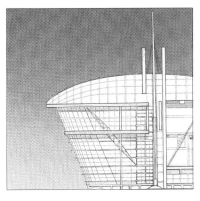

1. Using a scalpel and a metal straight edge, cut out a piece of film slightly larger than the area you wish to cover. Avoid cutting through the backing sheet.

2. Using the scalpel point, lift up one corner of the piece of cut film and carefully peel it away from the backing sheet.

3. Place the film over the surface of the artwork, carefully smoothing it out with the pad of a finger.

4. Trim away the excess film with a scalpel by carefully trace-cutting around the precise shape of the area to be toned.

5. Once the area has been toned, place a piece of paper (or a spare backing sheet) over it and, in order to achieve perfect adhesion, burnish the back of the paper with the base of a pencil, your finger or a spoon.

6. Note that since the tone is printed on the top surface of the film it is always possible, if necessary, to gently scrape away parts of it using the point of a scalpel.

drawing surface. However, aerosol spray work does demand a safety regimen: a well-ventilated room; a face mask covering mouth and nose; artwork positioned vertically, and the spray head not too close to the paper or deposits of pigment may run, sag and curtain.

Pressure Transfer Tones

Although expensive, sheets of pressure transfer tones are often introduced into architectural drawings in order to supply a range of both even and graduated screens of tiny dots bring a professional-looking and print-like touch to plan and section diagrams — especially those drafted for dyeline reproduction. When used exclusively in elevations and perspectives, tonal screens can project a sterile, mechanical appearance — one that is usually associated with the worst form of commercial art. However, when used freely to introduce contrasting areas of well-defined tone to otherwise loosely worked drawings, or when mixed with other mediums, as in a collage, the screens can bring an extra dimension to architectural graphics. Perhaps the best example of mixed-media tones is to be found in the lively, diagrammatic graphics of Hardy, Holzman and Pfeiffer, whose drawings are clinical but creative abstract representations of the spatial character of their design proposals.

Rather than purchasing ranges of sheets carrying different tones, begin by using one or two sheets; and produce darker sequences by overlaying one upon another. Pressure transfer pattern sheets are also available and can be applied in the same fashion as the tones, or placed on the artwork for directly transferring the pattern as you draw. When the sheet is lifted clear, the transfer is complete and ready for burnishing.

Finally, as tone is one of the three dimensions of colour, gaining experience of its graphic potential for creating visual interest and enhancing the spatial illusions of solidity and depth in architectural drawings makes a good introduction to working with colour mediums.

The Colour Makers

Although we are privileged with the faculty of colour vision, a traditional view of architectural design sees the creation of built form as a colourless science. Indeed, one popular misconception is that of a Modernist architecture conceived in black and white and expressed in gray concrete. However, despite his undeserved reputation as a creator of achromatic buildings, one of the great Modern Movement architects, Le Corbusier, used colour extensively in his architecture. Furthermore, when describing its value in his design process he once wrote: 'With colour you accentuate, you classify, you disentangle. With black you get stuck in the mud and you are lost. Always say to yourself: "Drawings must be easy to read." Colour will come to your rescue.'

Faced with a bewildering array of attractively packaged and spectrally arranged colour mediums, the beginner often finds it difficult, especially with a limited budget, to know what to buy. However, a good strategy is to purchase colour mediums either individually, or in basic sets when possible, and also to always buy the best. This strategy, rather than encouraging an indiscriminate use of colour, will allow the user to gradually build on a colour-mixing experience.

For example, my own introduction to colour mediums began with one week's experimentation using a palette comprising black, white and yellow gouache. Although extremely limited, this restriction forced me to push the admixture of these three colours to the limit. Also, as I stretched the palette by intermixing, I soon discovered that I could achieve a kind of green from mixing black and yellow. Once the potential of this palette was exhausted, I then added a blue and, later, a red, which provided the foundation for mixing an extensive range of colours. Beyond this, further ready-mixed colours were only added when demanded by a particular colour composition. A further advantage of a restricted palette is that successful architectural colour presentations are usually structured around a simple scheme based on one or two thematic hues.

A good way of discovering how an attractive colour scheme works is to carry out a simple analysis. This is done by counting the number of hues present, and assessing their incidence and area within a drawing. Even a cursory analysis will show that harmonic colour structures usually result from a juxtaposed arrangement of a family, or group, of related colours — such as blues, blue-greens, and greens.

Visual 'spice' can be introduced into a scheme by adding proportionally smaller areas of colour taken from another group of hues, such as reds, oranges or yellow. However, as complementary colours placed in close proximity will enhance, or heighten, each other's qualities, and therefore provide a visual stimulation that attracts the eye, they should only be inserted at points of compositional interest and importance. John Constable

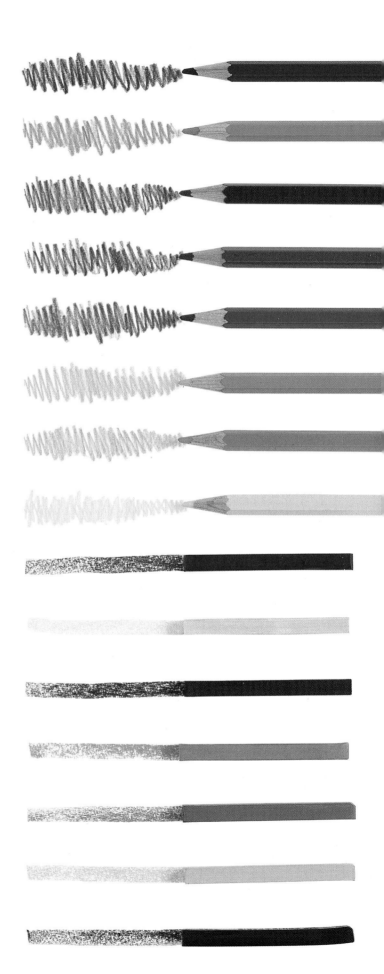

A selection of coloured pencils and pastels.

APPLYING A COLOURED PENCIL WASH

1. To colour mix with coloured pencils, begin by laying down a light, soft and smooth layer of colour. The base layer should be applied with strokes that all follow a single direction.

2. A second colour can now be applied directly over the first one. A lightness of touch during application will allow the lower colour to ghost through, and be filtered by, the one on top. Of course, this 'combination' of colours can be further modified by the application of more layers.

used to employ this technique, by adding a stab of vermilion into his fields of green and blue.

Although the basic principles of structuring colour remains constant, mediums do vary in their techniques of application and admixture. In this respect colour mediums fall into two basic categories: those that are applied in a liquid state; and those that introduced to the drawing surface in a dry state.

Coloured Pencils

Coloured pencils are made from a mixture of chemical pigment and kaolin. They are extremely popular for colouring-up architectural drawings because they represent an instantly accessible colour medium that is comparatively easy to use, and they provide a wide range of potential colour quality in graphite and ink-line drawings — from rich and full-blooded applications, to quieter and subtler colour graduations. They are also sensitive to, and work well on, a variety of papers, including white and yellow tracing paper and cartridge paper; and they are particularly suitable for colouring up dyeline and photocopied prints. Buying the best coloured pencils means selecting 'Artist' rather than 'Student' quality. Also, as some ranges are too hard, the pencils should be soft enough to obtain a gentle tonal graduation when held at a shallow angle to the paper, and yet hard enough to produce a crisp line, without snapping, when held almost perpendicular to the paper.

'Prismacolor' has become the generic term for coloured pencils in the USA, and the ranges made by Berol and Eagle represent the most widely used and softer varieties. Although also popular is the slightly harder range from Rexel Derwent.

The marks made by coloured pencils are permanent and, usually, can only be scraped away with a blade. However, a small range produced by Venus Col-erase can be removed with an eraser. Perhaps the most useful quality of coloured pencils is that they enable lines of one hue to be drawn over washes of another — although you should not combine too many in one drawing.

It is best to begin with a basic range; which might include three primary colours, an alternative green and a few neutrals. And when rendering, aim to follow a sequence of gradually building up colour tones by working the drawing with several layers of colour. When brought under control, this process permits subtle hue changes across the surface of the drawing. Also, you should remember to apply varying pressures to the pencil, as a light fist can imply a sensitivity to the atmospheric effect of distance on coloured forms, whilst a heavier fist can highlight particular areas, or bring foreground forms into sharp focus.

Coloured pencils can also be found playing supporting roles in drawings that employ mixed mediums. For instance, they can be used to sharpen the focus of foreground areas in watercolour washes and, as we shall see later on, play an important role in conjunction with markers.

Pastels

Made from powdered pigment bound with gum arabic or resin, and formed into square-section sticks, pastels represent a delicate, if not tricky, colour medium. Being a relatively crude medium, with colours being built up from open webbed layers, pastels are technically at their best when not overworked. Indeed, their charm lies in the delicacy of touch they require — which dictates a drawing style that focuses upon essentials whilst discarding unnecessary detail. For this reason, pastels are rarely seen in more formal architectural graphics, but they are sometimes used for sketch designing, and rapid sketching on the custom-tinted and textured papers. However, I have seen pastels used to good effect in night-time elevations worked over dark-coloured supports. This technique was prevalent in the 1930s, when cinema design elevations, outlined in graphite on black paper, employed a finger-rubbed pastel dust to simulate the aura of a coloured, ink-lined neon lighting.

Dry Transfer Colour

When large areas of flat colour are required in a drawing, architects will sometimes use self-adhesive, dry-ink colour sheets, or acetate colour-film overlay. The most common is the overlay film, as its transparency retains the integrity of the line drawing. Colour film is often used in orthographics and perspectives as a fast means of delicately colouring areas of sky, water, glazing or greenery. Apart from its occasional use in interior drawings, to show the precise colours of a scheme, another major use of film is the abstract colour-coding of diagrams. The two types of self-adhesive sheet colour are applied in different ways: overlay colour film is attached in the same fashion as pressure-transfer tone (see page 37); whilst the opaque dry-ink version (also available in transparent form) is burnished directly from the sheet.

Possibly the best-known range of dry transfer colour is that made by Pantone, which totals 743 hue variations in various types of finish. Essentially designed as a selector system for colour-matching and communicating precise colours between graphic designer and printer, the enormous range allows the architect to specify exact colours, and introduce atmosphere into three dimensional representations. Pantone also extends into a range of over 200 colour co-ordinated markers which are marketed with broad, fine and ultra-fine tips.

Coloured Papers

As an architectural graphic can often be assembled from many different colour mediums, the potential of coloured papers as elements in a collage should not be ignored. Extensive ranges of both subtle and vivid colours can be useful in presentations. And the various paper types include sugar, craft and art, together with the gloss, gum-backed 'Butterfly' paper.

Paints

One of the main differences between the graphic works of artists and designers is their choice of colour mediums. For example, artists tend to draw on a wide range of mediums — from the opacity of oil, tempera, gouache, and the new generation of versatile acrylic/polymer paints, to the transparency of watercolour. Whereas designers — especially architects — are attracted to mediums that work best in conjunction with line. Therefore, they tend to opt for the transparency of

Left: Fruit Salts.
An unusual textural effect can be achieved by sprinkling effervescent powder, such as indigestion fruit salts, over a freshly applied wash – the fizzing action of the powder causing minute 'explosions' of texture.

watercolour and inks. Before the advent of the marker, gouache rendering was used to some extent in presentation drawings, but the raw speed of markers has almost killed off the technique. However, gouache is still indispensable for producing highlights, and putting in very fine details and lettering where opacity is essential.

The medium traditionally associated with architectural rendering is watercolour — notably in the work of students at the *Ecole des Beaux Arts*. Although challenged in turn by the airbrush and the marker, watercolour is still used in presentation work.

Watercolour
Watercolour is made from refined, water-soluble pigments, and marketed in tablet and tube form. 'Artists' quality is more refined than the 'Student' version, and for beginners the former is recommended in the pocket-sized boxes which contain up to twelve tablets. Watercolour is ideal for making subtle colour renderings over pen or pencil drawings on textured papers and boards. The colour-mixing principle is the same as when using layers of colour film — in other words it creates an effect similar to that of peering through sheets of coloured glass.

Pools of liquid watercolour are built-up using one, two, or more different dilutions — each successive layer of tinted water acting to modify and darken those below it. The technique relies upon seeing the white of the support through the layers of colour. And the resulting colour impression is gained from light being reflected back from the white surface, through the layers of wash, and into the eye of the viewer. Consequently, the technique combines a delicacy of touch with a fairly rapid application. And as a rendering can easily be

overloaded and taken to a point of no return, the secret lies, as with most activities, in knowing when to stop.

Watercolour Special Effects
Beyond the basic techniques of applying large, shaped, flat and graduated washes there are other techniques that are particularly germane to architectural drawing:

Wet-in-Wet Technique
The application of pools of diluted colour into a still-wet wash of another colour causes a subtle bleeding effect. This blurring quality can be used to effect when painting skies, water and reflections.

Drybrush Technique
The drybrush technique produces an irregular textured effect when a colour-loaded, but almost dry, brush is dragged lightly across the surface of a different coloured wash. By exploiting the surface of the paper, this technique is ideal for suggesting the rough surfaces of materials, such as concrete and brickwork.

Highlights in Wet Colour
Highlights and lines can be 'cut' into a freshly-applied wash, using a round-ended blade or the end of a brush handle. The line is formed by pushing rather than pulling the instrument, and care should be taken not to groove or cut the paper. One of the more obvious applications of this technique is the insertion of mortar joints in elevations.

Highlights in Dry Colour
Once a wash is completely dry, highlights and broken lines can be gently scratched away using the corner of a razor blade. This technique can be used to simulate the glint of light on various reflective surfaces, including glazing and building materials with a polished finish.

Being transparent the watercolour medium is extremely difficult to correct. However, during application certain modifications can take place. For example, while a passage is still wet, it is possible to soak up most of the colour using a blotter or a paper tissue. Another method of removal involves soaking a sponge in clean water and then gently working it over the paper. However, this technique of 'sponging out' will never remove all the evidence of a wash and, by creating misty effects, can function as a watercolour technique in its own right. Most colourmen claim that their paint products do not represent a health hazard, and will label warnings when chemical products are potentially harmful. However, my

GUTTING A MARKER.

A marker felt that has been extracted from its holder is a very useful tool for quickly creating lines and bands of colour, of varying widths, over the drawing surface (see Using a Gutted Marker, page 45).

1. Firmly grip the base of the marker in one hand and, using a scalpel or craft knife, cut the plastic seal around the holder just below the rim of the cap. Apply a steady pressure on the blade and take great care to ensure that it doesn't slip and cut your fingers.

2. Once the plastic seal has been cut the cap can now be twisted off, to reveal the marker felt within the holder.

3. Grip the container firmly in one hand and, using the illustration as a guide, repeatedly knock both wrists together to dislodge the felt from inside the holder.

4. Once the tip of the marker felt has protruded from the neck of the holder it is a simple matter to grip it between thumb and forefinger and pull it clear.

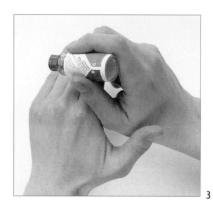

own habit of pointing a working brush in the mouth came to a sudden end when, on attending a colour technology class, I learned that Naples Yellow is derived in part from camel's urine!

Inks

Coloured drawing inks are based on brilliant dyes dissolved in a solution of shellac — which enables one colour to be superimposed easily upon another. This glazing process produces a characteristic vibrance of luminosity when dispensed with brush and airbrush. The recent formulation of brilliant watercolour inks and liquid acrylic in dropper-cap bottles, provides an even greater intensity of colour in around 40 water-soluble and transparent hues. Unlike its predecessors this type of ink can also be used in technical pens.

Brushes

Brushes for water-based pigments are manufactured in a variety of sizes (ranging from 0 to 14) and shapes (ranging from round and pointed to flat and dome shaped). Hair and bristles are taken from the squirrel, bear, pony, ox, hog and sable (although modern sable brushes are made mainly from Asiatic Kolinsky mink tail). Being the finest, sable brushes are the most expensive, but a good investment provided they are well treated. Brush maintenance involves never letting others borrow them, never leaving them point—down in water, and always rinsing them thoroughly after use. A suggested range of sable brushes

for beginners would include numbers 00, 2 and 4, and a size 12 for applying large areas of wash or loading airbrush tanks. Another useful brush is the round- and flat-ended stencil brush, which can be used for stippling beyond the stencil. However, before purchasing a high quality brush, it is the buyer's prerogative to check if it forms a point. To do so, simply ask if you can test the brush in water, or moisten its tip on the lips before shaping. If the point splits, reject it.

Colour Markers

The comparatively recent history of the colour marker in environmental design circles seems linked directly to that of architectural style. First used in a throw-away manner in the sixties as a rapid medium for schematically colouring diagrams and sketch designs, it took a decade of experimentation in other design disciplines to prove its worth. Meanwhile, interior and product designers had developed a refined marker technique which was not to go unnoticed. By the eighties a renewed interest in more variegated and colourful buildings had emerged, which caused architects for the first time to take this medium seriously and to use it in prestigious drawings. Generally, markers dispense two types of ink: permanent spirit-based ink, and water-soluble ink. Marker tips vary from the wide- and soft-felt tips, available in round, square, oblique and chisel shapes, through the conical, semi-soft bullet tips, and on to the fine-line and ultra-fine-line tips of the composition, nylon and fibre-tipped markers. From amid the bewildering range of manufactured sets, comprising palettes of a hundred or more colours, the Magic Marker emerges as the one that gave its name to this medium and is now almost generic. Despite its stubby, unergonomic shape it still has many advantages over its thinner rivals — except that it is now marketed in a long, 'slimgrip'-bodied form. Markers provide a transparent medium that, in many ways, resembles watercolour. In order to describe form, ranges of tone have to be established. However, as markers are neither mixed like paint, nor produce varying intensities of colour as a result of varied pressure on their tips, a different technique must be employed.

One method of application follows a 'painting by numbers' system, in which each individual marker plays its own colour role in a composition. This approach accounts for the extensive marker ranges in which different tints and shades of one colour are provided. They are applied in the same way as pastels — in other words laying down patches of colour one alongside another. An alternative method of application is to lay down a colour, and then modify it with a second wash of the same or another colour. Being similar to watercolouring, this process extends the range of tones and colours of a few markers, and accounts for the limited palettes used by many designers. However, the number of colour layers does depend upon the type of marker, and also the type of paper. For example, being absorbent, layout paper will take several layers of colour, while the non-absorbent bleed-proof papers quickly become saturated and will accept only two or three applications.

Textured Colour Washes

These custom-coated marker papers can be exploited by applying washes to both the front and the back of the sheet. Washes applied to the back give a textured effect in a muted colour. Textured washes can also be created on the front of the sheet by the addition of a light sprinkling of lighter fuel over the newly applied wash.

A typical marker drawing begins with a line drawing in pencil, technical pen or razor point marker. Areas of colour are then established, employing a co-ordinated scale of colour strength in order to fix the foreground, middleground and background (and using graded washes to indicate varying degrees of illumination on larger surfaces). To complete the illusion of three-dimensional modelling, shades and shadows are finally intensified with darker colours.

Faced with such a vast spectrum of marker ink colours, trial palettes are invariably tried on a scrap of paper. This is done to test the effect of individual colours, and to predict their colour impression when combined in washes. Such experimentation will lead to a greater awareness of colour, colour saturation (colour strength), and tonal value (degree of lightness) in colour drawing.

It is particularly important to develop an ability to modify colour strength, because this is the dimension of colour that promotes the illusion of depth and space. Therefore, each main hue within a palette should be accompanied by several markers whose inks will provide a desaturation (weakening) of colour as it is applied into the background of the drawing. There are several variations of this technique, one of which is the colour modification of marker washes using a range of light-coloured pencils.

Markers and Coloured Pencils

Having already mentioned that more restricted palettes of colour have the greatest impact, it is interesting to note that some architects will use as few as just three or four markers. These are employed to provide an almost neutral range of colours to describe building materials. On top of this, the colours of five or six coloured pencils are then applied, in order to elaborate the colour and tonal structure of the image. Pattern and textural effects are achieved by stippling, directional hatching and cross-hatching in response to the light source.

Airbrushes

Students often believe that an airbrush is the answer to their rendering problems and rush out and buy one, only to discover that it isn't. It is an expensive item, so make sure that you really need it and look for one which suits your needs. Stick to double-action brushes (down for air, back for paint) with a reasonable cup size. You will also need an air source, which will be either an air compressor or cans of air propellant. But ultimately your final choice will depend on how much you use an airbrush and how much you want to spend. In fact, if you are really interested in airbrushing, it is worth buying a book devoted exclusively to the subject and borrowing an airbrush to experiment with.

Spraymarker

The recent development of the spraymarker represents a new medium that bridges the gap between the marker and the airbrush. The Letrajet spraymarker is assembled by inserting a fine-line or ultra-fine Pantone marker into the custom holder, and attaching the hose to a source of compressed air. The resulting jet of air blown across the marker tip works in the same way as a traditional diffuser spray, whilst achieving pretty good airbrush effects. The system obviates the need for purchasing inks or paints and the mixing of colours is eliminated. This newfound ability to create instant airbrush effects, and to switch quickly between marker and spray, makes a welcome addition to the architect's array of mediums.

Another development is the electrostatic Spraypen, which produces a high quality fine spray that would be hard to match even with an airbrush. But because each ink particle is electrostatically charged it is attracted to the substrate, and the spray is deflected by items with an opposite electrostatic charge, such as plastic rulers, acetates, etc., which can lead to unpredictable results. Obviously experimentation will be necessary in the early days of this revolutionary product, but its potential for the architect-renderer is obvious: no external air source; compatability with marker colours; easy colour change-over with no cleaning; long battery life, and so on. Ultimately, it could displace the airbrush.

USING AN AIR MARKER

If you purchase an air marker it should come with fairly comprehensive instructions supplied by the manufacturer. However, the basic procedure is as follows:
1. Insert your chosen Letraset fine or ultra-fine tipped marker into the housing of the air-marker.

2. Attach the air hose either to a compressor or to an aerosol canister of compressed air. It is particularly important to strictly follow the manufacturer's instructions printed on the side of the latter — especially with regard to the safe disposal of empty or nearly empty canisters.

3. Having assembled the air-marker, simply depress the lever with your finger to blow colour from the jet onto the artwork. Learn how to control the direction and flow of the marker by practising on spare paper. The system illustrated above is designed to work at an air pressure of 60 psi (4.2kg/cm^2.)

USING A GUTTED MARKER.

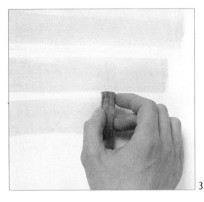

1. Having extracted the marker felt from its pen holder, grip it between thumb and forefinger and use the rim, or edge, of the tip to create a fine line on the drawing surface. Slight variations can be made in the width of the line by adjusting both the angle at which the edge of the felt meets the surface and the pressure on the tip.

2. Again by gripping the marker felt between thumb and forefinger, its round tip can be dragged flat across the drawing surface to create a broad strip of solid colour. Unlike the fine line described in step 1 above, the width of this strip can not be varied by changing the angle of, or the pressure on, the tip.

3. By gripping the sides of the marker felt between thumb, forefinger and index finger, it can be dragged back and forth across the drawing surface to create a wide band of colour. By continually re-charging the felt from the ink well of a Magic Marker quite large areas of colour can be filled in relatively quickly.

Basic Drafting

Beyond the more fluid, freehand phase of the design sequence — when an evolving concept needs to be dimensionally defined — comes the technical drawing phase. However, this stage is often synonymous with a wooden or sterile rendition, induced by an apparent formality that is associated with the use of drafting equipment. Therefore, the need to practise with the basic instruments becomes particularly important. Also, there is the need to approach technical drafting as an art form — that is, drawing that is capable of both dimensional accuracy and creative expression.

Pencil Lines

To begin the drafting experience start with a clean sheet of drawing paper on the board and with drawing instruments near to hand. Then, engage the T-square stock to the ebony edge of the board and slide the blade gently to the upper portion of the format. Using a sharp HB grade pencil, draw a line completely across the paper. Make this line consistent by retaining the same angle of address while gliding its point at a steady speed. The line should begin and end positively, and be executed crisply and evenly along its length. The main aim of this simple exercise is to develop a personal drafting touch — namely, one that avoids digging the pencil point into the paper, whilst ensuring the delineation is neither too faint nor tentative.

Meanwhile, this operation also involves the use of the free hand which ensures that the T-square stock is firmly secured to the edge of the drawing board.

Practise this drawing action by ruling a series of lines, each below the last. Once a crisp line has been achieved continue drawing lines, but this time rotate the pencil back and forth between forefinger and thumb along the entire length of the line. The slight backwards and forwards rotation aids the retention of a sharp pencil point whilst introducing a degree of tension to the line. **Linear tension** is an important ingredient in pencil drafting. It results from a line appearing 'stretched' between the two positive points of its beginning and end — an 'elastic' quality that can be found in the work of master draughtsmen and a major characteristic of delineation that separates their drawings from those of the insensitive hack.

The drafting experience should now be extended to some vertical and angled lines drawn with the aid of the set square. During this stage, sit the set-square on the blade of the T-square and use the free hand to lock the two into the required position. This use of the non-drawing hand to clamp drawing aids in position will feel strange at first but will soon seem quite natural.

Pen Lines

As the majority of architectural drawings are drafted in ink, it is also important to gain basic experience with the technical pen. After fitting the stylo, and making sure that the cartridge is filled with ink, begin with a small ritual intended to encourage the ink to flow. Either gently shake the barrel at a 45° angle, or stroke the drawing tip on a damp cloth. Either way, the flow of ink should always be checked on a scrap of paper before placing the

stylo on the drawing paper. Crisp and straight ink lines will result from assuming and maintaining a drawing angle of 80° to the horizontal — with the stylo held against the straight edges of T-squares and set squares. This drawing angle also helps to avoid irregular line widths and the danger of scratching the paper.

After drafting a series of lines, try 'planting' further lines directly over those pencil lines already established on the paper. This is important because just as freehand sketching is a two-stage process so technical drawing also begins with the initial lines of construction that guide the final drawing. However, unlike a sketch, a technical drawing to be finished in ink will begin with a preparatory pencil drawing worked as completely and with as much care as if it were the finished image.

Basic Construction

Beyond the fundamental experience of drafting lines is the need to become familiar with the actions and functions of other drawing aids, such as dividers and compasses. A start can be made with the construction of basic geometric figures. However, as more equipment comes into play, the need to establish a pattern of displacement around the drawing board becomes crucial. It is the learned dexterity in the handling, retrieval, interchanging and maintaining of drawing equipment that smooths the path for a speedy drafting operation. When drafting simple geometric figures, remember to mentally separate those marks made for construction purposes and those marks that will ultimately appear in the completed figure. This selective process of drafting construction lines will help to determine which lines and arcs — and which parts of lines and arcs — should be lightly drawn (and later discarded), and which lines will be required in the definitive drawing. In this way, any subsequent need for rubbing away redundant construction lines — together with the chance of damaging the drawing surface — will be obviated.

As almost all architectural drawings are drawn to a scale that is much smaller than the actual dimensions they represent, technical drafting demands a high degree of accuracy. Furthermore, the smaller the scale employed, the greater the degree of accuracy required. Many factors can contribute to degrees of error. These include the human element, and even inconsistent thickness of line. However, a major cause can be focusing on the accuracy of a part, rather than concentrating on the accuracy of the whole. In other words, it is more important that a drawing be consistently accurate to an approximation than that the parts be minutely accurate. However, the latter approach can become quite serious when small margins of error are multiplied by successive repetition. Consequently, a golden rule when drafting is never to accumulate dimensions as a means of plotting a length. Rather always enlist the principles of subdividing long lengths rather than employing a repetition of constituent short lengths. Other rules of thumb include: avoid touching the drawing paper; maintain immaculately clean drawing equipment and, when drafting, always make a clear connection between intersecting lines.

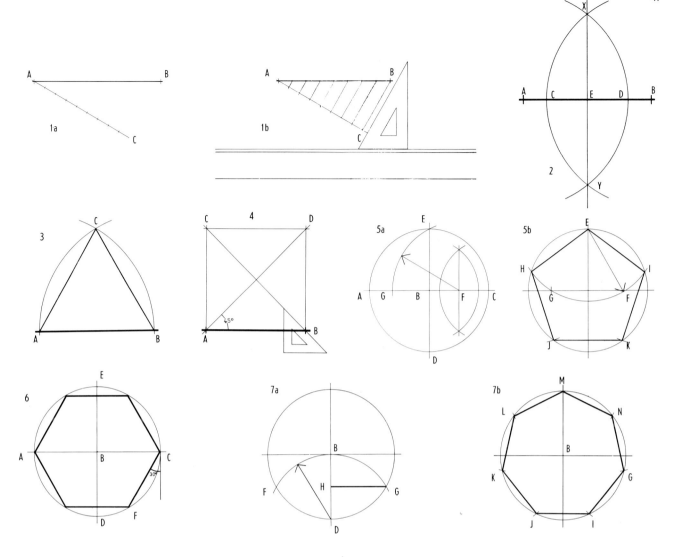

BASIC DRAFTING

To help you become proficient with the various drawing instruments, practice constructing the basic geometric figures shown below.

1. **Subdividing a Line: a.** To divide A-B into equal parts, draw A-C out from A at any angle between 10° and 90°. With a scale, mark-off equal divisions along A-C. **b.** Use a set-square on a T-square positioned below C and parallel to A-B to transfer, by a series of parallel lines, the points of subdivision on A-C to A-B.

2. **Bisecting a Line with a Compass:** To bisect A-B, draw an arc with A as its centre to bisect A-B at D. Now repeat with B as the centre, to bisect A-B at C. Then draw a line to bisect X and Y and bisect A-B at E.

3. **Constructing an equalateral triangle:** Draw A-B to required length. Set compass to length of A-B and draw arc with A as centre to bisect B. Repeat, with B as centre to bisect A. Arcs bisect each other at C. Finally, connect A-C and B-C to complete the triangle.

4. **Constructing the Square:** Using a set-square on a T-square below and parallel to A-B, project diagonals inwards at 45° from A and B respectively. Using a set-square, project lines at 90° out from A and B to cut the diagonals at C and D. Connect C-D to complete the square.

5. **Constructing a Pentagon: a.** Using a compass, draw a circle with B as its centre. Construct the diameter A-C to bisect B, using a straight edge. Then construct a second diameter D-E to bisect B at 90° to A-C. Bisect the radius B-C at F, using a compass and the method outlined for figure 2 above. Again using a compass, strike an arc with F as its centre through E, to bisect A-B at G. **b.** With E as its centre, strike an arc through G and F to bisect the circumference of the circle at H and I. Using a straight edge, connect H-E and E-I to form two sides of the pentagon. Set a compass to the length of H-E, then strike an arc with H as its centre to bisect the circumference at J, and connect H-J. Repeat this procedure to form J-K and, finally, K-I to form the 5 sides of the pentagon.

6. **Constructing the Hexagon:** Following the same procedure as for figure 5, construct a circle with B as its centre and project 2 diagonals through B at 90° to each other that bisect the circumference at A, C, D and E. Using a set-square positioned parallel to D-E and resting on a T-square that is below and parallel to A-C, project a line along the third side of the set-square at 60° out from C and the vertical of the set-square until it bisects the circumference at F. Then connect C-F, and repeat the procedure from F and so on around the circle until the hexagon is completed.

7. **Constructing the Septagon: a.** Construct a circle and two diameters that bisect each other at 90°, using the same method as outlined for figure 5. Strike an arc with D as its centre to bisect B and the circumference at F and G. Using a set-square project a line at 90° out from the radius B-D at H to bisect the circumference at G, and measure B-G. **b.** Set a compass or pair of dividers to the length of B-G and, starting at G, bisect the circumference at I, J, K, L, M and N in turn. Finally, connect up the points to form the Septagon.

Freehand Sketching

The distinction between a 'sketch' and a 'drawing' seems to stem from the speed and attitude of execution. The ability to draw quickly is a skill that most architects have to acquire because, with so much design time spent in the act of drawing, the need to rapidly communicate ideas — often against pressing deadlines — becomes paramount. This accounts for the incidence of one-day 'sketch design', or *esquise* projects in design schools, and it also explains the existence of a sketchbook experience behind the graphic skills of all the great architects.

Freehand sketching has a long architectural tradition stretching back to the Middle Ages, when wandering designers would make drawings of building details for future reference. More recently, designers such as Charles Rennie Mackintosh, Louis Kahn and Le Corbusier have also carried sketchpads on their European travels, and recorded the buildings that were to have such a profound influence on their later work. In this sense, a collection of sketches functions as a personal file of things and places seen and visited. Although almost replaced today by the instant photograph, the act of sketching is still one of the most valuable experiences for the designer, as it exercises a co-ordination between thinking, looking and drawing.

Using the Brain

Sketching is an extension of thinking because it often challenges our understanding of what we think things look like. In this way we learn about the spatial behaviour of forms in space. However, quite often the way we look at things can be over-ridden by the manner in which the mind's eye sees the world. For example, a common occurrence in beginners' sketches is the depiction of objects from higher viewpoints than that taken by the eye. In such drawings rooftops can be 'seen' graphically when, in reality, they are hidden from view. Therefore, sketching becomes a learning process through which we study what is before our eyes rather than a response to a stereotyped mental picture. In other words, the more we sketch, the more we develop a 'seeing eye' as well as a 'thinking eye'. From the outset try to avoid the hackneyed still-life set-piece, and choose instead subjects that are of real interest. Aim to draw objects *and* spaces, and select them for their richness of shape, variation in tonal range and variegation of texture. In this way, we engage a higher commitment from the brain. Also, when confronted by difficult and complicated forms, use the brain to visualize simplified 'boxes' into which the form may fit. The preliminary ghosting of a boxed framework makes the form much easier to draw.

Using the Eyes

Sketching also involves a kind of slow-motion looking process, in which the drawing point follows the line of the eye as it moves around the subject. However, as a sketch will not record every tiny detail that the eye sees — its lines reflecting only a synthesis of what is seen — the resultant drawing will appear as a reduced and selective extraction of what is viewed. Therefore, use the eyes to decide what is important, and then focus the sketch on these aspects. This should entail some time spent scrutinizing the subject before proceeding. Set a deadline for each sketch, to avoid labouring the work. And try to keep your eyes trained on the subject rather than watching the progress of the drawing. With experience the hand will gradually learn to respond quickly and sensitively to the roving eye.

Using the Hands

Artists described as possessing a 'good fist' receive praise from admirers of their drawings. Drawings that convey a delicacy of touch are often described as emanating from a 'light hand'. Conversely, 'heavy-handed' drawings display a boldness seen as lacking in finesse. These references to the drawing hand describe qualities of line that are, in part, a response to different degrees of pressure on the drawing surface. However, apart from regulating pressure as it steers the drawing tip around the paper, the hand can also function as an invaluable sketching aid. For instance, by using both hands with thumbs touching to form a right-angle with index fingers at 90°, an adjustable 'finger-frame' is formed. If this frame is held out and moved about in the line of sight, a view selected for sketching can be initially scanned to find the best possible composition. This is a convenient technique much-used by photographers and film directors to explore and isolate the potential of a cropped image, prior to shooting. The thumb and index finger can function as an accurate gauge during sketching to measure the dimensions of objects and spaces in the field of view. This method, however, relies upon the sketch being re-scaled on the pad at the size at which the subject is seen in the eye. Although some people sketch outside this scale, drawing at the perceived size is easier, more convenient and a natural way of transferring seeing into drawing.

To measure the height or width of an object, thumb and index finger are cupped and held out into the line of sight while squinting through one eye. Thumb and finger tips are then used as a gauge to register the sight-sized dimension before transferring it directly to the drawing surface for marking. This technique of checking and double-checking dimensions can also be used throughout the sketching sequence for measuring the spaces between objects. Moreover, difficult angles can be judged by ringing them inside a circle made by an 'okay' sign formed by the thumb and index finger. When viewed and imagined as a clock-face, the exact 'time' of angle inclinations can be estimated before their transfer into the sketch. While sketching, try different ways of handling the drawing instrument. For example, experience the crispness of lines drawn with a sharp pencil held vertically, and compare them with the broader, more diffuse lines produced when the pencil is held at a sloping angle of address. Try making lines while rotating the wrist from side to side, or rotating the pencil in the fingers. Above all, exploit the effects of applying pressure at important points in the line, and of withdrawing pressure at less-critical moments.

view from Lake Palace Hotel
Udaipur India.

Using the Drawing Instrument

The softer pencils are generally good for sketching, but this is by no means a golden rule because it is often effective to mix different grades of graphite in a single drawing. The first priority is to maintain their sharpness. This is particularly important for the softer grades — from 2B upwards — and for the thick charcoal and carbon pencils. Sketching with markers can produce magic results, especially when a fine-line fibre tip is used for outlines and tonally elaborated with two shades of gray. Some designers hang on to near-exhausted black markers expressly for the purpose of adding faded half-tones in rapid drawings. Although a little dusty, charcoal twigs and sticks of Conté crayon are ideal for lightning sketches. Both mediums respond quickly to the lightest of touches; application of their broadsides giving sweeping blocks of grainy tone. Alternatively, tone can be finger-printed as an adjunct to lines drawn with their tips. Already attuned to the rhythmical demands of handwriting, a fountain pen is also a responsive line-maker. Unlike the technical pen tip, fountain pen nibs

View from Lake Palace Hotel, Udaipur, India. Colin Stansfield Smith. An accomplished watercolour sketched in under thirty minutes on acid-free paper.

open and close in response to finger-pressure and produce lines that vary in weight and width along their run. When colour sketching with pencils, pastels or paints, work with a restricted palette comprising three or four basic hues. Working within this restriction, and having to mix colours, will help you to gain valuable experience. Finally, apart from being used to remove highlights, the eraser has no role in sketching. It is better to leave incorrect lines in place and to draw correct lines alongside them. This is a drawing technique that, when necessary, employs successive lines to 'carve-out' the definitive contour. However, as beginners will often strive for perfection in early sketches, they may consider that this process of 'linear refinement' makes drawings appear 'unfinished'. This is a mistake: the quick sketch is only intended to capture the essential essence and form of what the architect has just seen.

Experimenting with Mediums

The incorporation of several different mediums and graphic techniques in a single architectural drawing is not uncommon. Therefore, time spent away from the drawing board to experiment with the potential effects of unusual mediums, or of unconventional techniques using the traditional mediums, can lead to some surprising and stimulating results.

When studying at Liverpool College of Art in the sixties, I and my student colleagues were introduced to a project in which we had to assume that world stocks of artist's pigments had been depleted and that, for a week, our artwork would have to employ improvised mediums. The ensuing experiments led to some very unusual palettes which included, amongst others, the stains of mustard, coffee, ketchup and baked beans.

It was during this project that I stumbled upon the marvellously subtle colour effects that occur when household bleach is introduced into raw washes of permanent black fountain ink; effects that became even more subtle when the ink was subject to increasing

Above right: Show polishes, applied by tissue, provide an earthy colour palette for ink-line drawings.
Below: Seaside Pier. Ink and Bleach. Andrée Porter. 'Etched' effects were introduced into a fountain pen ink wash using dilutions of household bleach.

dilutions of the bleach. Another student, Stuart Sutcliffe (who, before his untimely death, went on to become a founder-member of the Beatles), exploited the marvels of a new-found palette of shoe polish. When tissue-applied to ink line drawings on cartridge paper, the polish acted as a transparent glaze, creating earthy and harmonic ranges of black, brown and tan. This short excursion into unconventional mediums (reminiscent of

Roland Searle's use of crushed plants, berries and blood to tint his drawings, during a World War Two internment) opened the door to a treasure-house of unusual and exciting graphic 'special effects'. And such an experiment is still valid today for evironmental design students, as a wide range of techniques can, with a little innovation, be incorporated to good effect in architectural renderings.

Applicators

The trial use of unconventional applicators can provide a refreshing, if slightly unpredictable alternative to the traditional drawing instruments. For instance, lines made using the side of an ink-loaded strip of card, or the marks resulting from dragging it sideways across the drawing surface, can be adapted for special effects. Also, the spidery lines of ink-primed matchsticks, twigs and sharpened bamboo or quill, together with the printed textures of sponge, wood end-grain and crushed paper could be examined for future use. And the stippling of stencil brushes and the splattering of ink, either flicked from a brush with a snap of the wrist, or 'sprayed' by scraping a blade over the ink-primed bristles of an old toothbrush, can produce explosive textured results.

Surfaces

Drawing surfaces can be modified to alter the impact of an applied medium. For example, a traditional water-colour technique involves scarring thicker papers with a scalpel, to create a serrated wash in which the floating particles of pigment become trapped in the incisions, and read as darker lines. Another technique involves the preliminary application of water — either in a pool or as a flat wash — into which raw pigment is allowed to bleed. Thicker papers can also be scored with a blunted point held against a straight-edge, before being rubbed over with soft graphite; which reveals the grooves as white, negative lines. This is very effective in pencil-rendered plans and elevations for simulating the lines of a floorscape, and for the junctions of building materials in roof and wall planes (see page 65).

Another special effect can be achieved by ruling a stack of tight, horizontal ink lines, through which a diagonal scratching made by the corner of a sharp blade will create the impression of light glinting on a reflective surface. An alternative version is obtained by using soft graphite on smooth paper which, after being finger-smudged into a thin film, receives the slash of apparent highlights from the corner of an eraser.

Yet another variation involves pastel dust — scraped from the side of a Conté crayon — being spread out as a liquid wash, with the aid of a little lighter fuel on a wad of cotton wool. This technique, after receiving highlights picked out by an eraser, has obvious uses in the rendition of reflective facades. Thinner papers can be overlayed on surfaces displaying small-scale and varie-gated textures (such as fine grade sandpaper, and the obverse of linoleum and hardboard), for a subsequent graphite rubbing which 'lifts' their impression (see page 131). It takes only a little imagination to appreciate the value of these marks for simulating building materials in plans and elevations.

Using white spirit as a solvent, these figures were pressure transferred from a colour magazine directly onto a presentation elevation drawing.

Resists and Solvents

Further textural effects can result from the application of coloured wax onto a water-based pigment which, on contact, separates into a multicoloured wash. Unusual effects also result from mixing inks with different resist agents, such as white spirit, mineral spirits and masking and pen cleaning fluid.

Solvents such as turpentine, mineral spirits, nail polish remover (acetone), or silk screen cleaning fluid, can be used to pressure-transfer blocks of colour selected from large magazine photographs printed on non-glossy papers. The technique relies upon matching the appropriate solvent to the print and, after coating the photograph, burnishing its back with a pencil to release its ink. This method can be extended to the transfer of trees and people directly into line drawings destined for a coloured pencil rendering (see page 79). However, the ultimate integration of transfer and rendering requires that the direction of the burnishing and the strokes of the subsequent rendering be synchronized. Whether made by accident or intent, every graphic mark should be viewed with a wit that visualizes its promise in the pictorial depiction of architecture. For instance, the stripes resulting from overlapping bands of marker ink (an embarrassment to some designers) finds a convincing role in the simulation of elevational brick-work and cladding. It is through this ability to recognize potential adaptation, and through a trial and error experimentation with the various mediums and tech-niques, that budding designers learn to push themselves to their limits; and in so doing, extend their individual graphic abilities.

2
ORTHOGRAPHIC
PROJECTION

In objective drawing and sketching we draw what the eye sees. However, in order to communicate the images
'seen' in the mind's eye, a mode of technical drawing has evolved to provide a fragmented but comprehensive
and related sequence of aerial, side and frontal views. Known as orthographic projection, this drawing system
(together with others) is employed throughout the design sequence — from conception to construction.

The primary architectural drawings are the plan, the section and the elevation, and each plays a specific role in design and communication, as well as following basic principles of arrangement and display on the drawing board — a process that is called orthographic projection, because each drawing type presents a right-angled view of the different surfaces that make up a building design.

First Angle Projection

The easiest way of visualizing orthographic projection is to imagine an object (which represents the design idea) as being suspended within a transparent box. The

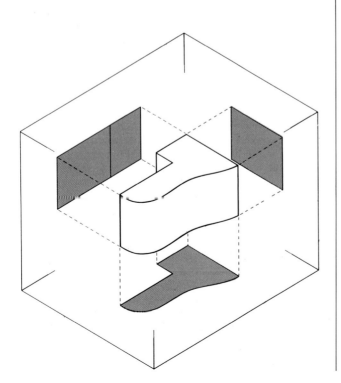

significant faces of this object are projected along straight parallel lines to reappear as though shadows of themselves on the inside planes of the box which are immediately behind them. When the planes of the box are 'flattened' out a separate view is provided of each of the object's vertical faces, or 'elevations', and horizontal faces, or 'plans' — the number of views projected corresponding to the complexity of information that will be required to fully explain/describe the object. The unfolded series of projections give a complete, scaled and dimensionally co-ordinated picture of the object; the inner lining of the box now representing the drawing surface.

This particular system of documenting and arranging a layout of drawings places the elevations above the plan, and is known as First Angle projection. It is the traditional system first devised by Gaspard Monge in 1746. And a method for literally unfolding true-to-scale elevations from a related plan can be found in many architects' drawings from around that period. The principle works for rooms, squares and atriums, and can still be found in use today. Of course the great advantage of this flattened drawing configuration is that the directly linked planes of a design can be drafted and viewed simultaneously.

Third Angle Projection

An alternative version of orthographic projection involves projecting the faces of the object through the planes of the transparent box, to appear on its outside. When the planes of this configuration are flattened, the arrangement of views — this time with the plan located

First Angle Projection is a way of graphically representing the precise form of an object. When opened out flat, the inner sides of the 'glass box' present the projected planes of the object in an arrangement which places the horizontal profile (plan) below the side and end profiles (elevations).

above the elevations — is a layout known as Third Angle projection. First adopted by American designers, this is the system most commonly used internationally in design.

Each view in orthographic projection is represented by a drawing 'type'. The view from above is known as the plan, and the views from the front and side are known as elevations and end elevations respectively. When we slice through the object in the vertical plane, we produce a section. Each drawing type also represents a different vantage point, specific viewing condition and design function.

Building plans can present aerial views of an architectural form complete with its roof. However, when used in the form of a horizontal slice, 'ground plans' and 'floor plans' are revealed that describe both the dimensional arrangement and the pattern of contained and surrounding space.

Building sections work in exactly the same way as floor plans, except that they function as selective cross-cuts made vertically through the solid and void of an

'Unfolded' wall plan for the Salon at Kimberley Park, Norfolk. John Sanderson, 1761. The basic principles of first angle projection are demonstrated in this pen and wash scale drawing in which a cubic interior space is simply flattened out to provide a simultaneous view of related planes – an orthographic layout technique popular with Neo-Palladian architects of the eighteenth century.

architectural idea in order to reveal the pattern of its internal workings.

Building elevations result from the same viewpoint as sections, but they describe the form as intact and complete. Regardless of the depth of their position in an elevation all visible planes appear on the same scale, and function to assess the all-round massing and silhouette of a designed form.

In supplying different aspects of information about a three-dimensional idea, the orthographic drawings must be viewed in a related way. When we use orthographics we take our mind's eye on a journey around the design. In this sense, they function as an abstract method of representing a future reality.

Scale

Because of the sheer size of building designs, orthographic drawings are always reduced in scale — using dimensions that are chosen by the designer to act as an appropriate fractional version of their equivalent full size. A set of orthographical views comprising plans, sections and elevations is usually drafted to the same scale so that their collective information can easily be cross-referenced, and a complete graphic picture of the building design assembled.

Selecting a scale for a drawing is the means of regulating both the size and the amount of detail that is required to describe the nature of the design. In other words, when choosing a scale, the designer is regulating the amount of distance between the mind's eye and the complexity of an idea. Therefore, the bigger the building concept, the smaller its size on the drawing board, and the further away it is from the designer's mind's eye. For example, small buildings, such as a house, may be drawn orthographically to a scale of 1:50, or even at the smaller scale of 1:100, but the increased scale of 1:20 will allow more detail to be revealed. Whereas increasingly larger buildings, and groups of buildings, have to be shrunk along the decreasing scales of 1:200 and 1:500. Thus, in regulating scale, we not only adjust the graphic distance

of an idea, but we also control its size in relation to a drawing board layout.

Architectural ideas are transferred into a scaled existence using the scale rule. This carries marks that represent the different scales — employing calibrations reduced in a consistent proportion. For example, a reduction of 1:50 is indicated by markings which, together with others, are etched at the ends of the rule. Along the edge of the rule calibrations will indicate 0, 2, 4, 6 and so on. These represent millimetres which, along the scale of 1:50, are each equal to 50 millimetres of real size. Although the scale of a design idea will tend to increase somewhat between the onset of designing to its conclusion in presentation drawings, this Gulliverian view of an evolving built form can place considerable distance between designer and idea. Indeed, the need to design and present in detail must necessitate a further fragmentation of designs into larger-scale study drawings. If they were not enlarged, the designer might never predict precisely nor realize the implications of the object's future existence. Moreover, the articulation of designs at the larger scales allows them to 'breathe', and brings about a confrontation in which the 'touch' and the 'smell' of a building's potential existence might be sensed. At the definitive drawing stage it is important to annotate orthographics with a clear indication of scale. This is commonly shown numerically, but can be illustrated using a graphic version of the scale rule.

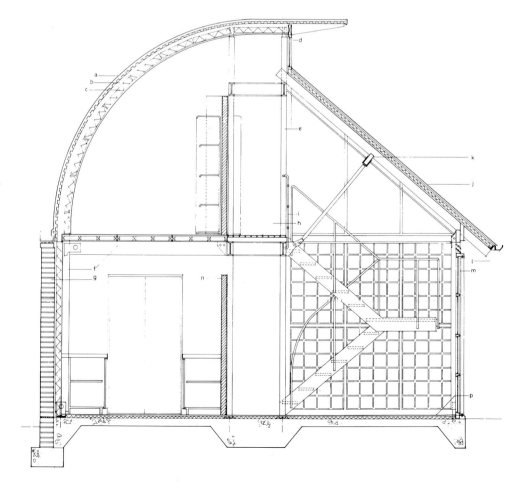

Isometric of the courtyard house. John Pardey. The basic difference between working drawings and presentation drawings is that the latter are primarily concerned with the appearance of a building, while the former, such as this 1:20 scale detail section, focus on the construction and assembly of the building fabric.

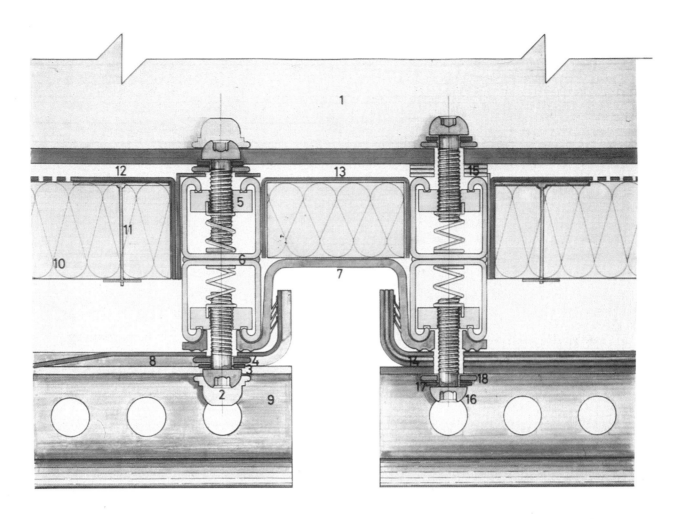

Working drawing. Nicholas Grimshaw and Partners.
An unusually colourful production drawing showing
working details from the cladding system used in Nicholas
Grimshaw's design for the Herman Miller Distribution Centre,
Chippenham, Wiltshire.

Insertion of this information is especially useful when drawings are to be resized at a later date.

Working Drawings and Presentation Drawings

At the end of the design process two quite different and distinct drawing types are produced in order to communicate a design intention: 'working drawings' and 'presentation drawings'. As the two are often confused it is important that the basic difference between their respective functions is understood.

Working drawings (also known as 'production drawings') demonstrate how a building is constructed, and comprise a vocabulary of dimensional precision through which the architect conveys a detailed and final proposal to the builder or contractor. A full set of working drawings will include complete and detailed graphics that co-ordinate component, assembly and locational drawings that, when appropriate to the complexity of construction being detailed, will involve a variety of scales. For example, larger scale drawings will be produced where the exact positioning and connection of relatively small components, such as bricks and tiles, is a vital part of the information to be conveyed.

Working drawings are rarely colour rendered. Rather, they remain in line, to communicate a total picture of the form, placement, structure and construction of a building design.

Presentation drawings (often referred to as 'design drawings') are produced to address those — such as the client or a group of clients — concerned with the ultimate experience of a design proposal. In contrast to working drawings, which focus exclusively on the orthographic slice through the building fabric in order to detail materials and connection methods, the presentation drawing deals with the space between and surrounding the slice. They are drawings that, primarily, make graphic predictions of the visual and spatial impact of a building. And as such they afford the opportunity of investigating more fully the spatial qualities of surface, light, volume and colour.

In conveying these impressions, many architects approach presentation graphics as 'selling' drawings — that is, as persuasive vehicles for the marketing of design ideas. Presentation drawings also have a promotional role, and often they will be drafted expressly for publication in the international design journals. Media exposure of this kind is considered extremely important as it brings the work of the designer into the architectural debate and, as in the case of several architects, such as Richard Eisenman, can bring an instant recognition.

Orthographic Conventions

The architectural plan is, in essence, an analytical drawing that functions as a mechanism for describing the pattern of spatial enclosure. Being concerned with clarity and detail, the plan enlists a conventional vocabulary of codes and symbols that combine to convey the nature of all its working parts.

Vocabulary and symbols

The building plan represents a scaled horizontal slice drafted to depict what would result from cutting through a structure at a particular point above the ground plane. The slice is usually cut through the solid and void of a design idea at around 1.5 metres (5ft) above floor level (average eye level). This is done, primarily, in order to expose all major openings, such as doors and windows. However, the height of the slice can be adjusted to provide the most informative section. Meanwhile, planes and objects seen below the level of the cut will, if important to the plan, also be shown.

As the plan describes what remains after the removal of that which exists above the level of the slice, a vocabulary of signs and symbols is brought into play to increase its power of spatial definition. One aspect of this vocabulary occurs along the sectional cut. For instance, doors are never left closed but, for reasons of clarity, shown open at 90° to the wall complete with the line of the arc of their swing. Also, the outline of sills is shown at window openings, as is, when scale allows, the sectioned window frame and its sheet of glass. Symbols exist for all types of door, including those that revolve, fold or slide, together with others that specifically denote lifts, ducts and columns. Staircases are delineated as they would appear from above. Those that start from below the level of the cut remain visible until they become hidden by the edge of openings in the floor plane through which they might pass as they descend to lower levels. Staircases that ascend past the level of the cut are broken off at that point; their severed ends being signified by a special section line. The use of an arrow on stairs and ramps always denotes an upward direction. This simple indicator avoids any confusion that might stem, say, from the abbreviation 'up', which could be misread for 'dn' if seen from the back of an inverted tracing paper drawing.

Another important dimension of the plan vocabulary is the symbolic use of broken lines. They are employed when part of an object or plane needs to be shown, but is hidden or partially hidden from view. When the hidden area occurs below the line of the cut, its shape is ghosted with a dashed line; whilst above the cut, overhead ceiling or structural features are given a phantom presence using dotted lines. This vocabulary of depth, using dots on the near side of the cut and dashes on the far side, permits the communication of sophisticated spatial information and can help untangle the most complicated of drawings. It is also applicable to the horizontal view of interior space as represented by the section.

Fixed furniture and fittings are always included in the plan, especially those connected to water and waste services. These are described from an aerial view, using a minimal, representative outline. Ready-cut stencils are

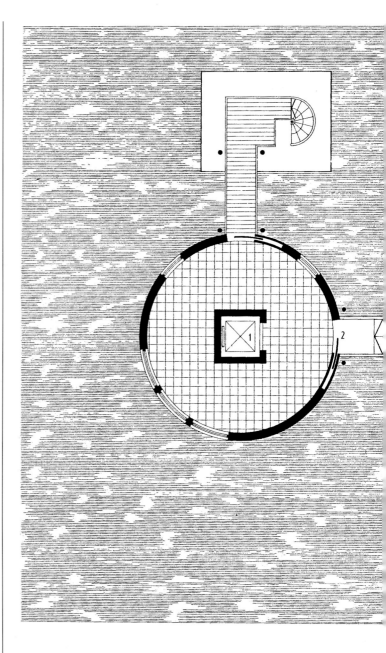

widely available and used for their rapid installation, but most architects tend to devise and stick to their own symbolic versions.

Loose furniture can also be included in plans and shown clearly with a minimum of fuss. This is considered 'good practice' by many designers, as the positioning of seating, tables, beds and cupboards, etc., is, in itself, a design exercise that tests the viability of the spaces that they will occupy. Fixed floor finishes and the outlines of loose floor coverings can also be included; and areas of paving and lawn can be shown outside the confines of the plan. Again, these are indicated simply and seen from an aerial view.

Meanwhile, trees are either shown in the outline of their foliage, or sliced to expose trunk and branches. However, within the outline of foliage a convention of time uses a dot to symbolize the trunks of existing trees,

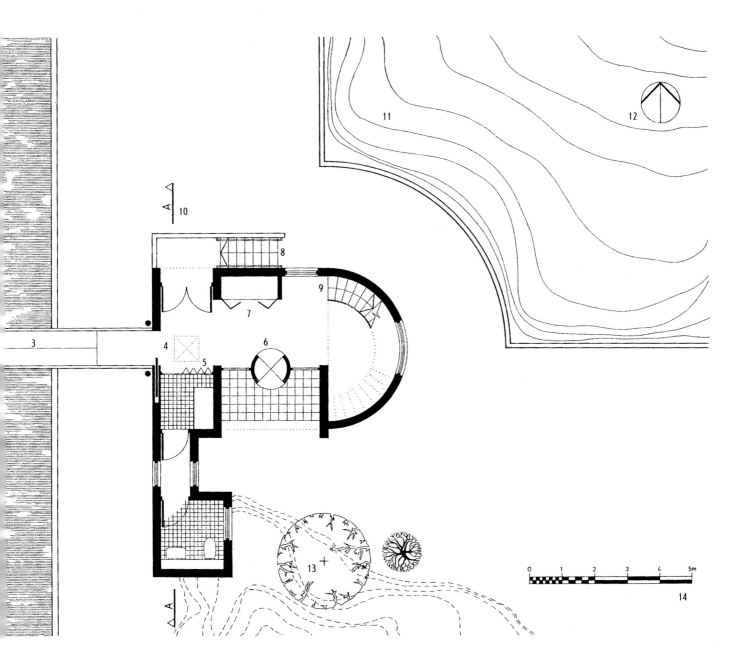

while new or proposed trees are symbolized with a cross. The outline of foliage of trees to be removed is shown as a broken line. Similarly, site boundaries are demarcated using bold broken lines, while existing contours, if shown, enlist a continuous line. On the other hand, the lines of any proposed contours are broken and dashed.

The conventional vocabulary of the plan would not be complete without an indication of its scale and, particularly, the addition of its northpoint. Traditional northpoints comprise an encircled arrowhead positioned prominently alongside the plan drawing and aimed at the north pole. They are included in order to orientate the viewer in relation to geographical features and to the orbit of the sun.

Another arrowed convention might be seen in plans if they are to be read in conjunction with an accompanying

Key to Conventions:
1. Lift. 2. Recess sliding, or pocket door. 3. Ramp.
4. Skylight. 5. Folding, or accordian doors. 6. Revolving door. 7. Bifold doors. 8. Stairs 'up'. 9. Stairs 'up' (above the horizontal section). 10. Symbol showing position of cut, direction of view and annotation of attendant section drawing.
11. Existing contours. 12. Northpoint. 13. Proposed tree above proposed contours. 14. Scale.

section. When this occurs it exists as a fine or broken line drawn across the face of the plan, in order to indicate the precise trajectory of the line of the cut represented in the attendant section drawing. Arrows positioned at each end of this line and outside the perimeter of the plan are connected at right-angles and point in the direction of the view.

3
THE PLAN AND THE SECTION

The addition of tone, texture or colour to a line-drafted plan or section usually signals a transition from the abstraction of a diagram towards a more pictorial rendition. The nature of this transition can be determined by several factors, such as whether the designer intends the drawings to reach a wider audience that includes those uninitiated in technical drawing; and whether he or she was, for example, to explore the design concept as an object seen against its setting, inhabited by people, bathed in sunlight, or examined in terms of the colours of its building materials.

There are several types of plan and section, each drawn to a scale that serves a particular function. For example, plan types include the smaller scale location plan, which pinpoints a site within a neighbourhood or regional context. An increase in scale finds the site plan which, when it includes the design proposal, illustrates its relationship to the immediate setting. Site plans commonly function as an aerial view in which the proposed architectural form is portrayed against the impact of surrounding and existing natural and man-made forms, together with evidence of a physical topology using the convention of contours. In this kind of plan the building design is usually shown as complete — i.e., as a roof plan. However, in drawings where scale is increased to bring us closer to the design, the building is sliced horizontally to expose its interior cells and, if the scale allows, rendered to show details of finishes, furniture, and fittings.

The site section provides a panoramic view of the building location — the breadth of which is regulated by the chosen scale of the drawing. Drawn to a smaller scale, and representing a horizontal view of the site topology, site sections may or may not include evidence of the proposed building. However, when they do so, they provide a useful design tool for examining the working relationship between the building's vertical mass and that of existing forms which occur along the trajectory of its slice. There are two basic ways of drawing site sections: one simply records the silhouette of forms along the route of the cut; the other slices forms

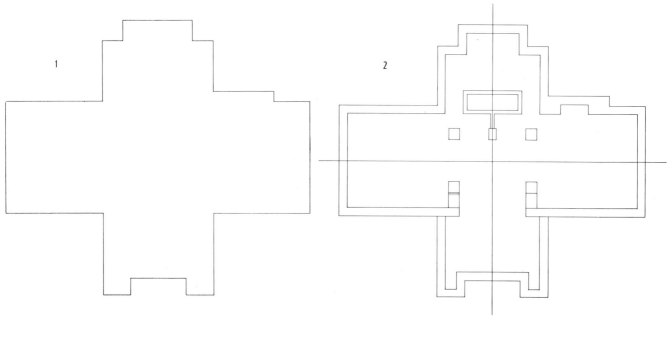

1

2

along the route of the cut, but also includes elevations of existing forms that occur behind the slice. Larger scale building sections focus on the interior cells of the architectural proposal in direct relationship to surrounding space. The scale of these sections often allows the designer to incorporate details which might appear on the rear, visible wall plane. When this interior wall plane is elaborated, these drawings are referred to as 'sectional-elevations'.

Drafting the plan

Definitive floor plans are usually transposed onto the drawing board by reference to the last in the sequence of schematic and sketch drawings produced during the design phase. At this point the design idea is converted into a dimensionally accurate and scaled representation of the former sketch. For building designs the size of a normal house a scale of 1:50 or 1:100 is most usually employed, and they are drafted with the aid of the T-square, set square, dividers or compasses and a scale rule.

Drafting the Section

By introducing verticality to the horizontal view provided by the plan, the section is constructed from known heights and to the same scale as that employed for the attendant plan. However, although the plan assumes a standardized height for its horizontal slice above the floor plane, the location and direction of the vertical cutting plane in sections is a matter left to the discretion of the designer. Therefore, whether the section is a cross-section (i.e., a cut across the width of a building), or a longitudinal section (i.e., a cut along the length of the building), the designer must plot a cutting plane that will represent an optimum exposure of the design.

The best sectional cut is one that exposes major

DRAFTING THE FLOOR PLAN

Preliminary construction of lines should always be worked in light pencil if the drawing is to be ultimately inked in – a decision that should be made at the outset.

1. After taping a sheet of drawing paper squarely on the drawing board, begin by roughing out all the general dimensions of the plan to the selected scale, so that its overall shape is well-balanced on the format. Make sure you leave room for any titles, headings and other lettering that will be later incorporated into the drawing.

2. Starting at one corner, and working systematically around the plan, block in its overall shape by transferring external dimensions into the scale of the drawing. Working from the outside in, add the thickness of internal load-bearing walls and partitions around centre lines.

3. Locate the position of the windows and doors by first plotting their centres and then establishing their widths. Add door and window symbols, together with those for staircases and any other elements exposed by the cutting edge.

4. This preliminary drawing now becomes the basis for a definitive, darker line – usualy drawn in ink – that converts the construction lines into the precision of the basic delineated plan. At this stage, an alternative method is to use the preliminary construction drawing as an underlay, on to which is taped a sheet of tracing paper. The definitive line drawing is then traced onto this and then removed, leaving the guidelines behind – allowing the latter to be used again, as or if required.

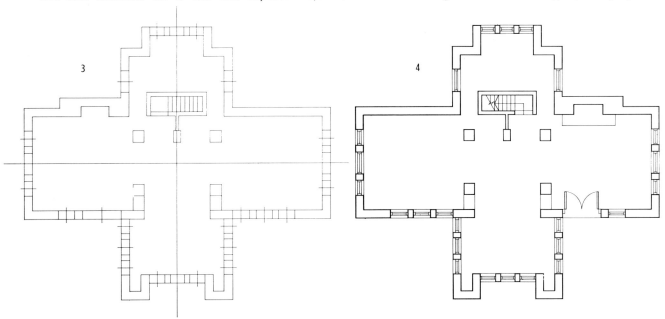

3

4

openings in walls and roof, together with floor levels and any other details important to the design of the architectural form. Also, to avoid any confusion, free-standing elements, such as columns, should never be incorporated in the slice as, when drafted, they can be misread as walls.

Line Weights

During the final delineation stage, and in order to invest both plan and section drawings with the illusion of depth, a system of graphite or ink line weights should now come into play. As part of this system the thickest, boldest line is always reserved for the nearest and most prominent element. This, of course, is the framework of the sectional cutting plane which — being drafted first — is delineated with two firm lines. These trace the inside and outside of walls, and other sliced areas of the mass, at the point where the edges of their planes meet the emptiness of contained and surrounding space. Once the skeletal framework of the plan and the section has been established, intermediate elements, such as doors and windows, that occur within the slice are drawn using a medium line weight.

In larger scale drawings the sequence of line weight is completed when features occurring on the floor plane in plans (or the rear facing wall plane in sections) are recorded using a fine line.

This simple exploitation of line thickness is a device that attempts to harness the inherent flatness of ortho-graphics to the way that we perceive space. In other words, the descending thickness of lines simulates our visual association of increasingly distant objects as appearing correspondingly less distinct.

The way plans and sections are drafted will be, in part, determined by the intended function of the drawing in presentation. For example, is the plan or section intended to act as a clinical, abstract diagram or is it meant to communicate a more literal interpretation of the design? Both 'styles' will affect differently the product of the ensuing stages. For example, the first step taken by some architects to get away from the mechanical appearance of a technically drafted plan involves the production of a freehand version of the diagram, which is made by making an ink line drawing directly on to an overlay placed on the preliminary graphite construction drawing. In this technique the apparent spontaneity of freehand lines is guided by the dimensional accuracy of the underlying drawing — the result conveying the quality of a sketch plan or section.

Rendering the Cutting Plane

When not left as a pure line drawing, the delineated thickness of sliced walls and other solid masses are, more often than not, shaded or filled-in with a dark tone or a solid black. Known as 'poché work' by American designers, this technique is applied to heighten the contrast between the diagrammatic slice and the resultant pattern of space. At the larger scales of 1:50 and 1:20, alternative treatments of the cut can be found. These include graphite shading, diagonal hatching and even spray tone.

DRAFTING THE SECTION

1. Begin by positioning and drawing the ground line – that is, the line describing the profile of the land mass on which the building stands. As with the plan, this should be established after roughly pre-determining the shape of the section in relation to the drawing format.

2. Now establish the thickness and extent of the floor slab in relation to the ground line, and measure upward in scale from this datum to find the points that will locate the line of the roof.

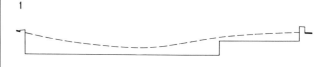

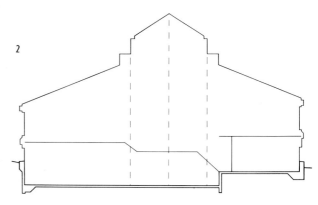

3. Working from out-to-in, establish exterior wall and partition thicknesses and, from established floor levels, plot the upper and lower extremities of windows and other exposed apertures.

4. Finally, add the thickness of the roof and any details – which if you wish can also include the end walls as seen in the sectional view.

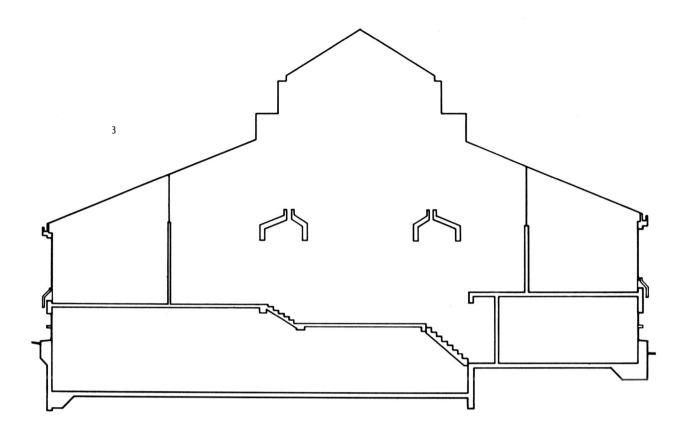

3

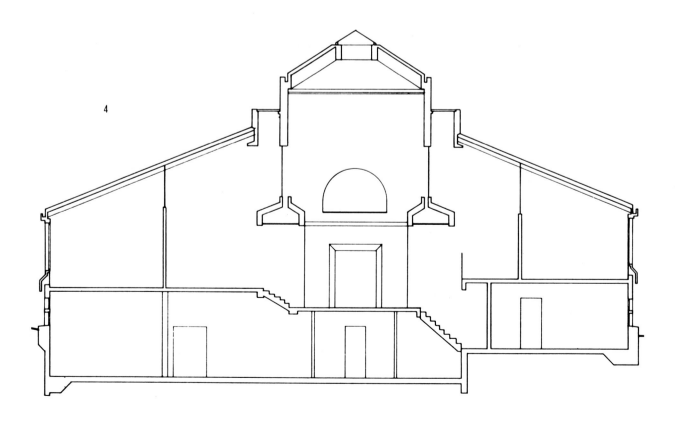

4

With regard to the treatment of the cutting slice, the basic difference between the plan and the section is the exent of tone in the latter: in sections the poche treatment can extend to the area below the profile of the ground line. This is because the ground line in sections represents a continuation of the vertical cut taken down through the earth below the building form. Therefore, this is often rendered in exactly the same manner as the wall thickness. This treatment has a twofold function: apart from emphasizing the silhouette of the immediate site topology, the rendered ground mass acts as a visual ledge on which the sectioned building is viewed.

Entourage

In order to increase the dimension of reality, plans and sections are often embellished with trees, figures, furniture and vehicles. Known as 'entourage', these ancillary elements function as props that can bring a sense of scale and animation to the diagram.

The Tree

The recurrent vertical element in plans is the tree. This is drawn in two ways: either appearing as a section which slices through the canopy to expose trunk, branches and, sometimes, foliage; or as a complete and aerial view — either with or without foliage. However, in smaller scale site and landscape plans, trees can be reduced to the simplicity of a circle or a single line which traces the edges of a whole group of trees.

When inserting trees in site sections it is a good idea to work outline drawings simply and directly from site photographs. Apart from bringing a strong sense of place, this method, in making an indirect reference to

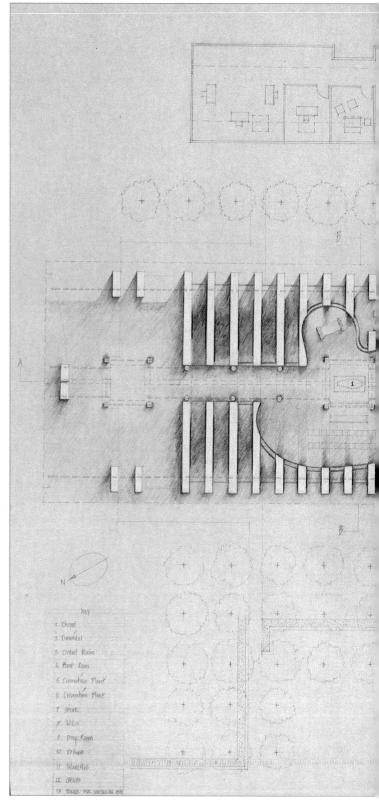

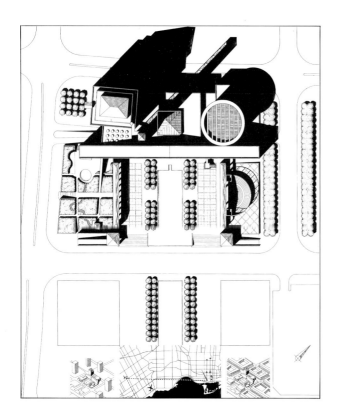

the actual appearance of trees, avoids the sterility of stereotype, and accounts for the sensitivity of their appearance in the work of many well-known architects.

Figures

Rarely seen in plans, figures tend to populate sections of all scales, but are always positioned so that their existence reinforces both the scale and function of the building design. Figures are used to interact with

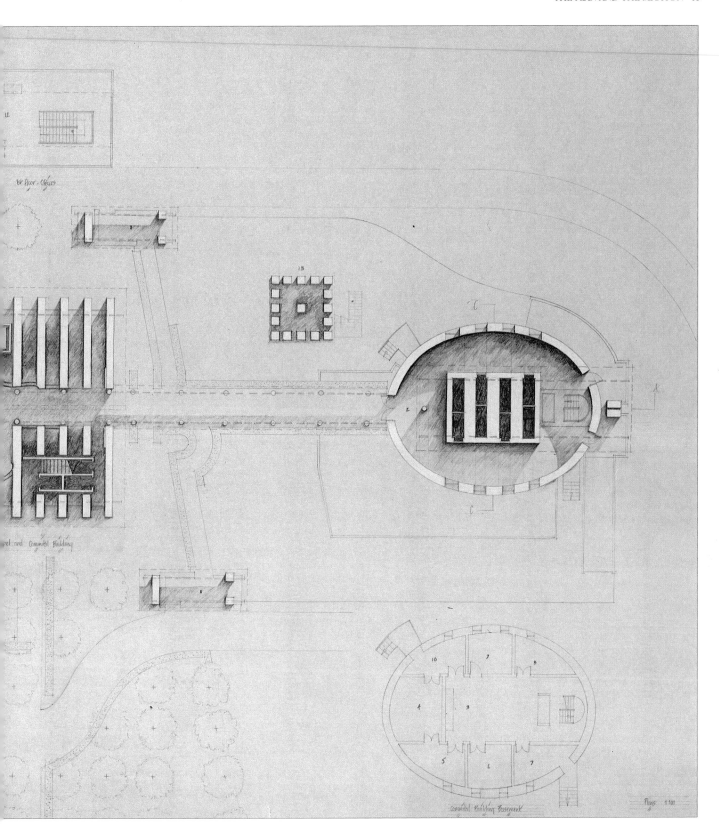

architectural space, and are often found climbing stairs, leaning over balconies, sitting, walking and standing in conversational groups. However, in animating the building, figures rarely act as focal points and remain in a simple and proportionally accurate outline. Therefore, many architects will use those taken from the scaled ranges of pressure transfer graphics, or merely develop their own personalized variations.

Opposite left: Building Plan, Mississauga City Hall, Toronto, Canada. Ed Jones. Ed Jones' roof-plan view uses the conventional direction for shadows – that is, with the sun's rays entering the drawing at 45° from the lower left corner.
***Above: Contextual Floor Plan, Crematorium in Norfolk. Simon Gill.** This award-winning graphite drawing illustrated the transformation, by shadows, of the diagrammatic nature of the plan into the apparent realism of an overhead view.*

FIRST FLOOR

SECOND FLOOR

GROUND FLOOR

ROBERT HUTSON ARCHITECTS   THE TITHE~BARN AT DUDDINGTON   THE WATSON HOUSE 1985

Additional items

Furniture and vehicles are also inserted in a simplified fashion. Again, these can be applied from the ranges provided by the custom sheets of pressure transfer graphics; or be outline delineations traced through commercial stencil templates, or exist as personalized freehand drawings.

Plans and Sections in Tone

The decision to introduce a tonal rendering into plans and sections is yet another step toward imbuing the diagram with pictorial emphasis. This usually involves the insertion of shadows to reinforce the significance of openings and apertures that occur within the envelope. As a response to a directional sunlight, shadows can also provide an invaluable clue to that dimension inherently missing from their linear delineation. For example, on the one hand shadows in plans can emphasize the illusion of mass, while indicating the extent of verticality. On the other hand, shadows in sections can reinforce the illusion of overlap and depth and bring a strong sense of atmosphere to the work.

Shadow Convention and Construction

The convention for shadows in plans sees the sun as projecting parallel rays at 45° upward from the lower left-hand corner of the drawing. However, this is a flexible rule of thumb and shadows can be projected from any convenient corner — their direction responding ultimately to which parts of the plan are required to remain in the light.

Tythe Barn Floor Plan at Duddington, Cambridgeshire.
Robert Hutson Architects. Paula Jackson used the scoring
technique (see opposite) to create the negative lines of the
mortar joints and thereby increase the sense of realism.

Sections

The convention for shadow projection in sections assumes a 45° line bearing from the top left of the drawing — i.e., over the left shoulder of the viewer. But again, depending upon how the resulting shadow pattern affects the final drawing, this direction can be switched to enter from the opposite side of the drawing.

Sciagraphy

The science of shadow projection is known as 'sciagraphy', and is a reasonably simple process of projection drawing involving the T-square and the set square. When the direction of light is established, 45° construction lines are projected from all the casting edges in the drawing, to a length that corresponds to the scaled height or width of the recesses or projecting planes from which they derive. However, the ability to construct shadows accurately depends upon a full working knowledge of the three-dimensional form of the building. Therefore, shadows in plans will often necessitate reference to both the section and the elevation, while shadows in sections will require reference to the plan and the elevation.

There are two types of shadow projection that affect plans and sections. The one associated with building plans involves projecting shadows to the height or width

THE SCORED PAPER TECHNIQUE.

1. Score thicker papers with a blunted point, such as the back edge of a knife or a stylus, pressed firmly against a straight edge. The scored lines can be used to simulate joints between floorscape modules or mortar joints in the vertical plane.

2. If you rub over the cuts/grooves with a soft pencil, they register as white, negative lines that can be put to many uses in plans and sections.

of the sectional cut. In other words, as the length of a shadow represents the corresponding length of the plane from which it is cast, shadows in floor plans are usually projected to a length of 1.5 metres (5 ft) — i.e., the conventional height of the cut. Meanwhile, the length of shadows in building sections denotes the scaled distance of the cutting plane from the plane receiving the shadow. The second version casts a shadow to the full height of the building to provide an informative silhouette of its mass. However, this is almost exclusively used in site plans where the building proposal is seen intact, complete with its roof plan.

As the projected edges of shadows are never shown

with a hard line, a good tip is to always plot their shape using a fine line. Also, always construct them on a tracing paper overlay placed on the original artwork. This avoids spoiling the original with a mass of construction lines.

Shadow mediums

Common mediums for rendering shadows include pencil shading, ink wash and pressure transfer tone — all capable of quickly creating a transparent film of tone. Of these, pencil has the advantage because, at a stroke, it can both produce transparency and simulate the direction of light.

Rendering Shadows

Shadows are best rendered as halftones, using a directional shading that coincides with the angle of sunlight. Apart from intensifying the illusion of illumination, the transparency of directional halftones also allows details of textured finishes to be indicated on the plane that receives the shadow.

However, when halftone shadows are introduced into building plans and sections, the sectional cut — especially at the larger scales — will often be left unrendered, so as to create a contrast between the white of the drawing paper and the pattern of the tonal treatment.

Shadows rendered as solid black are generally reserved for the smaller scales of site plans, where the area of their projection tends not to impede any significant information occuring on the ground plane.

Two strategies of halftone shadow rendering are widely used. *The first* seeks to suggest a hint of shadow, which is rendered — usually in graphite — in a dark-to-light tonal sequence from the casting plane. Meanwhile, the far edge of the shadow is allowed to fade away and blend in with the plane on to which it is projected. This technique requires very little construction, and merely assumes a 45° angle of sunlight streaming into rooms through external windows and doors. The result is a highly atmospheric and seductive drawing that appears — especially against the white of unrendered sectional cuts — to graphically hollow out an impression of internal space. *The second* version employs a shadow tone that progressively moves from light-to-dark from

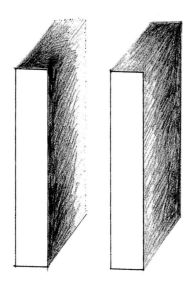

Shadow Rendering
Two methods may be used: either (left) a progressively lightening tone to emphasise the negative prominence of an unrendered sectional cut; or (right) a reversal of the tonal progression, to simulate reflected light within a shadow cast from a rendered sectional cut.

the casting plane. In recognizing the principles of reflected light, this technique requires that all the outer edges of the shadow projection be constructed to provide a crisp pattern of positive tone.

The principle of reflected light takes account of the effect caused when, in bright sunlight, a certain amount of illumination is assumed to be scattered back into shadows from adjacent right-angled planes receiving direct light. This effect is represented by rendering shadows in a graduated fashion that registers the shadow as having a slightly lighter casting edge with a darker extremity. This subtle tonal modulation can be quite stunning in larger drawings, as it functions to animate planes and creates a strong sense of three-dimensionality. It is also a technique used to good effect with pressure transfer tone by many architects who seek a greater degree of realism.

Textures

The representation of tone also raises the potential for indicating texture. An indication of surface finish in sections and, especially, in plans can be created by a simple range of technical pen or pencil techniques. For example, basic clusters of dots, line flecks, controlled scribble and hatching can produce a vast range of surface simulations. Clusters of dots, for example, are commonly used to suggest grass in site plans, but coarse aersosol spray and 'rubbings' taken directly from sheets of sandpaper (see page 131) can also be used.

However, when grass is depicted in larger scale plans the more laborious stippling and hatching techniques can be economized by concentrating their effect around the perimeter of shapes — a time-saving ploy that suggests the textural nature of the whole shape.

There is also the technique that confines a suggestion of texture to the tone of cast shadows. This is a sophisticated but nevertheless economical rendering of tone that simultaneously conveys the impression of light and surface.

Plans and Sections in Colour

The final step in the pictorialization of plans and sections is, of course, the use of colour. However, before proceeding we should consider a secondary use of colour in orthographics. That is, to its schematic use in diagramming the working parts of sections and in the zoning of spatial areas in plans. Here, colour is deployed symbolically, each hue being assigned to a meaning which is explained in an accompanying legend. Conversely, when used realistically colour is employed to explore the appearance of materials and surfaces as they might exist in the future architecture. This approach has to take account of the effect of distance: as the scale of the drawing is the means of regulating distance between viewer and graphic size so, too, the strength of colour must be also 'scaled' or muted in order to coincide with the implied distance. Failure to consider this spatial influence on colour can cause the common problem where the colour of rendered plans and sections appears 'nearer' than the drawing. The solution is to test intended palettes on a scrap of paper, and to dilute them

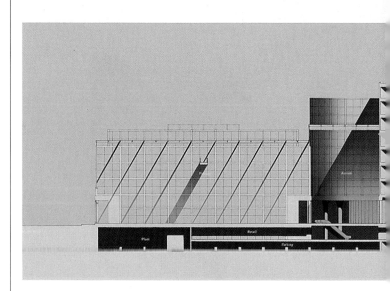

until they simulate the illusion of the intended distance. For example, as a 1:50 plan positions the viewer thirty times further away than a 1:20 version, a chromatic compensation should be made for the increased distance that the smaller scale imposes.

Degrees of Colour Rendering

Any survey of colour-rendered plans and sections reveals a series of steps in the extent of colour use.

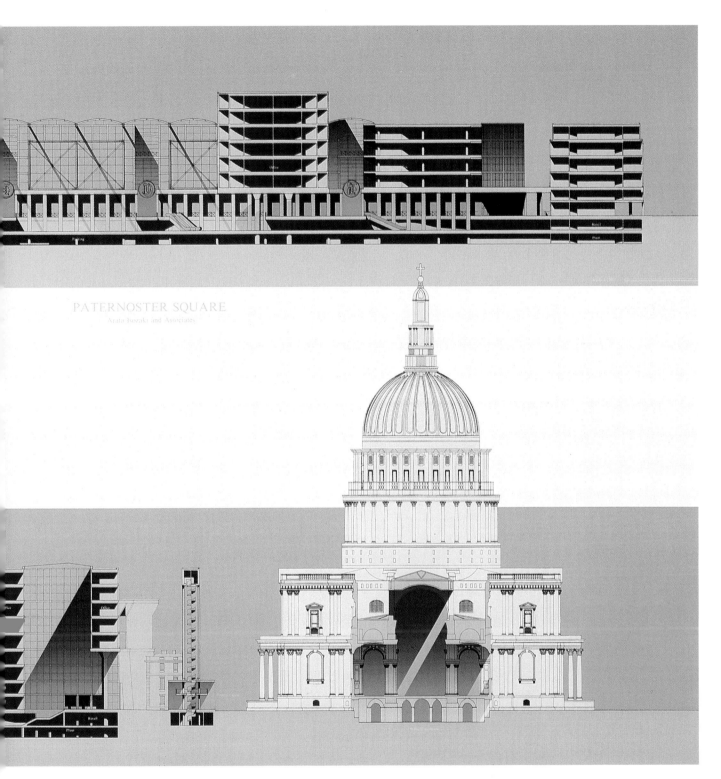

PATERNOSTER SQUARE
Arata Isozaki and Associates

Basically, colour can simply be applied exclusively to the sectional cut. Such minimal colour use can be most effective in increasing the positive-negative image of the diagram. This rendering strategy often finds a dark red, a deep blue, a neutral or a colour wash that makes reference to the building in use. An alternative use of colour sees the application washes of watercolour, coloured pencil, marker or pressure transfer colour film to the areas contained by the sectional cut. This technique

Paternoster Square Competition Section. Arato Isozaki & Associates. These two sections employ shadows to 'carve' out interior space and describe projections on visible planes. The shadows also display a graduated tone that suggests the incidence of reflected light.

draws the eye to the pattern of interior space — i.e., as a colour 'positive' against the unrendered white of the 'negative' of the cutting plane.

This figure-ground relationship is intensified when shadows are introduced. When not represented by a secondary wash of the same colour used to denote the wall or floor plane, shadows can be shown as a blue or a blue-gray when projected on to white or neutral surfaces. However, some designers use graphite shadows over colour washes, or use coloured pencils to make subtle changes of hue.

Another stage in the process of colour rendering is the colouration of the space within and surrounding the diagram of the cutting plane. This broader use of colour can be quite compelling as, by isolating the slice of the plan and the section as a negative footprint, a chromatic space appears to flow within, through and around the building design.

Realism

The more extensive uses of colour can also bring a considerable degree of realism. This results from several factors that, apart from a recognition of the basic principles of light, shade and shadow, include harnessing the textural appearance of mediums to the scale of the drawing, and operating within an organized and predetermined colour palette and structure of tone. For example, many site plans are structured by orchestrating the direction of the strokes of pointed mediums, such as coloured pencils and markers, to suggest the modelling of contours. The texture of these strokes, together with the grain of watercolour washes, will also be controlled by the texture of the paper in relation to the scale of the image. In other words, the smaller the scale of the plan or the section, the smoother the tooth of the paper and the finer the grain of the medium.

Also, when working with colour, a tonal structure is vital — colours should be organized into a scale of tonal steps to reinforce the illusion of depth. This can be simply sequenced if the sectional slice is seen to represent 'foreground' — i.e., it is nearest the viewer and either assigned the strongest colour, rendered in black or left as white.

Intermediate elements such as trees, figures, and furniture etc., are then viewed as occupying a 'middle-ground' space. When colour-rendered, such entourage should attract medium-weight colours.

Finally, the floorscape and groundspace of plans, and the visible end wall planes and surrounding site context in sections, are treated as 'background'. This application of colour-tone assumes a stage-like perception in which a progressive three-step muting of the tone of colours forms the basis for the impression of three dimensions in the graphic illusion. However, most important of all is the control of the colour range. Palettes should be restricted to essentials, and developed from an initial use of limited hues. These should then be exploited through their dimensions of lightness and darkness (tints and shades). As previously stated, colour restraint is vital if the finished rendering is not to divert the viewer from the architectural statement.

Sectional View of the Council Chamber, Mississauga City Hall, Toronto, Canada. Jones and Kirkland.
This superbly rendered section uses a range of hues, basically confined to the pinks and blues of coloured pencils. Blue-grey shadows play an important role in intensifying the illusion of both the curves of the ramps and the cylindrical chamber. Meanwhile, the abstraction of the sectional slice is emphasised by the gradual fading of shadows from the sharpness and strength of the casting edge. The rendering – which covers all parts of the drawing – is layered to emphasise the grain of the paper.

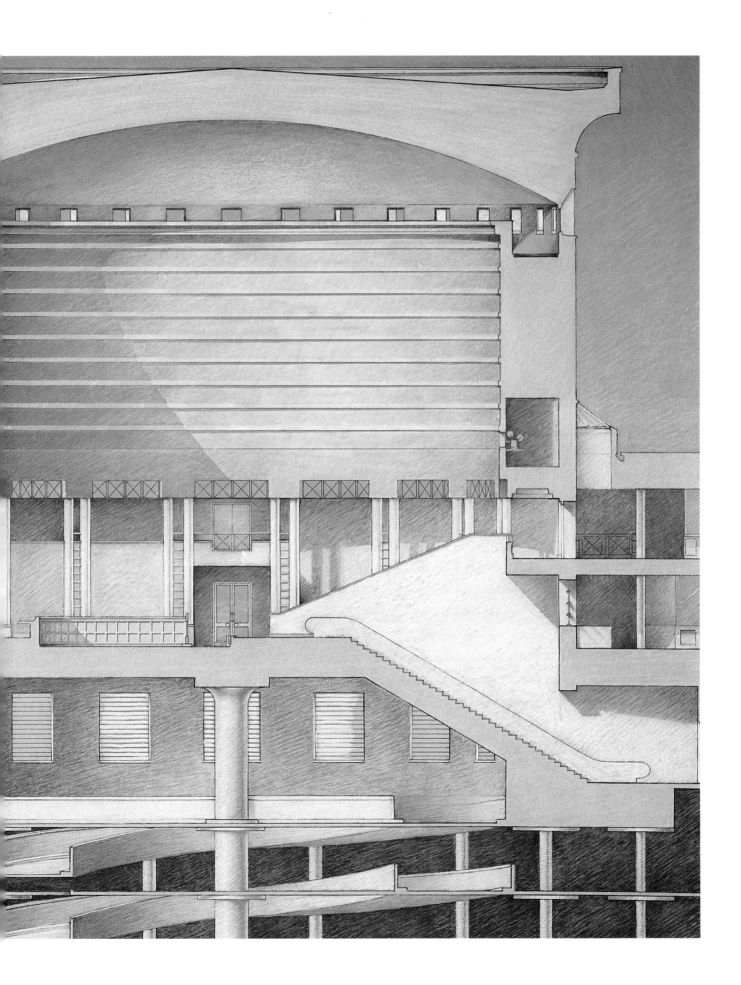

GALLERY

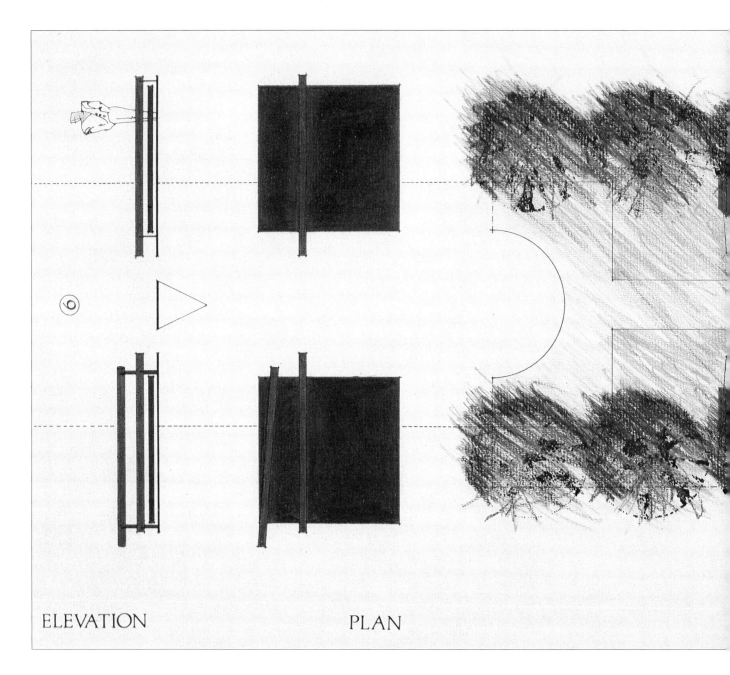

ELEVATION   PLAN

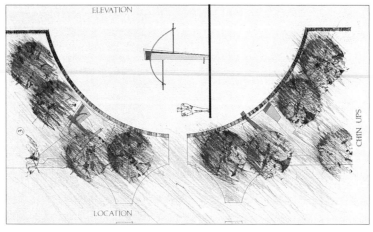

GALLERY

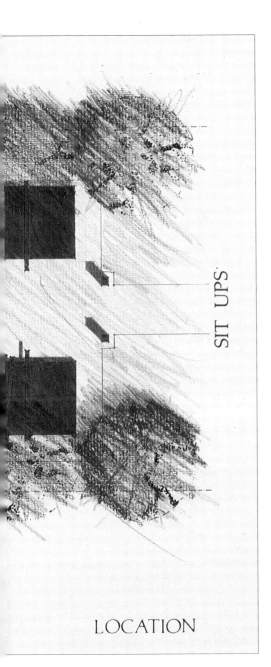

SIT UPS

LOCATION

*Below: **Contextual Floor Plan, Swindon Arts Centre. Murray Groves.** This highly elaborate student competition entry and award-winning design employs mixed mediums to produce a realistic aerial view of objects and surfaces on the floor plane, while highlighting the abstraction of the horizontal slice through the building design.*

*Left and left above: **Plan of 'Chin Ups' and 'Sit Ups' Exercise Stations, Trim Trail, Aztec West, Bristol. Bruce Gilbreth Architects.** Drawn by project architect, Iannis Zachariades these two 1:50 scale plans (with ancillary elevations) were rendered on an A3 size photocopy print made on off-white and slightly textured paper from the original drawing. Coloured pencil was applied in a left-handed diagonal application – the rapidity of strokes on areas of foliage establishing a strong contrast between the spontaneity of colour and the precision of the printed line.*

GALLERY

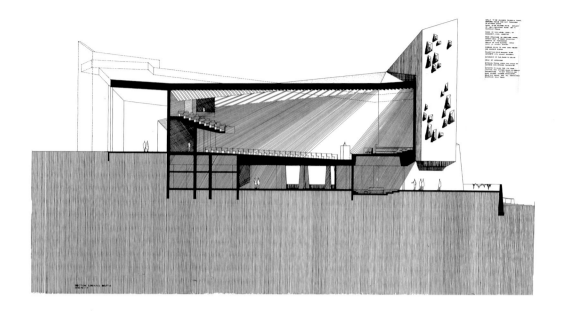

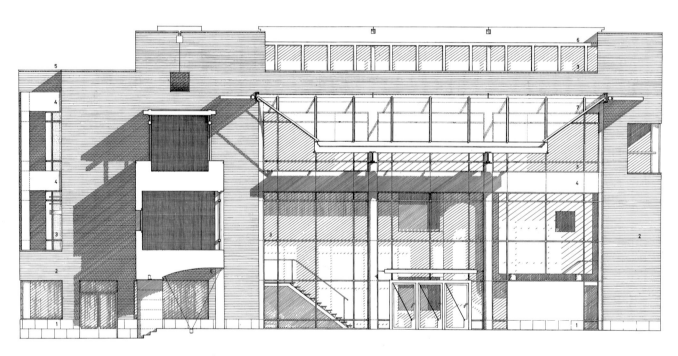

*Above top: Longitudenal Section, Chapel for Tuskegee
Institute, Alabama. Paul Rudolph. Rudolph's masterly use of
the technical pen is well known. Even in this less-elaborate
section drawing his distinctive technique is evident in the
highly effective use of hatching.*
*Above: Section, Aston University Competition. Allies and
Morrison. This prize-winning 1:50 scale section was drawn
through a gallery to show the entrance to the proposed
building – a controlled use of hardline hatching being
enlisted to illustrated the transparency of the space. The
original drawing was worked in ink on tracing paper before
being transformed into a dyeline print.*

GALLERY

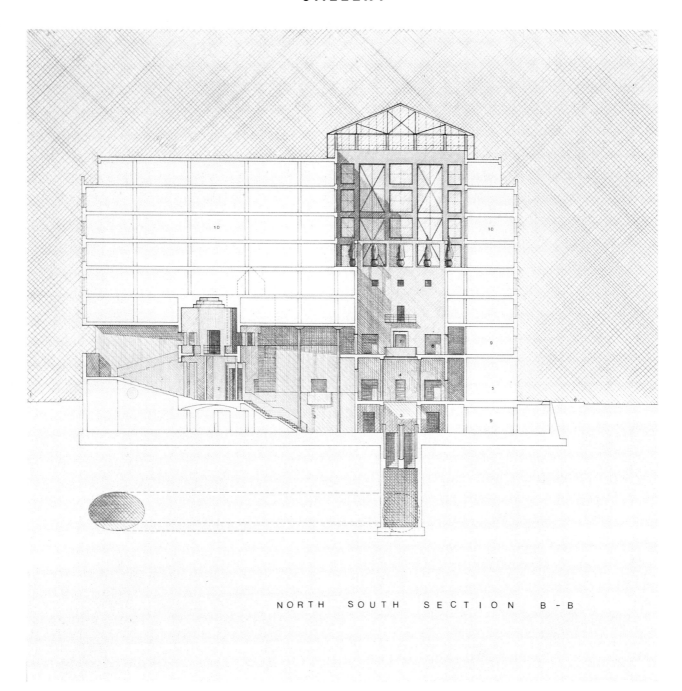

NORTH SOUTH SECTION B - B

Section, Grand Buildings Competition, Trafalgar Square, London. Rick Mather Architects. *This 1:200 scale section began as an ink line drawing before being developed using a distinctive method involving the hatched and cross-hatched lines of coloured pencils. This unusual technique is also found – albeit using coloured ink lines – in the work of Helmut Jahn. The effect relies upon the appropriate weight and combination of colour being assigned to the various solids and voids of the orthographic.*

4
THE ELEVATION

As an extension of the internal and spatial organizational aspects of the plan and the section, the elevation is the orthographic type which functions to explore the outward appearance of an architectural idea. Although, in reality, buildings are rarely seen in this format, the elevation provides a dimensionally accurate picture in which the silhouette, massing and fenestration of a design — together with its materials and context — are commonly assessed and communicated.

Just as the plan allows the position of any point to be determined in the horizontal plane, so too it becomes necessary to draw an elevation in order to determine a point in the vertical plane. Therefore, the plan and the elevation are usually drafted to the same scale so that a three-dimensional concept of a form can be easily cross-referenced. Elevations are combined with the plan to provide external views — which are usually drawn from the four compass points to show front, sides and rear facades of the building design. To do so, they graphically compress all the layers of spatial information into a single vertical plane. Therefore, all the forms seen on this plane that are parallel to the line of view, regardless of their position in space, retain their true-to-scale dimensions. As a result, all parts of the elevation, both in the background and in the foreground, are drafted to the same scale, and true measurements can be taken from anywhere in the finished drawing. For this reason they are, like the plan and section counterparts, quite easy to construct.

Drafting the Elevation

Elevations are quickly projected with direct reference to the plan — that is, the side of the floor plan that is to be elevated. Primary construction lines are created by projecting vertical lines from key points on the floor plan; horizontal points being plotted by measuring upward at scaled heights from the ground line.

Interior Elevations

Interior elevations are drafted when it becomes necessary to examine the detail of internal wall planes. They focus on the appearance of the wall plane as viewed from the centre of the room. It is a drawing type employed when the designer wants to explore the elevational effect of lighting and furniture, and also to indicate the colours and finish of materials. For this reason this particular graphic view is often associated with the work of the interior designer.

Line Weights

As the elevation makes no reference to the diminishing size of increasingly distant planes, it challenges the designer to create illusions of depth using other means. A good way to imply depth is to employ the simple system of decreasing line thickness, to acknowledge the

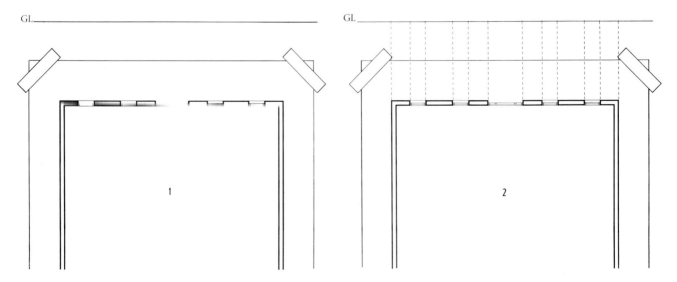

DRAFTING THE INTERIOR ELEVATION

Interior elevations are constructed in exactly the same way as exterior elevations (see below) – namely, guideline projections are made from the floor plan to find widths before the scaled heights are added. End wall features and furniture are then included with reference to the plan. Two versions of this graphic are commonly produced: one includes the sectional slice of walls and ceiling (see the 'Sectional-Elevation', on pages 92-3). The other simply isolates the wall elevation, without any evidence of the sectional cut, to focus on the detail of the interior wall plane.

DRAFTING THE EXTERIOR ELEVATION

1. *After taping a sheet of paper securely to the board, position the floor plan so that the side you wish to elevate vertically addresses the sheet. Then lightly tape the plan to the drawing surface, before pencilling in the ground line (GL). The GL should be parallel to the side of the plan to be elevated.*
2. *Using a set-square and a T-square, vertically transfer all the key points – including corners, projections and recesses, changes in plane, window and door widths etc. – from the plan to the GL.*
3. *Measure up in scale from the ground line along projected vertical lines, to plot the height of eaves, roof line, windows, doors and other horizontal features.*

4. *Once all the primary lines have been established, develop the outlines of the elevation from their vertical and horizontal intersections. The outline and details of roof, doors, windows, together with an indication of materials and context can also be inserted using the appropriate line weights.*
Note: *a shortcut in the transfer process can be employed when working on tracing paper: position the plan under the tracing paper. Widths are then directly transferred, with heights being plotted with reference to a section – provided one exists.*

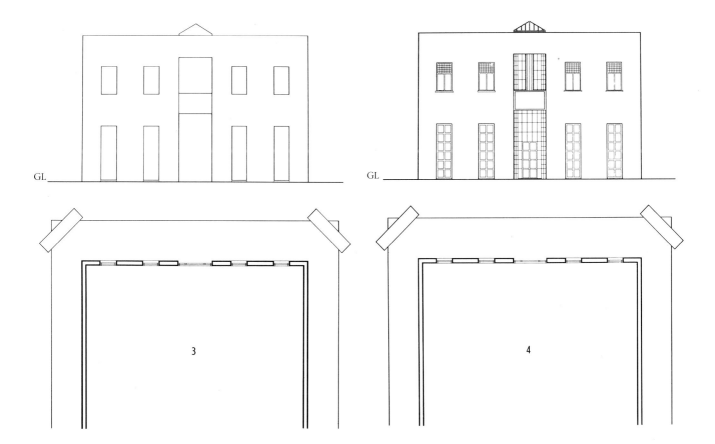

perceptual phasing of line strength with increasing distance. However, the strongest line weight should be reserved to denote the ground line. This is a convention that, like its counterpart in the section, visually fixes the building facade to the ground mass and graphically anchors the elevation drawing to the sheet of paper.

Main Picture: Elevation of Oxford Street Mall Project, London. Avery Associates. Drawn in ink on tracing paper by Bryan Avery and Allan Camp, this 1:200 scale elevation of a design proposal for central London is embellished with a well-drafted entourage. The latter provides a sense of realism and (urban) activity that transcends the static emptiness usually associated with such an orthographic view.

Detail: Transparent Trees. When trees occur forward of a facade their foliage can be 'dissolved' in order to retain visual access to the area behind that would otherwise be obscured. Here, the outline of the foliage remains intact whilst the lines of the facade appear to coexist within it.

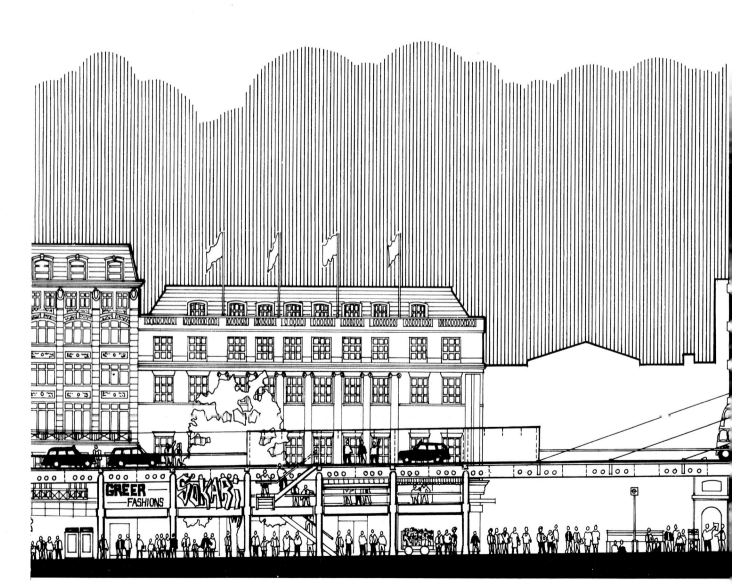

Materials in Line

Increasing the scale of an elevation drawing affords a corresponding increase in the opportunity for describing the pattern and surface appearance of building materials. However, a bland and consistently mechanical delineation should be avoided, as this can cause a 'toytown' effect in which the elevation drawing takes on the appearance of a small model. This distortion of apparent scale can be obviated by a graphic sensitivity to the distance implied by the particular scale in use, and by an understanding of construction methods. To help understand the spatial effect on the appearance of materials, a useful exercise is to make freehand sketches of various materials as observed along a scale of distance. This kind of first-hand experience will be a useful guide as to which lines should be retained and which lines should be left out in progressively distant views. Obviously, the act of sketching will also help in the understanding of how the various materials are assembled in construction. Many architects have evolved their own selective techniques for indicating materials. These involve a combination of line weight, emphasis of line and a mixture of freehand and hardline delineations.

Particular techniques include the singular lining of horizontal courses in small scale elevations which, when a greater scale allows, introduces the selective suggestion of vertical modular elements.

There is also the broken line depiction of brickwork, blockwork and tiles. This is a subtle deployment of line emphasis which, while focusing on the points of inter-section between vertical and horizontal connections, responds intermittently in line weight to the assumed direction of light. This technique is easy to develop and follows a simple principle — namely, that the edges of shadow-casting planes receive a slightly thicker line.

Another method of avoiding a mechanical looking drawing is to work mortar joints in freehand lines. This is especially effective when, in conjunction with a ruled line drawing, two different types of material occur in the same elevation, such as stone and brickwork or timber and steel. By hinting at the contrast between these materials in line, a dimension of visual interest is added.

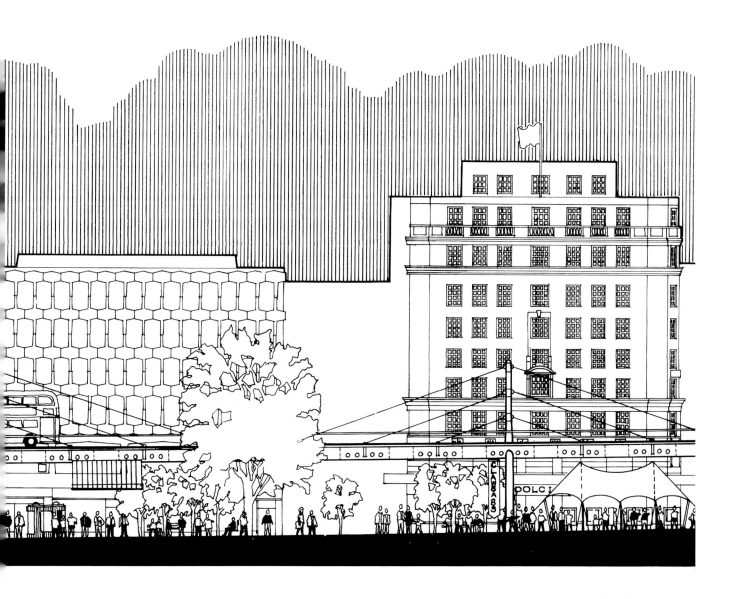

Also, in larger elevational planes, every detail of a material need not be represented. Rather, a selective area of pattern and surface texture can be suggested.

Contextual Entourage

Elevations also create the opportunity to present a building facade set against a background of the site, with existing or proposed features included on either side. Together with the outline of existing buildings in the vicinity, the presence of trees can induce a sense of place, scale and season. For example, trees can be depicted either with or without foliage, shown as species that are indigenous to the locality and, when relevant, include the identifiable forms of existing specimens already on site. Tree delineation should be simple, economical and, at all costs, avoid the anonymity of a stereotype. Indeed, most elevations — even when fully rendered — show trees and shrubs in an unelaborated line. The aim is to exploit the fluidity of line inherent in freehand drawing and create a softer contrast to the graphic lines of the building facade, without visually detracting from it. Trees are also used as compositional devices, and deployed to enhance an illusion of depth. For example, when appearing from behind building planes the overlap clue is exploited. Also, a varying skyline of trees can exploit the modulation of topology and, in some cases, they can appear both behind and in front of the elevation. However, when trees occur forward of the facade, a whole series of techniques are employed to dissolve their mass and enable a view

PHOTO TRANSFER TECHNIQUE

1. Having cut out the area of the photo you wish to transfer, place it face-up on a clean sheet of paper. Then coat the image liberally with a solvent, such as white spirit, acetone or methylated spirits.

2. When it has been thoroughly soaked with the solvent, transfer the photo face-down onto the appropriate area of the elevation.

3. Holding it in position, rub briskly and reasonably firmly over the back of the photo (or the section of it you wish to transfer) with the point of a pencil or ballpoint pen.

4. Carefully peel back one edge or side of the photo to check if the image has been successfully transferred. Each line of pressure exerted when rubbing should result in a corresponding line of released printing ink. If sections of the image are a bit patchy, reposition the edge or side of the photo and repeat the rubbing process.

5. Finally peel back the entire photo to reveal the complete image.

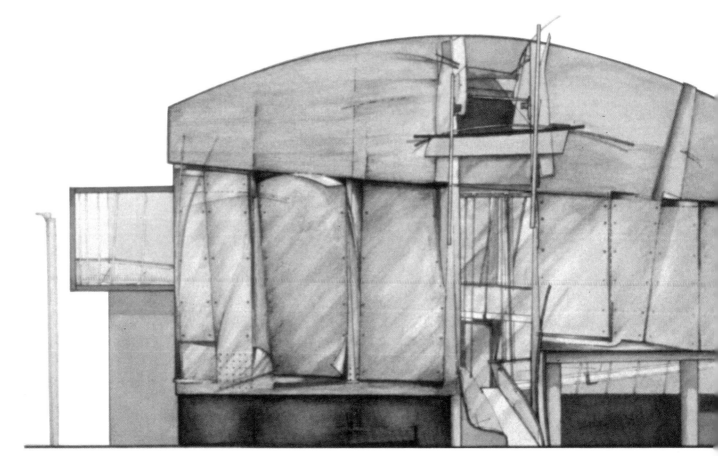

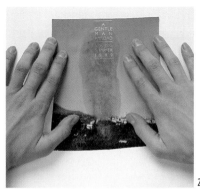
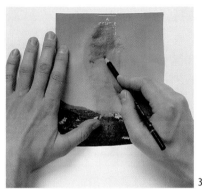

through to the detail of the building. Human figures tend to appear in elevations more than sections. However, like trees, they should be deployed to animate the facade without distracting from the architecture.

The distraction of entourage is much more likely to occur at the larger scale, when an emphasis on their depiction, or badly drawn versions, can pull the eye away from the central message of the drawing. Meanwhile, at the smaller scales, there are many examples of line-drawn urban elevations which literally teem with people, bustle with vehicles, and are filled with trees and plantings both on and around the building facade.

Shadows in Elevations
Line-drawn elevations can be further enlivened

Left: Elevation of the Langen Museum. Peter Cook and Christine Hawley. Drawing on a muted colour palette, this crayon and watercolour rendered pencil drawing on cartridge paper evokes a figurative and atmospheric quality that, hitherto, has not been associated with the influential graphics of Cook and Hawley.

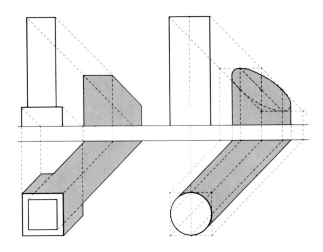

Above: Simple Projections and Recesses.
*By corresponding to average daylight conditions, the 45°
shadow convention appears convincing in elevations. And, as
the dimensions of shadows are generally the same as objects
from which they are cast, construction is easy using T- and set-
squares and compasses.*

Above: Freestanding Columns.
*When plotting the shadows of columns standing forward of
an elevation, 45° projections from the casting edges of both
auxilliary plan and elevation make contact in the vertical
plane to find the outline of the shadow. Notice the shadow
construction of the top of the vertical column – boxing it into
a rectangle aids accurate drafting.*

and pictorially enhanced by the inclusion of shadows.
However, apart from increasing the illusion of depth,
shadows also provide a searching examination of the
quality of a building design. This stems from their ability
to emphasize the displacement of form, and to describe
the shape and surface inclination of planes. In this sense,
shadow rendering functions as a design tool that allows
the designer to assess the composition of architectural
massing and explore patterns of fenestration.

In order to construct accurate shadow projections, the
designer must also be fully conversant with the three-
dimensional nature of the design. Furthermore, he or
she should be prepared for the fact that a projection of
shadows is a process of analysis that will illuminate
design defects, rather than obscure them. As in sections,
the convention for shadows in elevations sees light as
falling over the left shoulder of the viewer, and consequently entering the drawing from the top left-hand
corner to strike the architectural form diagonally along
an angle of 45°. Although the option is always present for
other angles of bearing, this 45° convention has two
positive advantages. First, in plans and elevations it
greatly simplifies the problem of their cross-referenced
construction. Second, the width and length of shadows
will be of the same dimension as the horizontal form or
protrusion from which they are cast. This means that the
majority of shadows in an elevation can often be plotted
with the aid of the plan or the section.

Simple Projections and Recesses

The plotting of shadows from protruding rectilinear
elements, such as eaves, balconies and overhangs, is
simply a 45° projection of their horizontal mass as seen

Below Left and Right: Dormer and Chimney.
*To plot the shadow cast by a dormer window, first project lines
at 45° back from the casting points on the side elevations to
the roof. Then transfer the points of intersection horizontally
to the front elevation. Where these make contact with
equivalent projections cast from the elevational view, the
outline of the shadow is formed. To plot a shadow cast by a
chimney enlist the help of an auxilliary side elevation to find
the point at which the shadow cast from the top of the chimney
strikes the inclined plane.*

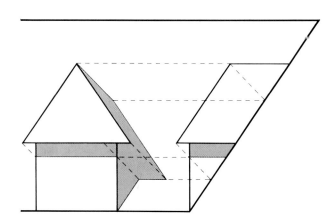

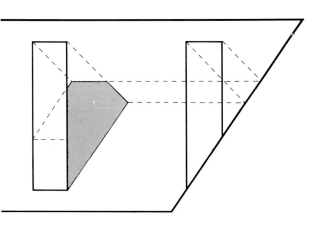

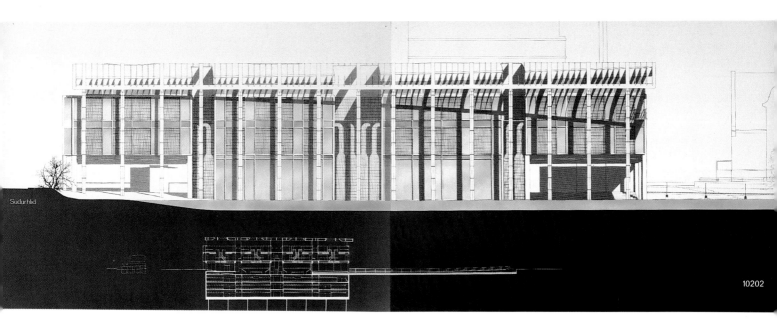

Sudurhlid

10202

in the plan. Similarly, shadows cast into rectangular, circular, and other shaped recesses exist simply as evidence of their unseen right-angled plane as revealed in the plan. In other words, shadows cast from lines parallel to the plane receiving them are quickly constructed by 'sliding' the casting edge along a 45° angle to a length corresponding to the depth of the recess or the projection.

Freestanding Columns

Vertical elements, such as columns, that are situated forward of the building plane cast shadows that are

Above: City Hall Elevation, Reykjavik, Iceland. Margaret Hardardoffir and Steve Christer. A good example of how shadows can create an illusion of solidity and mass in architectural graphics.

plotted with reference to the plan. When these elements stand clear of the wall, part of their shadow will fall on the ground and part on the wall. Therefore, beginners should follow their construction stages by plotting shadows point by point in sequence from plan into elevation. This cross-referencing experience will form the basis of a three-dimensional understanding of sciagraphy, and will minimize the chance of any details being fudged or omitted.

Dormer and Chimney

The dormer window and the chimney stack represent recurrent architectural forms. Their shadow projection is a comparatively simple task but, as and when sloping roofs are involved, they will require reference to a side elevation or a section. The main principle to remember here is that shadows cast from vertical forms and corners will remain parallel to the slope of the roof.

Shade and Shadow

Up until this point we have been discussing shadows only, but when dealing with curved surfaces it becomes

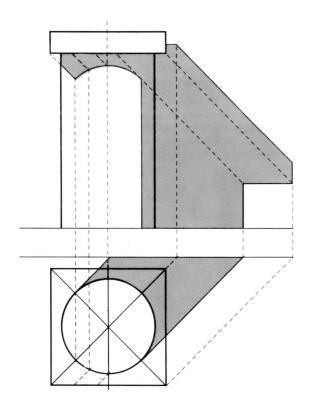

Cylinder and Block
The shadow of the corner of the block is plotted on the surface of the cylinder with reference to the plan. A number of convenient points are then similarly plotted along the lower casting edge of the front of the block, and connected up to find the curve of the shadow on the cylinder. The resulting projection defines shade and shadow. Render the former with a soft inner edge to fade it back into the illuminated portion of the column.

necessary to differentiate between 'shadow' and 'shade'. A shadow is created when an object interrupts the path of light between the source of illumination and a plane. Whereas shade is caused by the absence of light on the surface of a form or a plane — i.e., that part of a form or a plane that is turned away from the light source. Furthermore, no shadows will fall on surfaces that are already in shade.

Cylinder and Block
Casting shade and shadow from a block above a cylindrical column is a traditional sciagraphy exercise that, due to their fascination with Classicism, has its roots in the projects of the *Ecole des Beaux Arts*.

Spheres and Hollow Spheres
The precise areas of shade on a sphere and a hollow sphere can be plotted with the aid of section lines. These are drawn both on plan and elevation at regular intervals, and at an angle corresponding to that of the path of light. The section lines then generate contours on which tangents are drawn at 45° to the section lines. These give points from which the line of the shade can be plotted. Once these simple principles have been grasped, they form the basis for plotting many related spherical surfaces. For instance, the sphere suggests the

construction for shades on domes, while the hollow sphere construction suggests the shade of semi-domes, as often seen in sections.

The best way of developing an understanding of shade and shadow is to allow light to play across architectural forms at all stages of their evolution — even when making thumbnail design sketches. If this practice is backed-up with studies made directly from nature, and from scale models placed in various positions under a strong illumination, sciagraphic principles will rapidly become second nature.

Tonal Rendering
Tonal shading comes to the rescue when curvilinear planes need to be emphasized against the inherent flatness of the elevation. Often, in order to reinforce this contrast, a predominant cylindrical form on a building will be the only formal element to receive tone. For example, in an elevation by Jones and Kirkland (see opposite), three tonal techniques are simultaneously employed to express the concept of roundness. These include a ruled diagonal hatching, a system of freehand line flecks and another of stippled dots. These three shading techniques form the basis of a tonal vocabulary for buildings shown at a scale of 1:200. It is interesting to compare these techniques for expressing curves in elevation with those used by other architects when drawing to different scales. Indeed, the use of bar shading, which employs different line thicknesses as well as interval differential and other types of tonal rendering, can create highly convincing drawings — especially when applied with a working knowledge of reflected light (see Chapter 3). However, the main consideration when tonal rendering materials in elevations is to harness the scale of the technique to that of the drawing. Pen and pencil hatching, together with ink washes, represent the traditional techniques for simulating the surface of the building. An exploitation of the various types of hatching, such as single-directional, multi-directional, and those 'decomposed' by broken lines, will establish tonal structures that can be adapted to different scales for a range of visual effects. In turn, these techniques can simulate a wide range of building materials with flat, shaped, textured, matt, reflective and shadowed planes. When the drawing scale increases, a textural simulation can move the elevation to new heights of pictorialism. However, the difference between a texture that is created by the tooth of the drawing surface and one created by the point of the pencil is a distinction exemplified in a comparison between the techniques of Michael Graves and Jorge Silvetti. In the former, the technique is 'accidental', while in the latter it is carefully constructed using a premeditated structure of assembled graphite strokes.

Techniques for Hatching Glazing
Whilst eighteenth century designers employed a solid ink wash to simulate glass — giving the impression of 'eyeless' facades — here is a range of more modern linear techniques that employ freehand and ruled hatching.

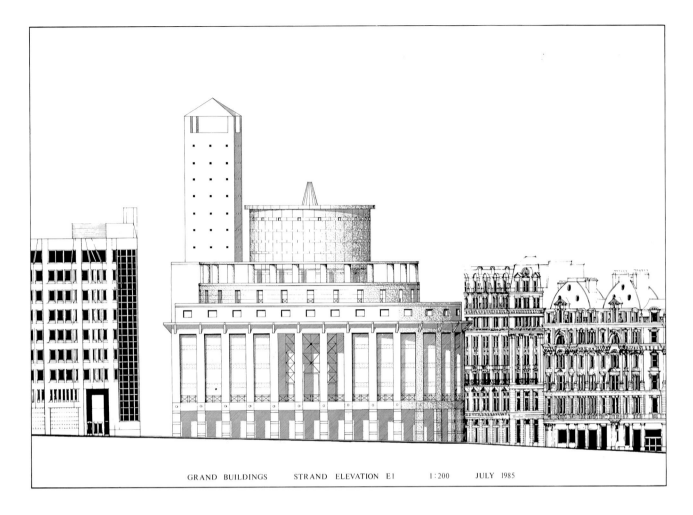

GRAND BUILDINGS   STRAND ELEVATION E1   1:200   JULY 1985

But much more problematic for architects is the rendition of glass and glazing. When not left blank, or subjected to the banality of two or three line flecks to suggest reflection, windows are traditionally washed in gray ink or graphite, or filled-in with solid black. This darkening of glazed apertures is a response to their appearance in reality. However, larger scale drawings can include a suggestion of their reflective quality, but should be rendered in a more realistic fashion. There are several techniques that can be exploited to this end. These not only enlist a contrast between the techniques used for recess shadow and illuminated glass, but also include a highlight inserted using an eraser or a razor blade.

A general strategy for elevations is to assemble them in calculated layers of tone. Clear steps of value can progress from foreground to background — either increasing or decreasing in weight as they emphasize the overlapping of planes. In some cases, the ground line will profile a sectional slice which will be hatched or painted to appear as the darkest (or the lightest) tone in the range.

Occasionally, a hint of sky will be suggested to complete the pictorial illusion; simplified cloud formations being rendered in line or in graphite dust. When they occur immediately behind the facades of especially tall buildings, sky tones will function

Strand Elevation, Grand Buildings Competition. Jones and Kirkland. This fine 1:200 scale ink drawing demonstrates the subtle modelling, using a selectively applied and highly organised structure of dots and line flecks, of a cylindrical form within the inherent flatness of the elevation.

compositionally to counterchange the tone of the plane. However, when not left blank, or rendered in a graduated tonal wash, sky treatments are positioned above and clear of the design, so as to avoid conflict with the architectural message.

Colour Rendered Elevations
When a perspective is absent from a design presentation, the onus for conveying the atmospheric or emotional content of the space surrounding a building proposal will often fall to the colour-rendered elevation.

Flat Colour Washes
The most fundamental colour-rendered elevation is a line drawing embellished with the colour washes of markers, coloured pencils or watercolour. In this basic but highly effective form, the elevation at different scales exists as a colour-tinted drawing; the transparency of wash functioning to reinforce the line drawing, while

hinting at the intended hues of materials. Although created by simple means, this time-saving approach does involve a latitude of technique from which a whole gamut of distinctive drawing styles emerge. On the one hand, the grain of coloured pencils can evoke the character of surface associated with traditional building materials — especially when rendered in conjunction with a freehand line drawing. On the other hand, bland watercolour washes over a black ink line hold the potential of a more machine-like aesthetic, associated with the slickness of high technological buildings.

This affiliation of certain colour mediums with particular architects and their drawing styles provides an interesting study. Compare, for example, the highly polished architecture emanating from the cool marker colour washes on Nicholas Grimshaw's hardline drawings, with the playful charm of Terry Farrell's crayon, coloured pencil and freehand line enthusiasm for Art Deco. Both techniques, although quite different, rely on economy of application and simplicity of colour range. Often a highly successful elevation will be rendered in a single hue — the range, if elaborated, being extended by the addition of neutrals or colours of a closely related hue. Indeed, the majority of elevations rarely involve more than three or four basic colours. A good way of checking this imposed restraint is to simply count the number of colour changes in the elevations illustrated on pages 86-7.

Selective Colour Rendering

When working to pressing deadlines, some designers will adopt an even greater colour minimalism. There are many examples of elevations in which pre-selected elements are targeted with a colour, and those where pigment is applied exclusively to the facade against an unrendered, line-drawn background.

Another time-saving technique popular with students, is the colouring of a representative strip of a strategically placed circle on the face of the drawing. By offering a

Right: Facade Study, Grand Buildings Competition. Alan Phillips Associates. A superb pen and ink drawing rendered in airbrush with diluted washes of ink – a subtle exercise in sciagraphic projection.

glimpse of the intended colours, this partial rendering is applied with the notion that it is better to convey evidence, albeit fragmented, of this important design dimension rather than none at all.

Multi-layered Rendering

When time permits, highly modelled elevations can be achieved. These are developed from layers of rendering that are built up to represent the phenomena of light, shade and shadow, and also to exploit considerations such as materials, surface and texture. As part of this colour-layering process, several mediums can be used in different parts of the drawing, and also one on top of another. For example, a frequent combination is ink and graphite with coloured pencils, and also watercolour and/or marker washes under modifying layers of coloured pencil. And other mixed mediums combine photomontage with airbrush and watercolour.

However, although diverse in their graphic colour effects, all are bound by an unpretentious simplicity of colour — each medium or combination of mediums being enlisted for their ability to provide a specific colour effect. Basic colour techniques, such as those illustrated below and opposite, should be practised by the beginner, who should develop the skills of simulating the colour nuance and surface quality of various materials. Notice how the depiction of masonry, glazing, steelwork and incidental entourage, etc., is modified to respond to different orthographic scales. It is the development of such graphic effects, together with their harnessing to scale, that forms the basis of a proficient colour-rendering vocabulary.

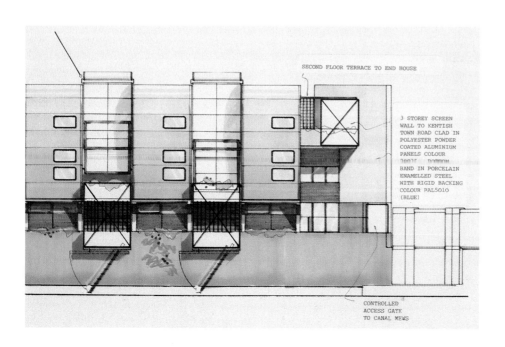

SECOND FLOOR TERRACE TO END HOUSE

3 STOREY SCREEN
WALL TO KENTISH
TOWN ROAD CLAD IN
POLYESTER POWDER
COATED ALUMINIUM
PANELS COLOUR
3003F RO???ON
BAND IN PORCELAIN
ENAMELLED STEEL
WITH RIGID BACKING
COLOUR RAL5010
(BLUE)

CONTROLLED
ACCESS GATE
TO CANAL MEWS

Elevation Detail of Canalside Housing, Camden, London. Nicholas Grimshaw and Partners. An ink line drawing by Neven Sidor was printed onto Ozalux (a high contrast glossy dyeline print paper) before receiving flat marker washes in a limited colour range.

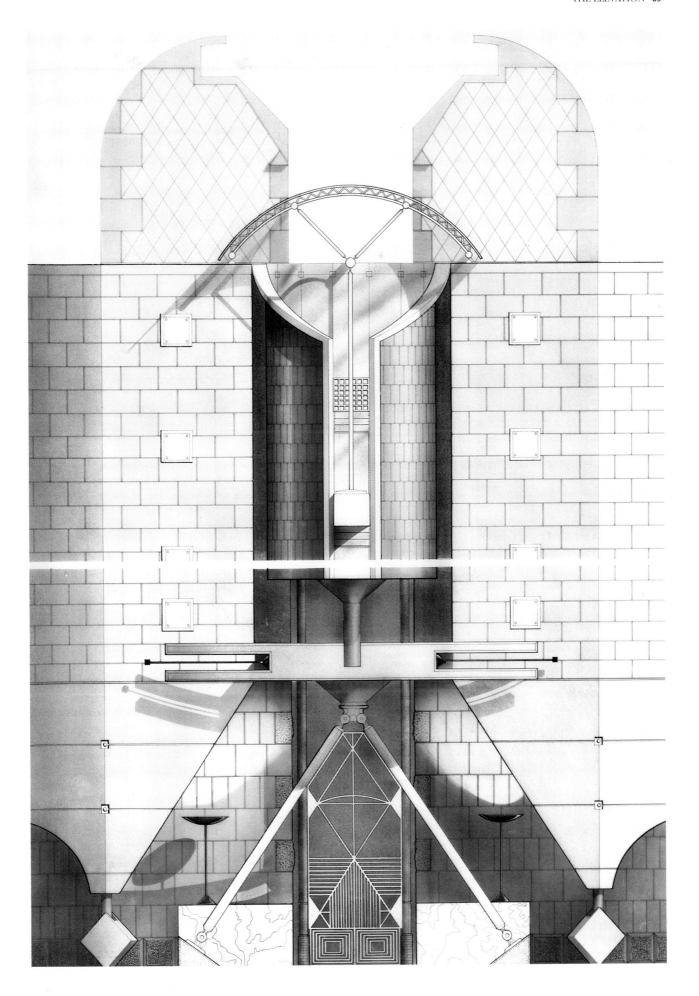

GALLERY

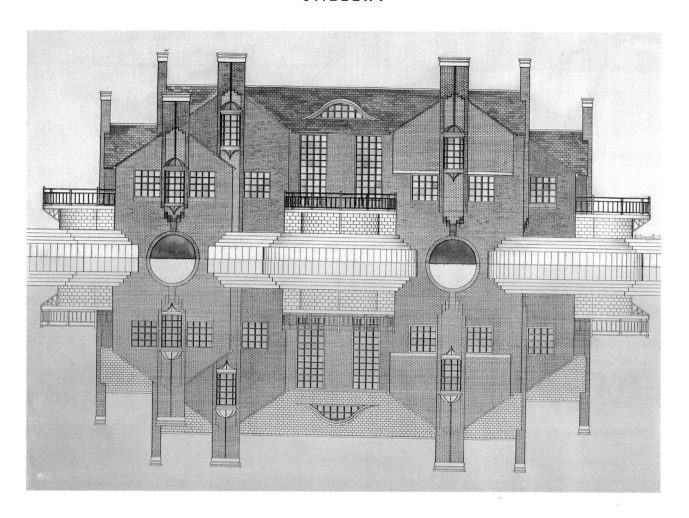

Above: Elevation of Church Island House, Staines, Middlesex. Basil Al-Bayati. *By exploiting its waterside setting and casting its reflection in the river, this 1:50 scale coloured pencil and watercolour drawing represents the first step away from the dimensionless space of the elevation. The implication of a space forward of the facade moves the drawing towards the illusion of a psuedo-perspective.*

Left: Elevation of Oxford Motor Museum Project. Nigel Spawton. *This presentation drawing shows how coloured pencils can describe subtle variations in the colour (and texture) of building materials.*

Right: Bayswater Road Elevation, 1-2 Porchester Gate, London. Green Lloyd Architects. *One of a series of modified elevations drawn to a scale of 1:50 by Sam Lloyd. Five Derwent pencils were employed to colour-up a dyeline print made on stout paper. Graphite shading was used to add weight to the shadows and gouache was brush-applied to indicate highlights.*

GALLERY

5
THREE-DIMENSIONAL
ORTHOGRAPHICS

This book cannot hope to cover perspective drawing in as much detail as would a specialist book on the subject. However, if we apply some of its basic principles we can, coupled with a simple understanding of the rudiments of one-point perspective, quickly give the inherent flatness of plans, sections and elevations the convincing illusions of pictorial depth.

When simple perspective co-ordinates are superimposed on the plan and the section, surprisingly realistic drawings can be produced. This is simply a method of projecting orthographics into three dimensions, and it is often used when a design idea is to be presented to a client or when projects are to be published for consumption by a wider audience.

Being quicker to produce than a detailed and time-consuming perspective construction, its application to, for example, elevations can rapidly convert the orthographic into a view of a building as seen in the context of its three-dimensional setting. Often this transformation is made simply by indicating the horizontal ground-plane forward of the face of the elevation; or by drawing

a scaled and overlapping object, such as a vehicle or a figure, in front of it.

Elevation Perspective

Such a basic intervention assumes a foreground space (non-existent in orthographics) with the facade occupying a middle-distance. Moreover, when a skyline or a tree-line is introduced behind the elevation, a background space is assumed. This illusory exploitation of horizontal spatial zones in terms of foreground, middleground, and background enlists two powerful depth clues that are not available to the elevation: namely, overlap (the partial obscuring of farther objects by nearer objects) and diminishing size. Designers adopt

Modified Elevation, Sale de Galas, Monaco. Ron Herron. This photomontage was produced in 1972 by one of the members of the enormously influential Archigram group. The image results from the skilful assemblage of photographic elements to create an elevational view of a structure complete with foreground space. The illusion of this space is generated by the scaled positioning of figures together with an indication of diminishing lines. This spatial extension of the elevation is commonly employed by designers to circumvent the time spent in constructing perspectives.

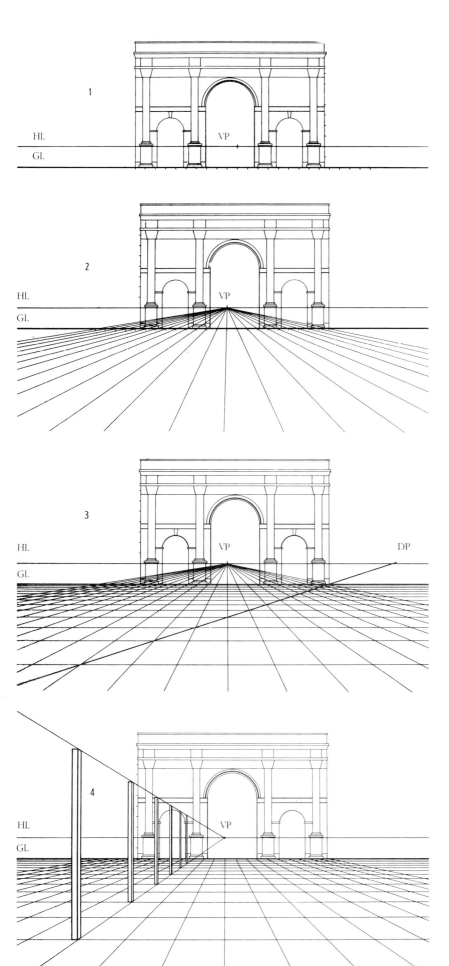

ELEVATION-PERSPECTIVE

1. Insert an horizon line (HL) at a scaled height above the ground line (GL), the base line of the elevation. The HL should be drawn to represent a standard viewing height, eg. 1.5 mts (5 ft). Insert a vanishing point (VP) at a position on the HL that will angle the resultant perspective drawing to an important feature in the design (eg. the entrance). Tick off increments along the GL and up one side of the elevation using a scale small enough to determine the width of paving slabs etc.

2. Project a series of lines from the VP so that they radiate out towards the viewer, and each intersects the scaled increments along the ground line. **Note:** *the ground line increments can be extended out to the right or left of the facade so that the complete width of the newly-formed horizontal foreground plane can be filled with lines of convergence. This extension will be required for frontal objects outside the projection of the facade.*

3. Now locate a diagonal point (DP) on the HL and out to the extreme left or right side of the facade. This point is very important as it represents the viewing distance of the observer; the further away from the side of the elevation the more distant and less acute the resulting angle of view. Then strike a line from the DP so that it bisects the nearest, lower corner of the facade at the GL. The points at which this diagonal cuts the radiating lines in the foreground give scaled units of perspective depth in the horizontal plane, which appear to increase progressively as they near the viewer Use these points to draw a diminishing sequence of horizontal lines, and to complete a perspective grid for guiding the location of the plan-shapes, forms and lines of objects at any prescribed point forward of the facade.

4. To plot the height of these objects, plot their scaled height on the facade at a point above their location in the horizontal plane. Project a line from the VP and through the point of the scaled height to find the same perspective height at any point along its length forward of the facade. The result is a perspective drawing with an illusion of foreground space – a stage for props and 'players', their position and relative size controlled by converging lines of linear perspective.

this visual trick for creating sham perspectives because it requires no premeditated construction. By merely drawing within the given scale of the elevation a foreground terrain, reflections from waterside buildings, trees and figures, etc., plus a hint of background, it is possible to create a compelling 'perspective' entirely acceptable to the viewer. However, with the addition of a little basic geometry more elaborate and dimensionally accurate elevation perspectives can be created.

The transformation begins with the elevation in outline which, for the purposes of its conversion, is assumed to represent the picture plane, i.e., the plane on which depth measurements can be scaled (for method see previous page).

Perspective-Section

Projecting a section into a perspective-section is one of the most popular drawing types because it provides a three-dimensional view of interior spaces as they would appear behind the slice of their cutting plane. In this transformation the picture plane, represented previously by the elevation, is now replaced with a section. However, in this case the edge of the picture plane is represented by the inside edge of the sectional cut — i.e., the inner line of the cut that denotes the point at which the building fabric meets its contained space.

When converting building sections portraying more than one internal space, the process remains the same — except that it is wise to spot the vanishing point inside a major room-space or a representative floor level.

Perspective-Plan

Using the same principles, floor plans can also be quickly projected into the overhead view of a one-point perspective. As in the section, the picture plane is framed by the inner line of the slice of the cut. But this time an alternative method of projection will be used in which the measuring scale is moved clear of the drawing area.

Basic Perspective Co-ordinates

A review of the perspective co-ordinates used in the three converted orthographics should explain a little

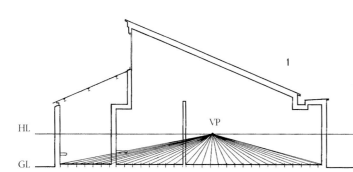

PERSPECTIVE SECTION.
1. To demonstrate this conversion, the same horizon line (HL), complete with its vanishing point (VP), used in the elevation is retained. However, before proceeding insert the scale of measurement along the bottom of the picture plane – each increment being projected back to the VP.

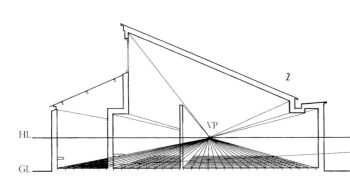

2. Complete the perspective grid by striking a line from the diagonal point (DP) to bisect the further, lower inside corner of the section. Where this line cuts each of the radiating lines, a diminishing scale of depth is achieved 'inside' the space of the section. Now connect each corner of the section back to the VP using lines that add the converging planes of walls and ceiling to that of the floor.

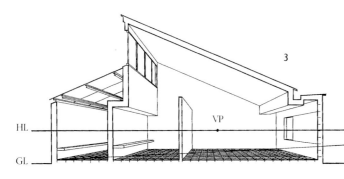

3. Plot the location of interior features (windows doors etc.) by extending the scale up the inside wall of the building section. Position and size of furniture, people etc. can also be established, as can outside objects, by extending the increments along the GL and taking a line from the VP through the appropriate increments on the side wall scale.

PERSPECTIVE-PLAN

1. Spot the vanishing point (VP) on its horizon line (HL) inside the plan – in response to the required angle of view. Then establish the diagonal point (DP) on the HL, outside the perimeter of the plan at a distance of approx the width of the plan. Draw a second HL above (or below), but clear of the plan. This will function as the measuring line (ML). Finally, strike a vertical from the inside wall nearest the DP, until it intersects the ML at X.

2. Measure off an increment scale along the ML from X and project a line from the VP to cut X on the ML.

3. Project a series of radiating lines from the DP to cut through the increments on the ML. Where each radiating line cuts the line VP-X, a scale of diminishing depth is established.

4. With all the co-ordinates installed, the perspective scale can be transferred into the plan after connecting the inside corners in the plan back to the VP – the height of the cutaway ceiling then being transferred from the measuring scale. This and other heights are dropped into the plan before being transferred around its invisible walls.

5. Plot any vertical or horizontal points both on the walls and, after using the picture plane increment scale, at any point on the floor.

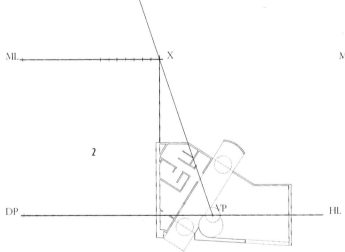

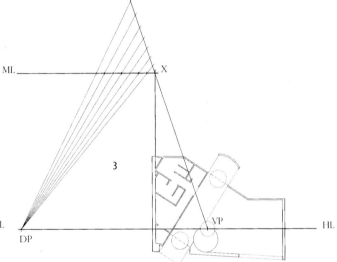

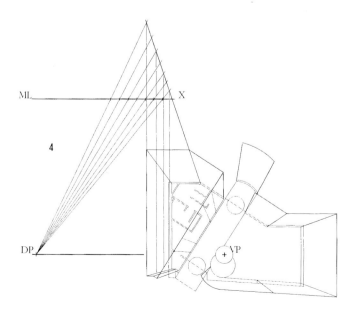

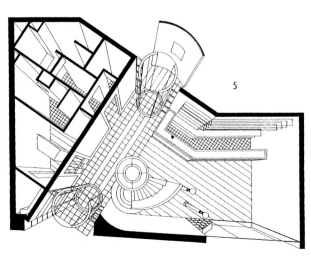

more of their functions. For example, the vanishing point controls the direction of view. Move this point up and above normal eye level and we create an aerial or overhead view; move it down and below normal eye level and a lower or worm's-eye view results.

However, lateral movement of the vanishing point causes quite different impressions. For example, location to the left will bring the right-hand vertical planes into greater prominence, and vice-versa if it is moved to the right. In other words, when the vanishing point is registered on its horizon line it corresponds to the sightline of the viewer as fixed on the picture plane.

The picture plane is an imaginary and transparent two-dimensional plane that is perpendicular to the viewer's line of sight, and onto which measurements are made before their projection back (or forward) into perspective space. Usually imagined as being coincident with the drawing surface, the planes of the face of the elevation, the cutting line of the section and the floor of the plan became the 'picture plane' for the purpose of their conversion. In representing the bottom edge of the picture plane, the ground line (in the elevation and section) defines the line of intersection between the ground plane and the picture plane.

Finally, the diagonal point simulates the scaled distance of the viewer from the object in view; the farther away its position, the more distance is assumed and the more foreshortened the resultant perspective. For example, the same diagonal point was used for both elevation- and section-perspective. Usually, however, the diagonal point is located nearer to the side of the section, i.e., at a distance approximately equivalent to that of the overall width of the section. From this position a more revealing view of interior floor planes is obtained.

Once the basic principles of one-point perspective have been understood, construction lines can be quickly worked on to a sheet of drawing paper which, when drafted, can be overlayed with tracing paper or clear film for a final drawing which can be worked directly in ink.

An alternative method is to construct the perspective in non-reproducing blue pencil. A subsequent ink drawing on the same surface will provide an original for a dyeline or a photocopy print which selectively reproduces only the ink drawing.

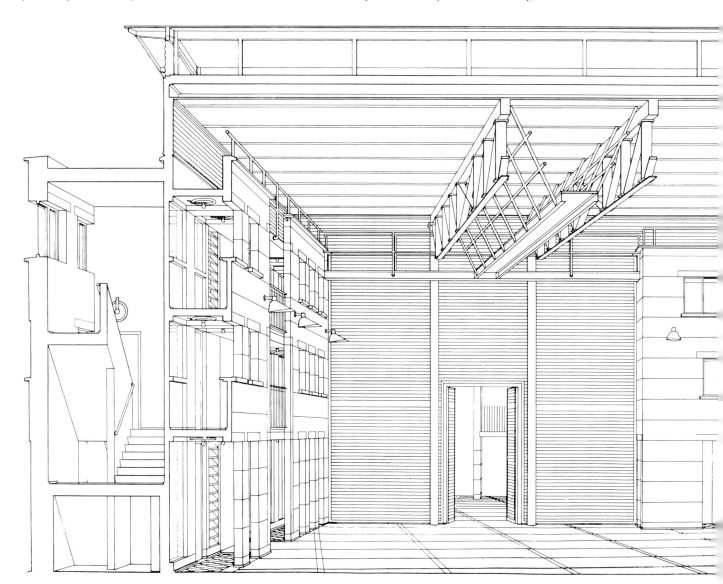

Above: Section-Perspective of Workshop for the Mentally Handicapped, Westoning, Bedfordshire. Edward Cullinan Architects. Apart from its projection of the section into the illusory space of a perspective drawing, this modified orthographic is yet another example of a drawing resulting from a team effort. In this case the artwork was produced by Robin Nicholson, Michael Chassay and Giles Oliver.

Left: Sectional Perspective View of the Interior of the Main Auditorium, Half Moon Theatre, London. Architect: Florian Beigel, Architectural Bureau. This ink drawing by Hendric Welp, on A0 size tracing paper, was deliberately delineated without atmospherics to show the disposition of architectural elements in outline. The combination of perspective and section was chosen because it best depicted the working parts of the auditorium. These include the two facing 'housefronts' situated under a hovering ceiling, with curtain-like walls hanging between the 'facades' and the roof structure. The layering of these vertical planes is explained by the sectional device, while the perspective component of the drawing describes horizontal space appearing to exist beyond the limits of the graphic as a route defined by roof structure and floorscape pattern.

GALLERY

Left: Modified Elevation, University of East Anglia New Buildings. Rick Mather Architects. This elevation departs from its inherent flatness to present a visual conundrum. For example, within the colour-hatched drawing several scales of depth are implied. On the left the sky becomes a near plane on which the extruded facade casts its shadow; on the right a far greater distance is suggested by the scale of the tree. The visual game is further developed by the plan seen as reflected in facade glazing, while small plan and axonometric fragments appear in a much reduced scale to occupy the foreground space.

Right: Psuedo Perspective, Waterfront House in Rotherhythe, Kent. Timpson Manley Deans Design Group. Drawn by ex-Oxford student Mick Timpson, this technical pen rendering was worked on heavy-duty tracing paper to produce an array of subtle line effects against ink-sprayed sky. The richness of this treatment – especially in the background – does little to erode the strong sense of distance generated by the foreground addition of silhouetted objects.

Right: Elevation-Perspective of Hostel at Priestley Road, Basingstoke. Edward Cullinan Architects. In contrast to the psuedo perspective opposite, this elevation projects its elevational planes backward and into a one-point perspective. Drawn by Sunand Prasad to a scale of 1:20, the resulting projection was rendered with approximately 15 coloured pencils and some additional airbrush work in the background. A layered use of the coloured pencils began with the yellow of the sun and ended with the darkness of the shadows – the latter being filled with reflected light.

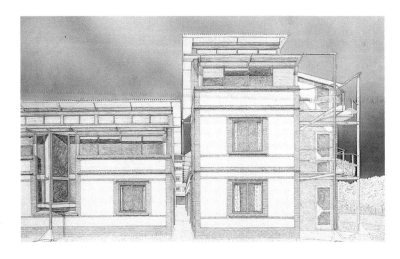

GALLERY

6
PARALINE PROJECTION DRAWINGS

The combination of the plan, section and elevation in a single projection creates a drawing type with a genealogy that reaches back far beyond the advent of perspective. Much-loved by Modernist architects, and still very much in evidence today, the paraline drawing is one of most widely used architectural graphics. This is due to the ease of its construction and the effectiveness of its overhead pictorial view. Compared with the flatness of orthographic views, most lay people find paraline drawings easier to understand since their spatial illusion comes somewhat closer to a natural perception of a three-dimensional object. For this reason, architects group them together with perspectives as 'three-dimensional' drawings.

Essentially, paraline drawings fall into two distinct categories: oblique projections and isometric projections. Oblique projections also subdivide into two groups depending on whether or not the plan or the elevation is projected.

Plan Oblique Projections
Commonly known as an 'axonometric', the plan oblique is by far the most popular of all the paraline drawings. Its construction begins with a ready-drawn, true-to-scale plan that is either projected vertically upward to find the ceiling or roof height, or downward to find the floor plane. As all vertical projections remain true, once a scaled height or width is plotted using the scale of the plan, the dimension can, unlike perspective projection, be transferred to all similar heights or widths that occur at any point within the volume of the projection. This is because scale and size ratios remain constant in both

horizontal and vertical directions. When drafting the plan oblique, the plan is usually rotated and tilted with one corner nearest the viewer. However, a preliminary rotation of the plan will find the best orientation to suit the required angle of view. The most common angle is 45° which presents equal views of the two visible perpendicular planes. When required, however, emphasis can be given to one plane by, for example, tilting the plan to an angle of 30/60° to the horizontal. The quickest method of drafting paralines is via direct plan projection. This entails placing a transparent overlay sheet on the tilted plan and projecting its key co-ordinates up into orthogonal space. During this extrusion, it is helpful to draft the projection as a 'glass box' construction — that is, drawing all lines regardless of the fact that some of them will remain hidden in the ultimate drawing. The construction phase should be ghosted in light pencil so that, when completed, the final delineation can be over-worked in ink or, if preferred, a second overlay added to produce a tracing of a clean and construction-free drawing. A variation of this drafting procedure can be executed when producing simple plan projections with cutaway roof planes. Using a transparent overlay sheet, the plan is traced, before sliding downward to the scaled dimension of room height before a second floor plan tracing is connected with vertical lines to its upper counterpart. The plan oblique

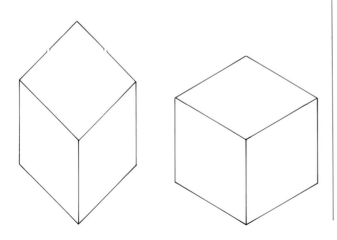

Paraline Drawing Types.
There are two basic types of paraline drawing: the axonometric (the most popular) and the isometric – each providing a slightly different viewpoint from which to visualise a new idea.

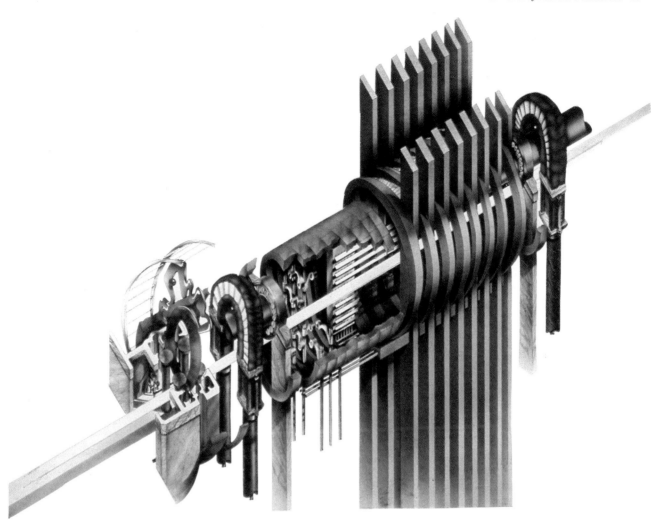

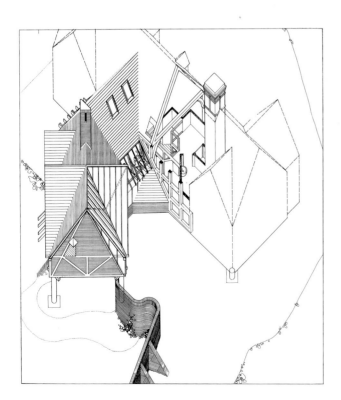

Above: The Macrophone. An Axononmetric by Jeremie Frank. Collection: Architectural Association. This splendid true plan projection of a highly inventive conceptual form explores with breathtaking clarity the impact of light, shade and shadow on its polished surface. To do so, its author has skilfully employed the airbrush medium to bring a convincing realism to her drawing. The medium also gives credence to the designer's fascination with a symbolic and theatrical architecture derived from parodied gadgets and filled with a spontaneous machine aesthetic.

Left: Axonometric of the House by Bushley, Gloucestershire. Benthall Potter Associates. Rather than simply being tilted and poised symmetrically on one corner, axonometric drawings can be positioned at any appropriate viewing angle. For instance, three viewing options are illustrated in Maxim Benthall's drawing of a house design in which the three basic forms are seen as occupying different angles in relation to the viewer.

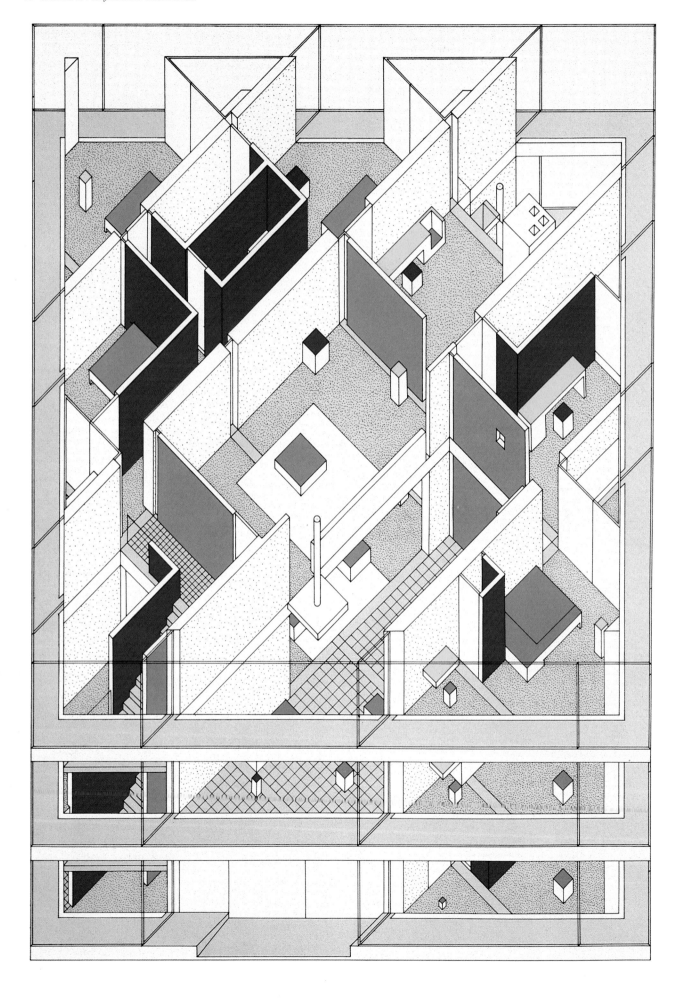

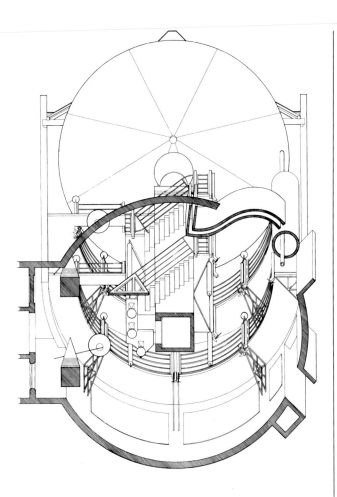

Above: Up-View Axonometric of the Diorama Arts Centre, Regents Park, London. Alan Phillips Associates. By looking upward into a staircase tower, this 1:50 scale ink on tracing paper drawing explores the interior space of a design idea, using a drawing mode that was first used in the nineteenth century by August Choisy. More recently this means of viewing internal volume has enjoyed something of a revival.

Left: Vertical Projection (Axonometric) of Project B House, Third Level Projection. John Hejduk. This kind of projection is currently enjoying a degree of popularity amongst some designers. It is used here by Hejduk to provide a conceptual exploration of an architecture of orthographic space in the manner of the Cubist painters. The plan is placed parallel to the picture plane before being extruded upwards into the illusion of orthographic space. Although few depth cues appear, the spatial power of this version of the axonometric is undeniable. For example, even the insertion of a flat and de Stijl-like colour – used to diagram structural and self-supporting elements and to define horizontal from vertical – reinforces rather than detracts from the strong impression of depth in the projection.

is completed when all the scaled thicknesses of enclosing and partition walls and recessed thicknesses of visible openings in the envelope have been inserted.

These two basic methods of projection respond to two discrete functions of the plan oblique. The drafting of a complete building invites the viewer to look *at* the architecture with its roof on; while a cutaway version — that is, with its 'lid' removed and either with or without portions of exterior walls — invites a simultaneous view *at* and *in* a building design. The cutaway version can exist as a highly sophisticated graphic which, for more searching views of its interior spaces, can enlist the conventional spatial vocabulary of dotted and dashed lines to dissolve planes and ghost hidden forms. While larger scaled versions of plan obliques are enlisted for a closer inspection of interior detail, such as furniture and finishes, and tend to attract a realistic colour rendition.

Two common variations on the plan oblique are worthy of mention. The first positions one of its true-plan sides parallel to the picture plane for its vertical projection up into a true elevation and — when not a cutaway 'shoe-box' plan view of interior rooms — into a true roof plan. Known as a 'planometric', this drawing type provides little evidence of the third dimension and relies almost exclusively on the power of overlap to convey its highly distorted sense of volume. The other variation of the plan oblique is the 'worm's-eye' or 'up-view paraline' drawing. To produce this projection, the true plan is flipped upside down and tilted at 45° for an extrusion that allows an upward view from below the framework of the plan to the walls and ceiling. First used in the nineteenth century to illustrate primarily the spatial and structural organization of buildings, this use of an impossible subterranean viewpoint is interesting because, in contrast to the more traditional bird's-eye view, it comes somewhat closer to the way we actually perceive architecture. The more recent revival of this rather unusual method of depicting designs is found mainly in the work of Mario Botta and Stirling and Wilford.

Elevation Oblique Projection
To construct an elevation oblique drawing, the true plan is simply substituted for a true elevation that is projected back into orthogonal space. The angles of this projection can be 30°, 45° or 60°, each successive angle representing an increasingly higher vantage point. In this projection the distortion experienced in the vertical sides of the plan projection now effect the horizontal planes — a deformation that does not afford easy access to cutaway views of internal spaces. Furthermore, as this projection can appear distended by elongation in the horizontal plane, it is a less-popular drawing type. When used, however, building designs are usually depicted with their longest or most irregular sides facing the viewer; their function being reserved mainly for studying the two visible elevations in relation to the roof plan.

Isometric Projection
The isometric projection drawing was first devised by an English contemporary of Monge, Sir William Farish, who wished to provide an alternative drawing system that

would help to make technical drawings appear more like a perspective. Unlike oblique projections, isometric drawings present none of their planes in a true shape. Therefore, an isometric plan has to be redrawn from scratch in order to comply with the tilted foreshortening of its 30° axis. For this reason, this drawing system is more time-consuming to construct but, in exhibiting less distortion, and with its three visible planes depicted with equal emphasis, the resulting projection combines a lower eye level with a more realistic pictorial impression. The lower vantage point tends to make the isometric more useful when dealing (economically) with low buildings that occupy a greater horizontal surface area.

A variation of the isometric is known as a dimetric projection that, to achieve a more life-like depiction, swivels the isometric into a non-symmetrical position in relation to the picture plane. However, in featuring one of its two vertical faces, and enlisting two scales of measurement for the purpose, the dimetric is rarely seen in architectural design. In linear form, the oblique and isometric projections appear devoid of all clues as to depth, apart from that of overlap, but they do compel powerful sensations of volume. This compulsion is in our mind's eye and results from its conditioning to the parallelogram or rhombus — not as a flat shape, but as a rectangle seen as occupying three-dimensional space. When we add colour, surface texture and pattern, and shade and shadow, this illusion is intensified.

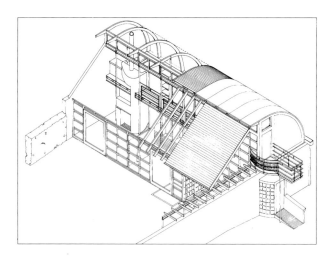

Above: Isometric of the Courtyard House. John Pardey. In comparison to the higher viewpoint dictated by axonometrics, isometrics become useful when dealing (economically) with forms that occupy greater horizontal surface areas – or when the view of a roof plane requires a greater prominence than that afforded by a true plan projection.
Right: 'Worm's-Eye' View Isometric of the Mississauga City Great Hall, Toronto, Canada. Jones and Kirkland. By providing a lower viewing angle and less spatial information than the axonometric, a beautifully rendered isometric drawing such as this is seldom employed for both upward and downward cutaway views of interior space.

7
TWO-POINT PERSPECTIVE DRAWING

By offering the most realistic view of all the pictorial graphics, the function of perspective in architectural design is immense. However, the true value of a perspective illusion is registered — especially with those uninitiated in design — not in the mechanical geometry used to construct it, but in the conviction of the resultant artwork. Therefore, rather than blind the reader with science, this chapter aims to introduce a sound, fast and accurate method of generating exterior and interior views from plans that can be immediately understood and adopted by the beginner.

There are several shortcuts which are used to avoid the routine of setting up a perspective from scratch. One is to use an existing photograph of a similar design form and to enlarge it to a suitable size for its traced adaptation. This can be achieved by overlaying a grid on the print, and drawing each individual box of information into a larger version of the same grid on the drawing board. Alternative methods of enlargement include projecting the print onto a drawing paper screen, using an episcope, a PMT machine, a Grant enlarger or a photocopier.

Another shortcut is to draw perspective views directly from sketch models made earlier in the design sequence; or to make Polaroid photographs from them for their later enlargement and adaptation into drawings. If none of these methods is available or suitable then, using the plan, a perspective construction drawing will have to be produced from scratch. The method shown here is a two-stage one that requires only a T-square and a set square. The method short-circuits the traditional process of rotating the plan on the drawing board — a cumbersome operation that is usually associated with setting up two point perspective drawings.

The next step is to determine the direction of view you wish the perspective drawing to illustrate. The location of this angle of view is important because ultimately it will influence the difference between a static or symmetrical composition and whether or not it is pictorially interesting or unusual. The best way of finding a representative and imaginative vantage point is to make reference to the three dimensional form in the mind's eye. Then make a mental journey around the elevations before selecting the general direction of the view. Apart from approaching a building design from the 'front', and including a sight of the main entrance, the majority of architectural perspectives seek to establish a viewing direction that best summarizes the form in relation to its immediate setting.

However, it is most important to avoid a viewing direction that, especially when dealing with square or

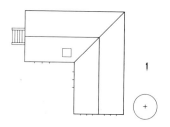

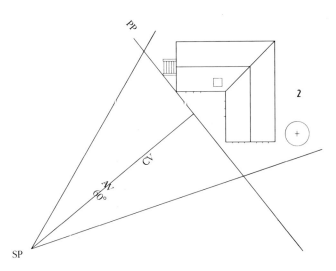

TWO POINT PERSPECTIVE DRAWING – STAGE ONE
Note: the step-by-step sequence should be followed in conjunction with the accompanying main text.

1. Tracing the Plan
Having taped the design plan squarely onto the board, and taped a large sheet of tracing paper over the top, trace the exterior outline of the plan together with any features or details that will appear in its immediate setting, such as roadways, existing buildings, mature trees etc. Next trace the position and width of all doors and window openings, together with roof details, such as the position of the ridge and chimney etc.

2. Locating the Station Point, Centre of Vision, Angle of Vision and the Picture Plane.
The station point (SP) represents the position of the observer in relation to the object in view. Place it approx three times the height of the building away from the desired focal point. Establish the Centre of Vision (CV) by projecting a line from the SP towards, and slightly offset from, the desired focal point of the drawing. Now form the angle of vision (AV), using a protractor and a straight edge, by projecting two lines from the SP towards the object in view, so that they both strike out at an angle of 30° to the CV, thereby forming an AV of 60°. In order to avoid distortion in the resulting projection, the AV should not exceed 60° or be less than 40°. The picture plane (PP) should then be inserted, again using a protractor and a straight edge, at an angle of 90° to the CV, and projected to cut the lines that form the AV. For our purposes the PP has been located forward of the plan, but just touching the near corner of the building. This is a convenient location because, as we experienced when converting orthographics into one-point perspectives (see pages 88-95), the picture plane is also the plane from which all scale measurements can be taken. Therefore, this contact with the angle in the plan will provide a true-to-scale height line from which all known heights can be later plotted.

3. Establishing the Vanishing Points.
To record the vanishing points (VP) for any given plane, simply project a line from the station point (SP) parallel to the adjacent side plane of the building plan. The point at which this projection intersects the picture plane is the VP. By being drawn parallel to the side plane of the building, the VP functions both for this plane and any other plane in the architectural form that is parallel to it. Now insert a second VP on the other side.

4. Transferring the Angles.
Connect the SP with all the angles of the plan, together with all information that was ticked off around its edge. Only those features seen within the angle of vision and facing the SP need be connected, and as this information is to be transferred onto the PP it is not necessary to rule these connecting lines beyond the plan and the PP. Finally, heights of plan elements, such as ridge line, chimney and any vertical forms seen in the immediate plan setting, are transformed by projecting lines out from their line/edge in the plan parallel to the nearest angle of the building until they cut the picture plane.

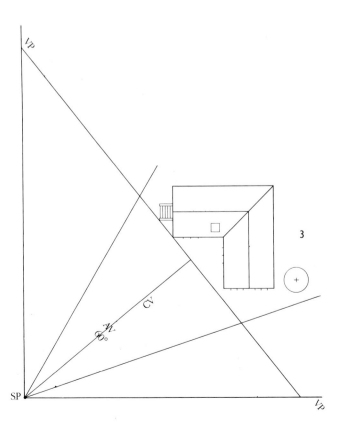

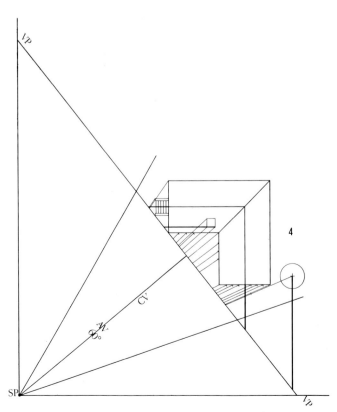

rectangular plans, is aimed at the corner of a cubic form. Otherwise, not only will the projected corner appear overly distorted, but the duplicity of converging side planes will lose any potential for a visual contrast. Instead, you should aim for the variety given by two receding planes that differ in their angles of perspective.

Station Point and Angle of Vision

Fixing the direction of perspective view involves the location of the station point and the range of the angle of vision. The station point represents the position of the observer in relation to the object in view. A useful rule of thumb when constructing exterior views of building designs is to locate this point at a distance approximately three times the height of the building. Although this guideline should not inhibit experiments with different distances, it does obviate any pictorial distortion that may occur when the station point is moved too close to the architectural form.

Centre of Vision and Picture Plane

Another way of visualizing this geometry, at this stage, is to imagine that the station point is replaced by the lens of a slide projector, and that the angle of vision is now described by the edges of its beam of light. In order to achieve a true and undistorted image projection, the centre of the light beam will have to be at right angles to the screen. For instance, if the screen was tilted away from the line of projection, a distorted image projection would result.

In perspective drawing the projection screen is replaced by the picture plane. The latter is represented in perspective geometry by a line which, when drawn across the plan at right angles to the centre of vision, functions as the 'screen' on to which the perspective will be cast.

Before locating the line of the picture plane, however, we should return to our analogy of slide projection. For example, if we move this line (acting as the screen) forward of the object (and nearer to the projector lens) a smaller image would result. Conversely, if we move the line back and away from the projector, the image would increase in format size. Therefore, in fixing the line of the picture plane, we also fix the physical size of the drawing. Furthermore, by moving the line backward and forward, the final position of the picture plane — and here the analogy with the projector ends — in relation to the object will also affect the amount of contextual information seen in the resulting perspective projection.

Vanishing Points

Usually in rectangular plans only two vanishing points are necessary. But if a plane were to exist in the plan at an angle, say, of 30°, it would become necessary to

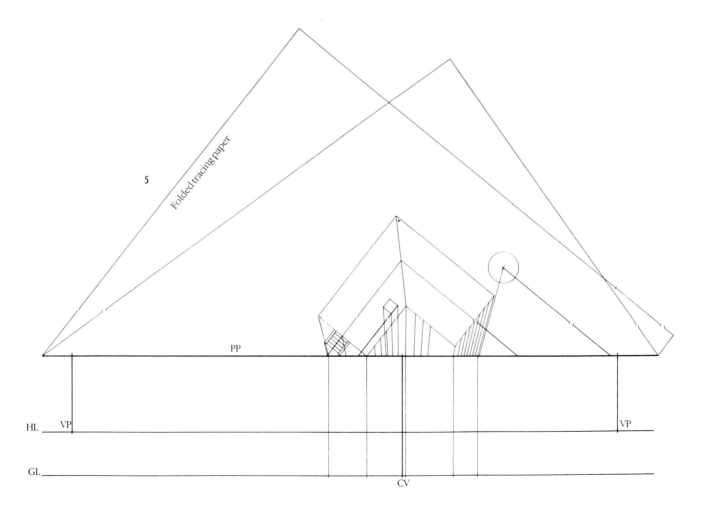

TWO POINT PERSPECTIVE DRAWING – STAGE TWO
Note: as with Stage One, the step-by-step sequence should be followed in conjunction with the accompanying main text.

5. Constructing the Perspective.
Having transferred all the basic co-ordinates into the scale along the line of the PP, remove the tracing paper overlay with the original drawing of the plan from the drawing board. Then tape a clean sheet of drawing paper to the board. This will act as the support for the perspective construction. Next carefully fold the tracing paper sheet along the line of the PP and tape it to the board with the PP (now represented by the fold) below the plan and in a horizontal position.

Begin the perspective drawing by marking a horizontal line below and clear of the PP across the bottom of the drawing sheet. This represents the Ground Line (GL) from which height measurements will later be projected.

Then draw a second horizontal line so that it corresponds, in distance from the GL, to the height of an average person (approx 167 cm (5ft 6in). This line represents eye level, or the horizon line (HL). Using the folded tracing paper as reference, first drop a vertical from the mark where the CV cuts the PP so that it cuts both the HL and the GL.

Next drop verticals from the respective VPs on the PP and record these on the HL. Continue by dropping verticals from those marks that represent all the main angles and projections in the plan.

6. Constructing Height Lines for Eaves.
The vertical line representing the point at which the plan touches the PP becomes the Vertical Measuring Line (VML). Measure the height of the VML up from the GL to the height of the eaves, using the measurement scale employed in the plan. The top and bottom edges of the two planes which this line defines can now be projected back to their respective VPs. To obtain all the related heights of other planes in the vertical plane, project their receding lines through the appropriate point on the height line and back to the VP. Thus the co-ordinates required to construct the perspective view are now in place. Note: to check which vanishing point the converging lines should be drawn to, simply consult the plan and note the direction of the plane in question.

7. Constructing Lines for Ridges.
The points at which the ridge lines cut the picture plane are now dropped vertically to the GL. These verticals become height lines on which their scale height is found, before projecting them back to the VP which serves them.

8. Adding Details.
After constructing the basic outlines, add details such as windows, chimneys and other features like the tree using exactly the same transfer process.

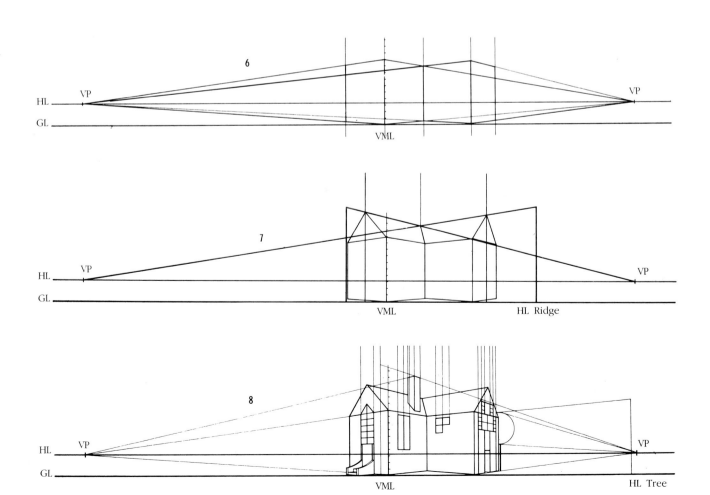

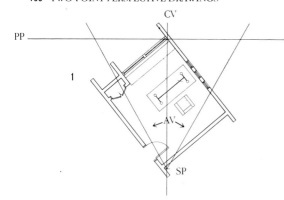

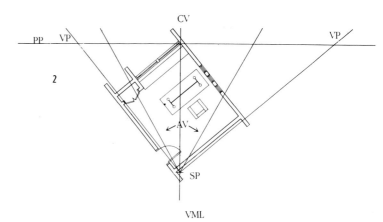

INTERIOR PERSPECTIVE – PLAN ROTATION METHOD
Note: again, the step-by-step sequence should be read in conjunction with the accompanying main text.
The procedure entails the rotation of a floor plan into a vertical alignment to give the best possible angle of view. This is achieved by drawing the 60° angle of vision on a separate sheet of tracing paper, which can then be manoeuvred around the plan until the most interesting viewpoint is found. The floor plan is then taped to the upper portion of the drawing board so that the direction of selected view point is to the top edge of the board.

1. Tape a sheet of tracing paper over the floor plan and lower portion of the board. Then position the Station Point (SP), the Centre of Visiion (CV), the angle of vision (AV) and the Picture Plane (PP) – (for method, see pages 102-103). The PP has been positioned to touch the far side corner of the floor plan – and thus provide a true-to-scale line for finding scaled heights in the contruction.

2. Next locate the two Vanishing Points (VPs) by projecting lines from the SP parallel to the angled wall planes – (for method, see pages 102-103).

3. Drop the line of the far corner of the room (the height line) vertically. Its scaled height is taken from the plan, and it will now function as the Vertical Measuring Line (VML). Use the VML to insert the horizontal line (HL) at the eye level of a seated or standing figure from the floor. Finally, drop the two VPs and record them on the HL.

4. The interior perspective can now be constructed. To find dimensions of objects in the horizontal plane project their angles in the plan back from the SP until they cut the PP. Then drop these lines vertically into the perspective space of the room. The heights of these planes are found by projecting lines from the appropriate VP and through their scaled height on the height line. Where these cut the required vertical denotes the scaled height at that point in the drawing.

project a third line from the station point parallel to this angle. This projection would then provide an ancillary vanishing point on the picture plane that would accommodate the singular convergence of this plane.

Sometimes vanishing points exist off the edge of the drawing sheet. In this event a paper strip appendage can be taped to the appropriate edge of the drawing paper and the vanishing point recorded.

Picture Plane Scale
Once transferred to the line of the picture frame, all the required points and features in the plan have now become reduced proportionally into a new scale. Being proportionally related to the scale of the plan, this scale will dictate the size of the perspective drawing.

Ground Line and Eye Level (Horizon Line)
Although we will proceed with the eye level set at 'normal' eye level above the ground, it is worth pausing to consider the implications of this when constructing perspectives. The position of the eye level should be a response to the type of building design on the board, and also to the characteristics of its site topology. For example, if a landscape setting exhibited ground features that needed to be conveyed in the perspective, the eye level, in order for the features to come into view, would have to be raised. Another design might find the building elevated on a mound or sited on a slope. In this case the eye level might be lowered below the

horizon in order to communicate this relationship more 'dramatically'.

However, whether a bird's eye view or a worm's eye view, the resulting perspective is arrived at using the same principles. The only general rule worthy of note is to avoid fixing the eye level at a height that will coincide with any prominent horizontal feature in elevation — such as a parapet, ridge, eaves line, etc. — as this, when seen in perspective, would appear as a horizontal line, despite any directional change in the planes.

Constructing the Perspective
Having established the basic perspective geometry, it should be decided whether or not to employ this construction drawing as the basis for a subsequent rendering. Generally, designers like to escape from the mechanical appearance of such drawings and to transform the key co-ordinates into another drawing support. A good method of leaving behind traces of the construction drawing is to trace off the required architectural form in perspective; which can then be easily rendered or photocopied onto a sheet of opaque drawing paper.

Another technique for avoiding construction lines is to work Stage Two of this process (see page 105) in a blue non-print pencil and record all the required lines in ink or graphite. The construction sheet can then be photocopied and, if required, resized into a new rendering surface.

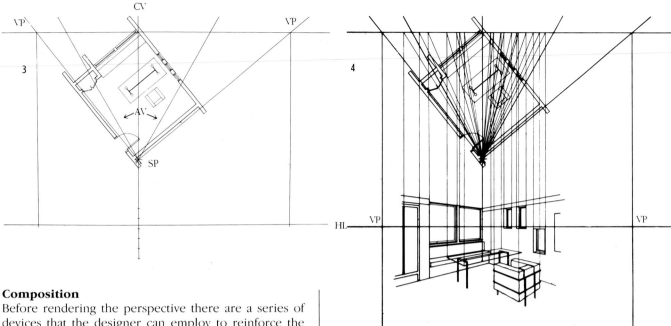

Composition

Before rendering the perspective there are a series of devices that the designer can employ to reinforce the drawing's visual message:

Cropping the Drawing

The relationship of the border to the projected architectural form is an important compositional issue. One golden rule is to avoid cropping the image so that the object/building occupies the centre of the format. Also, avoid horizontal lines halfway down the format, as such a location will divide the composition into two portions and thereby dilute the focus of visual interest.

It is the imaginative use of cropping, the interplay of foreground and background and the animation of the setting which transport the basic construction into a compelling illusion of space.

A good way of establishing the frame is to first review the characteristics of the architectural form in relation to its setting. For example, a tall, thin format will emphasize the verticality of a tower-like structure, while a frame with lateral emphasis will reinforce a horizontal mass.

A practical device that will help in the cropping of drawings is formed by two L-shaped pieces of cardboard. When used to form a frame, they allow subtle adjustments to the size and extent of the finished format.

Animating the Foreground

Extension of the lower edge of the picture frame will infer a greater depth between the picture plane (represented by the surface of the drawing paper) and the object-building. The resulting illusion of an increased foreground space can be animated using elements such as people, trees, and vehicles etc., which will, in turn, intensify the illusion of depth.

However, when designing foreground figure arrangements they should be grouped into overlapping clusters — as they would be seen in reality. Also, they should be compositionally structured in groups that do not create a symmetrical composition or block the message area. Moreover, foreground elements should appear to be true to the scale of the building. To establish foreground scale we need to return to the plan in order to determine some simple co-ordinates.

If a group of figures is to be positioned in the perspective drawing, first mark their location on the plan. Then draw a line parallel to one of the planes for which there is a vanishing point — from the group to the plane. This gives the height line. Now draw a line on the plan from the station point, through the group to the picture plane. This will give the vertical position of the group when the point is dropped into the perspective. As our eye level was taken to be 1650mm (63ins), the horizon line can be assumed as the height of a person. Therefore, if a line is drawn from the appropriate vanishing point and through the height line at ground level, the correct height is obtained in perspective. In fact, anywhere between this point and the height line the group will be true to scale in perspective.

Direction of Light

Another important issue that will have an impact on the composition is the direction of illumination. Prior to the rendering phase it is worth considering both the upper left and upper right as the location of the source of light. Each should be considered against the compositional pattern of shade and shadow that they generate together with their ability to illuminate the building form.

Interior Perspective

The two stage method of perspective projection can also be employed to produce adequate three-dimensional drawings of interior spaces. However it should be mentioned that there is often an important difference between the construction of exterior and interior perspectives — especially on those occasions when it is necessary to position the station point outside of the space being drawn. In this event, and in order to provide a representative and distortion-free interior view, the near end wall is 'removed' — an acceptable convention that allows visual access from outside the confines of the room. Using exactly the same principles as those outlined for plotting the exterior view of an architectural form, we can now enlist the more common method of interior perspective construction — the plan rotation method (see above).

COLOURED PENCIL RENDERING: JUAN CARLOS CALDERÓN

The sequence below depicts four stages in the development of a coloured pencil rendering of a perspective depicting the design for a private house in La Paz, by Bolivian architect Juan Carlos Calderón. His palette comprised, in the main, a selection of hues from the Berol Prismacolor range – including Raw Umber 941, Light Flesh 927, Flesh 939 and touches of Castell's Brown Ochre 182 for stonework and Olive Green 911 for foliage. The sky was built up from True Blue 903 and Castell's Blue Violet 137 with layers of Slate Gray 936 – the latter, together with hints of Pink 929, Orange 918 and

Black, being used throughout the perspective as a colour modifying agent.

1. The original line drawing was worked in pencil on tracing paper and copied on a dyeline printer – the print being over-exposed to achieve a clean, whitish background and leave a faint outline. However, the printed line drawing was, in parts, enhanced before rendering with a sharpened, black Prismacolor pencil.

2. Colour rendering began with a faint application of trial colours across the entire format of the drawing, using dull-

1

2

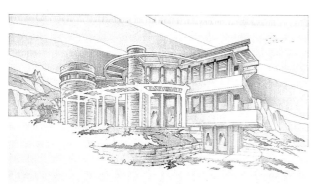

3

4

pointed pencils. The colour was applied using little pressure, the pencil point being allowed to glide over the paper and always worked in the same direction – in this case, vertically. Extreme care was taken to ensure that the lines of the strokes would not show; if they did, they were smoothed over lightly with a pad of soft tissue.

3. The process continued with the gradual building-up of the intensity of all the hues in a layer-by-layer fashion. Throughout, a lightness of touch was rigorously maintained and, as each layer of colour modified the one below it, a deliberate fading-off of each colour began. This systematic tonal graduation of colour is characteristic of Calderón's renderings. It is his means of introducing a spatial dynamic to the drawing and of emphasising the formal quality of the building design.

4. Finally, the addition of deeper tones involved the application of touches of pink and orange to warm-up the overall image. Also, to introduce a little more weight and 'tonal drama' an application of delicate films of black was made to the dark end of faded passages. The rendering was concluded with a last-minute delineation from a sharp, black Prismacolor. This was employed to develop a hierarchy of line weight in which thicker lines defined forms separated by greater distance. For example, within Calderón's hierarchy the contour separating the building from the sky receives the thickest line.

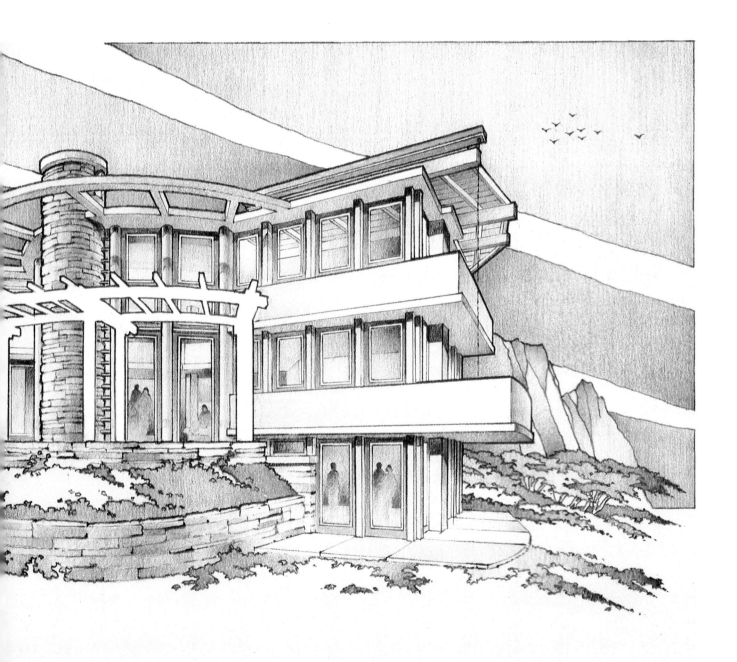

GALLERY

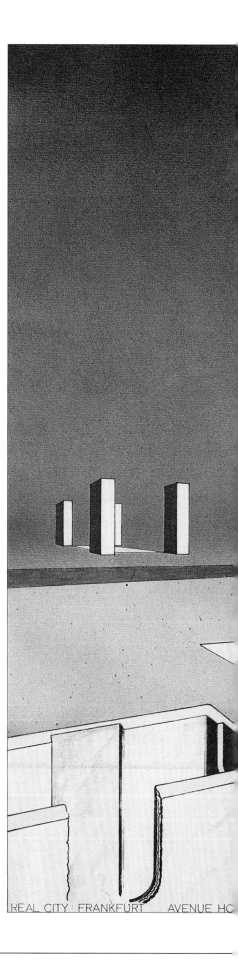

Above: Aerial Perspective from River, Cross Ness Housing, Thamesmead. Allies and Morrison. This perspective was constructed by one designer, reproduced via the photocopier onto plan paper, and the resulting print rendered, by a second designer, using Caran D'Ache pencils. Note the softness and evenness of the layered application – a skilful technique that recognises the atmospheric modification of colours by distance.

Left: Foyer Approach, Museum of the Moving Image, London. Avery Associates. A comparatively rare nightime sketch perspective used early in the design process and intended to explore the effect of the museum entrance area complete with its proto-constructivist neon tower.

Right: Perspective of Real City 'Villa'. Peter Cook. This dramatic perspective is typical of the artwork of Peter Cook. Worked in crayon and airbrush, flat, strong primary hues become starkly muted on shaded planes to create an image that embodies striking composition and great visual impact.

REAL CITY : FRANKFURT   AVENUE HO

GALLERY

PERSPECTIVE OF FUNDAMENTAL 'GUT' HULK & FACILITY GROUND   PETER COOK 1986

CASE STUDY · 1

FIFTIETH FLOOR INTERIOR OF THE SINGAPORE MINISTRY OF FINANCE BUILDING

INTERIOR DESIGNERS · B D P DESIGN

Based on a concept developed by the American architect, Hugh Stubbins, the design of the Ministry of Finance buildings was supervised by a Singapore design group known as Architects 61. Its interior design, however, was the subject of an international competition – BDP Design's preliminary entry being selected for its unassailable logic.

BDP Design is a London-based branch of The Building Design Partnership (BDP), the largest architectural practice in Europe. Headed by senior partner Rodney Cooper, they specialise in space planning and interior design. At the heart of their operation is an Acropolis computer-aided design system, capable of genrating all kinds of graphics in response to the complex and varied needs of modern commercial design.

Forty-nine of the fifty circular shaped floors of the Ministry of Finance building were space-planned using the Acropolis CAD system. After being fed with a corporate brief the machine identified the departmental structure for each floor, transposed the strucural diagram into planned blocks of allocated space and then converted this into a schedule of work-station components. At this point the pattern of fixed elements, such as partitions, filing frames, word processors, power and telecommunications outlets etc., had been established. Moreover, as the Acropolis is a true 3-D modelling system, this pattern could be reshuffled at will to respond to any modifications of the layout, and any aspect of the layout could be graphically generated in any drawing type and any colour combination, and be seen from any desired angle and to any scale.

However, as the top floor of the building was to house the offices of the Ministers of Trade and Industry, it required a special work environment. Consequently, and despite the sophistication of the computer-generated images, BDP decided to switch back to the drawing board

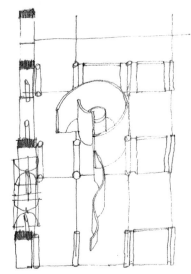

1. Left: The Singapore Ministry of Finance Building.   2. Above: BDP's Acropolis computer-aided space planning study for the fiftieth floor.   3. Above right: Preliminary axonometric projection visualised in fibre-tipped pen on detail paper.
4. Below: Developing concepts in ink-drawn perspective vignettes, by Martin Cook.

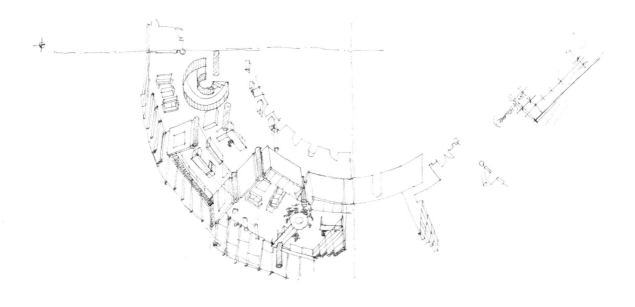

because, as Rodney Cooper explains, ultimately the creative process comes 'through the pencil and not through the machine'.

The original concept for the interior – with its strong play of radial and column forms – was developed on an intensive site visit to Singapore by the job team under the direction of John Barker. The basic plan ('footprint') separated the four ministerial offices from the central atrium containing a landscaped sculptured court with a circular indoor 'street' – the latter being approached from the floor below via a large, elegant spiral staircase (later abandoned due to security problems).

However, the most significant development to emerge from the visit was the discovery of *Feng Shui* – an oriental discipline that raised a range of cultural objections which meant that some wood-grains and certain colours were unacceptable to the clients and that personal assistants would not allow themselves to be seated facing towards office doors!

Having taken these factors on board, and formulated a basic idea that met with the client's approval, a more detailed design stage now began back in London – a process that was to involve a team of twelve designers working over a period of two years. Some of the initial sketches produced by Associate Designer, Martin Cook strongly indicate the design vocabulary the team wished to develop. The drawings trace the evolution of the project from the initial concepts imported from Singapore and exhibit an immediate concern for 3-dimensional space. The preliminary thumbnail sketches diagram the conceptual and curvilinear dynamic in relation to the four main office areas. These are then re-examined in greater detail via an exhaustive sequence of orthographics, comprised mainly of vertically projected axonometrics. Worked in fibre-tipped pen on detail paper, these drawings flesh out the initial ideas with remarkable clarity and purpose, and occasionally the aerial views represented by these projections are brought down to eye-level via clusters of perspective vignettes.

Cook describes his thumbnail sketches as 'exploring 3-dimensional form in a crude way'. The drawings are essentially 2-dimensional but they represent a means of 'feeling out' something that is not yet tangible – if you like, a way of fleshing-out an idea. However, he is quick to point out that this exploratory activity is not conducted in isolation. Success is invariably the product of a close working relationship within the team.

As the design for the fiftieth floor evolved and as scale increased, the thumbnail sketches were transformed into a summary of othographics which centred on the plan. This in turn triggered another drawing stage – represented by hundreds of working drawings and full-sized details – that recognised all the main formal elements of the interior in terms of materials, colours and methods of assembly – ie. they described in graphic detail how the design proposal could, in reality, be constructed.

The communication of the finalised design to the client took the form of a series of large presentation boards plus sample boards displaying actual materials and fittings. These boards were also reproduced for reduction into a brochure so that the client could retain a record of the entire scheme.

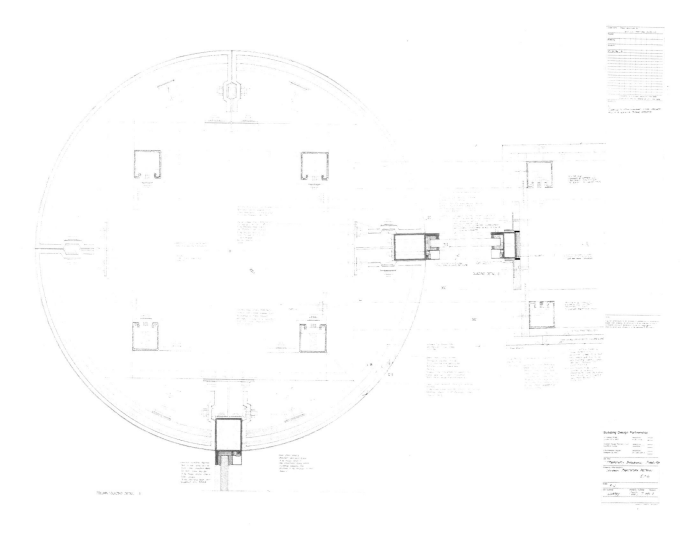

5. *Above opposite: The visualization process enlists a more distant viewpoint from which the mind's eye can evaluate the evolving design.*   6. *Above: The onset of working drawings reflects the clarity of the definitive design stage.*
7. *Below: Interior view of the completed fiftieth floor.*

CASE STUDY · 2

HENLEY ROYAL REGATTA HEADQUARTERS

ARCHITECTS · TERRY FARRELL & COMPANY

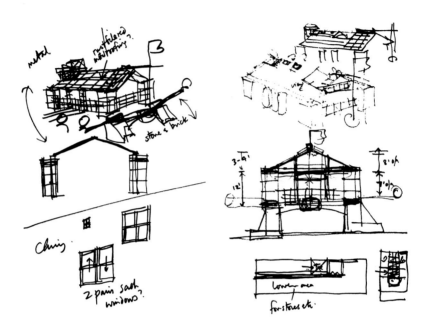

The widely published architecture and distinctive graphic style of Terry Farrell is internationally well known. Less known, however, is his use of drawing within the process of design. For example, in the London-based practice of Terry Farrell and Company, high priority is rarely given to graphics that depict a finished architecture as a built event. Rather, much greater emphasis is given to sketches and drawings that represent the essential spirit of a design concept. Therefore, in order to demonstrate how different drawing types function along a design sequence, this chapter retraces the paper trail of graphics leading the Farrell's design for the Headquarters of the Henley Royal Regatta on the River Thames.

From the outset of the project a profusion of sketch drawings focused on embryonic ideas in 3-dimensional forms. Projected from freehand plans and elevations, they were drawn in ink on detail and tracing paper. The sketch axonometrics also received a selective colour rendering from coloured pencils and Magic Markers. However, at this stage colour was not used to describe surface appearance, but employed to highlight form and to intensify the 3-dimensional illusion of the graphics.

Project architects, Doug Streeter and John Letherland explain their design process as always combining orthographics with 3-dimensional drawings – a multi-dimensional approach which allows the problems of shape and massing to be addressed at an early stage. Moreover, they describe their initial use of black and white drawings as having a neutralising effect on all but the emphasis of architectural form. When colour is introduced its function is to enhance a formal modelling. Thus, decisions concerning the actual colour of the building are withheld until a much later stage.

This initial graphic modelling of the developing 3-dimensional concept also involved small-scale models. However, the most significant development was the sequence of prophetic doodles by Terry Farrell. By crystalising his initial response to the scheme, these small ink drawings came to act as an iconic and continuous point of reference throughout the design process.

The sketches immediately identified a clear structural diagram, comprising the profile of a shed-like roof above a central arch, as seen from the river, and this established the main design statement at a very early stage. In so doing they triggered a chain of evolving drawings and provided a kind of check against which ensuing and thematic variations could be tested, and they exerted a powerful influence over all other aspects of the developing architectural form. For instance, in order to emphasise the strongly axial form of the building planning on all three levels, the elevation and its shed roof were graphically extruded back into the site against a grid to be sliced into a series of progressive sectional cuts.

As the design moved toward a greater sense of reality, subsequent drawings increased in scale and, as a consequence, more definitive orthographics were drafted on tracing paper and acetate to address the form in detail.

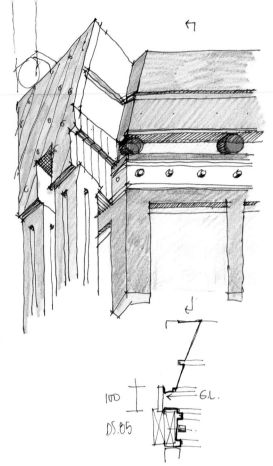

1. Left: Terry Farrell's ink sketches – 'the driving force of the spirit of the design' – represent his initial and prophetic reaction to the brief. 2. Above: embryonic axonometric projections, in marker and coloured pencil, focus on an evolving 3-D form. 3. Below: Early elevation study in coloured ink and pencil on detail paper.

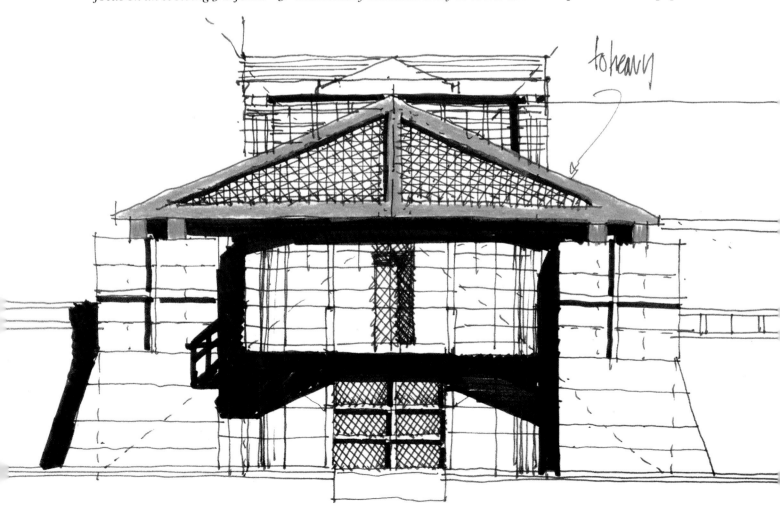

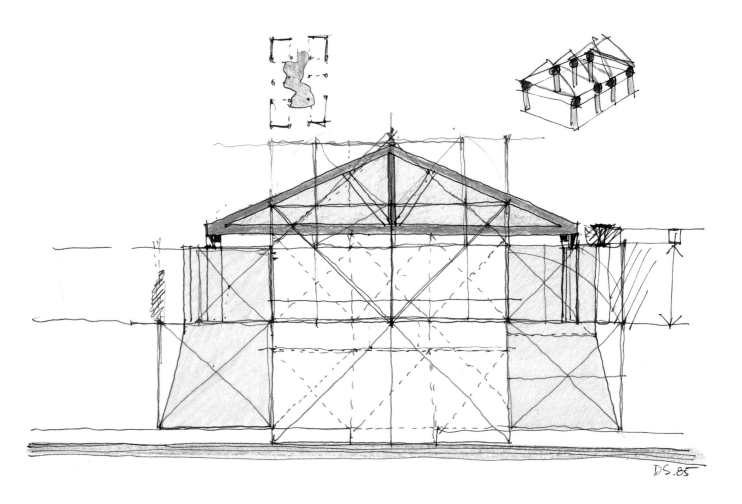

DS.85

However, this first excursion into a magnified scale was to be profoundly influenced by another crucial drawing.

This emerged when The Times Newspapers Ltd., requested a drawing, to illustrate an article they were planning on the project, that was 'hard-hitting' in detail whilst epitomising the richness of the original concept. In order to meet a tight deadline this was produced quickly in a freehand line, whilst shadow rendering was worked on an overlay placed on top of an earlier, large, hardline elevation. However, more importantly, its creation, by making direct reference to Farrell's sketch, performed a kind of reappraisal of the scheme. As a result, an additional layer of decoration – lost in the previous magnification of scale – supplemented that of the original sketch. The urns, rustification and battered piers etc. now came clearly into focus and, as building materials became fixed, architectural colour became an issue.

This closer examination of the building involved several layers and types of drawings. These included exploded orthographic projections of the front elevation that studied the 3-dimensional relationships between the building cross-section as an extrusion of the main river elevation. Also, a series of intensive design sessions focused on the resolution of details such as the subtle geometry of the staircase – a phase that paved the way for the definitive working drawings.

Later, a set of finalised design orthographics worked in pencil to a scale of 1:50 were employed to review all the known forms, proportions and materials intended for the project. In order to devise a colour palette which would both recognise and extend the hues of selected building materials, these drawings were worked on in coloured pencil by Terry Farrell.

However, after this, drawings ceased to be the central decision-making tool and many final choices as to colour and decoration were made on site. While the building was nearing completion, large swatches of colour were actually placed over it so that they could be judged *in situ*. Fine-tuning of the decoration was completed in exactly the same manner – timber stencil mock-ups painted blue being mounted on the building to facilitate a more thorough assessment of the wave motif frieze.

Finally, throughout the twelve month duration of the project there were regular, informal meetings with the clients — the Chairman and Secretary of the Henley Regatta – in which the raw sketches, supported by plans and elevations, were used to illustrate the progress of the design. This constant contact between client and designers meant few formal presentation drawings were produced. However, one of them – an elevation – was coloured-up for presentation to the Regatta Committee for installation in the completed building.

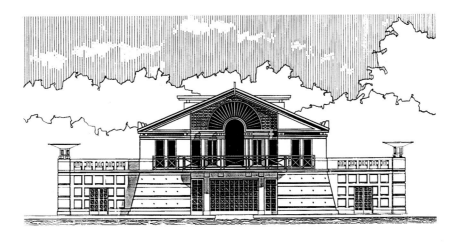

HENLEY ROYAL REGATTA HEADQUARTERS

4. Left: Diagrammatic study in coloured pencil, ink and marker on detail paper employs an abstraction of line and colour to review the proportional relationships in the riverside facade. 5. Above: Doug Streeter's technical pen drawing on tracing paper produced for The Times. The graphic version of the building was to revive Farrell's original and more richly decorated concept. 6. Below: Thames-side view of the Henley Royal Regatta Headquarters.

8
PRESENTATION

The presentation phase represents the second stage of an evolving design concept. At this point in the design sequence the idea usually becomes transformed into a new graphic form for its communication to others. The onset of this phase, however, is often also signalled by a completely different drawing attitude. This involves not only converting the paper trail of design into a formal definition of the architectural form, but also trying to make a profound impression on the viewer.

In reality the presentation phase represents an artificial juncture in the design process. This is because the need to transpose the design concept into a format for sharing with others is a consideration that has already been evolving in tandem with the design. The only real difference is that the graphic types, used hitherto as design tools, now find new roles as vehicles for communicating spatial ideas. However, the influence of the design on the mode of its presentation represents only one of three components that make up the chain of communication. Namely: the presenter, the design concept and the audience.

The Presenter
At one end of the chain is the designer-presenter. Graphically, a presentation has to be created within the competence of his or her graphic skills. Therefore, a choice has to be made against this competence as to which series of drawings are to be produced and which presentation mode will best convey the design project. Moreover, this decision will also be calculated against the available time-scale. Obviously these considerations should occur early in the design process.

The Design Concept
One important facet of communicating architectural ideas is that of emotional response. For example, compare the graphic rendition of a design for a log cabin with that of a high-tech building. Immediately, the notion of each architectural form suggests its own line quality — in other words, a freehand line for the former, and a hardline treatment for the latter. This language of emotional response can also be extended. For example, while thinking of the two buildings you should designate drawing mediums, colour rendering mediums, lettering styles and drawing surfaces for each imaginary present-ation. The fact that the two resulting lists can provide quite different responses is significant. This is because the various mediums and drawing techniques can, in themselves, impart emotional characteristics particular to their use. In presentation it is the orchestration of these mediums and techniques that can enhance or detract from the meaning of the communication.

The Audience
Some knowledge of the audience is the third factor in the communication chain. For example, a presentation strategy aimed at a panel of professional designers would be quite different to one aimed at a lay audience. In the case of the latter, the pictorialism of perspectives, paraline projections and, to an extent, elevations would be more in evidence — because non-designers often experience difficulty visualizing three-dimensional space from orthographic diagrams. Other issues that affect the form of communication include the presentation setting, the size of the audience and whether or not the designer is to be present. So, presenting a package requires an awareness of the presentation environment and a degree of control over it in order to enhance communication.

Presentation Types
Traditional wall displays represent the most common form of design communication. They usually comprise drawings, photographs and written material, but are often augmented with slide presentations, video films, reports and scale models. Presentation commonly takes place with the designer offering a verbal commentary that guides the audience along a linear route through the exhibited material. This audio-visual path follows a chronological sequence that shadows the design sequence. It begins with a review of salient issues, objectives, site analysis and the development of the design response and climaxes in the definitive design; the ensuing criticism often functioning to 'test' the proposal against the stated aims. However, there are occasions, such as in design competitions, when a wall display has to function autonomously. It has to be designed to speak for itself, providing a total exposure of information in which all the graphic components are simultaneously visible.

By way of contrast, there are two other forms of presentation which disclose content in sequential fragments. These methods rely heavily on the memory of the audience to reconstruct a comprehensive picture of the design:

Slide presentations have numerous advantages over wall displays. For example, the audience remains captive within a darkened room — their concentration being focused on the projected image. Also, information in a slide package is disclosed in a predetermined sequence, with its order and timing under the control of the presenter. Moreover, such presentations allow single, double and multiple images to be projected at any one time, and can also be presented by remote control. And finally, spoken commentaries can be tape-recorded to synchronize with automatic projections and, by adding background music or sound effects, specific moods can be evoked.

Reports function as miniature exhibitions that, like slide presentations, reveal their information sequentially. Usually produced with a greater emphasis on written material, the book format is portable and can be used to communicate ideas to larger and dispersed audiences.

Presentation 'Psychology'

As a result of numerous communication workshops with students at Oxford, it has become apparent that, apart from the need to draw convincingly, the notion of 'presenting a building design' is synonymous with 'marketing a product'. In other words, in the mind of the student, communicating design intentions involves a need to attract, to impress and to sell. This promotional attitude involves the search for visually compelling images and graphic displays that exhibit not only the quality of the design, but also the graphic prowess of the designer. As a follow-up to these workshops, students have — while themselves being assessed — conducted their own observational studies on the reactions of critical audiences. From the ensuing feedback the following pointers emerged:

1. In wall displays, a primary need is to clearly design and rehearse a visual and verbal path through the exhibition. A good impression was made when the 'history' of the design route was explained at the outset of presentation. This was particularly well-received when illustrated with the original concept graphics mounted directly into the display.

2. The strategic deployment of colour and contrast was found to play a key role in highlighting important stages along the display route. For example, stabs of colour in achromatic presentations, or intensified hues in colour-rendered displays, attracted the eye to major points of interest. This interplay of contrast was also seen to extend to the size and techniques used in drawings. For example, not only did changes in technique create focal points within an individual image, but variations in the size of images avoided the blandness of their being regularly ordered and repetitively-sized.

3. Drawing size was particularly important — larger drawings being judged as more potent than smaller drawings. This aspect of communication was exploited fully by one second year student who, wishing to make her mark, drafted a section of her design proposal to full scale. Confronted with such a huge drawing her panel of critics had to examine its content using a ladder! Indeed, in challenging the traditional convenience of scale, she not only echoed Le Corbusier's occasional need to produce a full-sized sectional drawing, but had also challenged her tutors. The result created a memorable event, and elicited a favourable response.

4. Graphic format size also regulates the viewing distance of an image — an important issue when communicating to larger groups of people. So, anticipate the size of audience, and then design the presentation accordingly. A common error amongst beginners is to ignore the viewing distance and spend hours producing drawings at too small a scale or in mediums too faint to read. However, a simple experiment can establish the viewing distance of various line weights and graphite grades: simply arrange the different lines on a sheet of paper pinned to a wall. Then measure their visibility over distance, and the viewpoints at which they become 'invisible'.

5. Students see distraction as the main enemy of presentation. Disruption in the flow of information can easily occur, and two common examples were cited: the disorientation caused when northpoints, together with their attendant drawings, faced different directions; and when displays mounted to address the eye level of a standing audience found a seated one, and vice-versa. Above all, was the distraction caused by the natural fascination for scale models. When elaborate models were shown in conjunction with drawings, the former became the preoccupying focus of attention — which has led to the practice of disclosing models only at the appropriate moment in the sequence of presentation.

One interesting facet of these student observations is the firm belief that people react quite individually to different graphic mediums and supports. Generally speaking, students believe that part of an audience reaction concerns the perceived length of time spent on a drawing. In other words, that a quick sketch would not command the same respect as a more formal drawing (a view challenged by tutors). In addition, there is an assumption that a drawing made in charcoal would not receive the same attention as if it had been worked in ink, and that a drawing produced on high quality paper is given more credence than one worked on tissue or newsprint. As a result, the quest for prestigious presentations has triggered the fashion for displaying colour-rendered ink drawings under glass — an expensive operation rooted in the notion that a layer of transparent material can elevate the graphic to an art form.

However, despite this search for more visually compelling forms of presentation, there is no doubt that — especially within a society literally bombarded with images — rich and variegated graphic displays do grab longer attention spans than bland displays. Also, that within a display individual drawings should be both clear and honest in their message. Therefore, in order to complete the chain of communication, a 'good' drawing is one that earns commitment and empathy in the viewing. Conversely, drawings that are weak, insensitive or inconsequential invite instant visual rejection.

Presentation: Layout and Lettering

An ability to present architectural projects is simply an extension of a basic design skill. As such, it should be approached with the same care and attention given to its appearance and structure as that given to the building design.

Layout is a design discipline that involves the composing of all the fragmented bits of information into a co-ordinated and logical communication system. In wall displays this layout will function on two perceptual levels: on the one hand, it will have to work visually as a total format; on the other, it must also function in detail. The former requirement concerns the initial impact of factors such as proportion, balance and cohesion; while the latter represents the communication stage, when drawings, diagrams and supporting annotation are read sequentially and cross-referenced in order to accumulate a total picture of the design proposal.

A good way of understanding this dual perception of layout is to examine the layout design of a newspaper. For instance, if we scan a newspaper front page from a few feet away we realize its overall structure. Certain graphic elements such as headline, lead photograph and the name of the paper emerge from the hierarchy of the layout as a result of size, boldness and contrast. However, when we move closer to read the paper, another and more detailed layer of information comes into view. At this close range the hitherto gray blocks of text become discernible in detail, as do a whole range of smaller images and graphic devices. Underlying and controlling this arrangement of pictures and words is an invisible structural framework. In order to detect the pattern of this structure we have to adopt a perception that momentarily switches off from reading the printed matter and switches on to 'reading' the unprinted white areas of the format. It is this pattern of so-called 'negative space' that is so important in layout design, and it is a design element that should be under the control of the designer. For example, we exercise this control when we arrange letters to form words; without this arrangement their message would be meaningless.

Similarly, the space surrounding drawings should also be controlled within a planned, overall pattern of negative space involving the entire format of a presentation. If we apply this double-functioning view of positive and negative space to the positioning of a drawing on a sheet we can begin to appreciate the idea of a small drawing appearing lost against a vast expanse of background. Conversely, we can also appreciate the point of graphic overload when an overcrowded display loses impact amid a visual confusion.

One important factor in perception is the eye's search for stability and this can be demonstrated using a simple figure-ground experiment. For example, if we place a black square at the dead centre of a white retangular

Depths in metres

KEY PLAN

JUNE 1986

Mark B. Artus

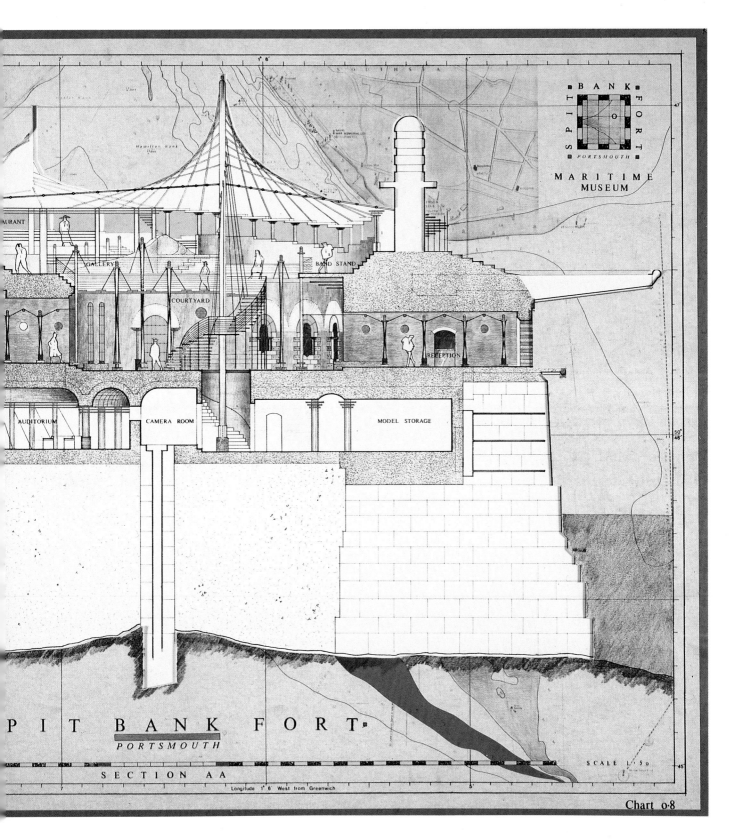

*Spit Bank Fort Conversion, River Solent, Nr Portsmouth. Mark Artus. A
student's compact presentation section drawn, on a scale of 1:50, to
communicate the rehabilitation of a river fort as a maritime museum.
Notice how the title, scale and section annotation form a plinth for the
overall composition.*

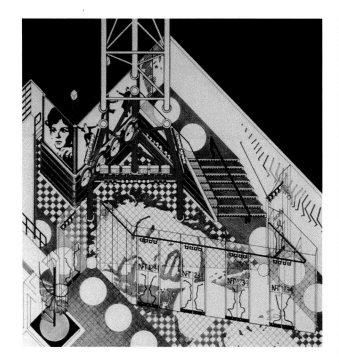

Left: Concept Axonometric of the Museum of the Moving Image and the National Film Theatre Foyer. Avery Associates. Its visual impact derives from intense detail set against a bland background and selective use of colour to reinforce the focal point.
Right: Elevation of the Holt House. Batey and Mack. The distinctive graphics of Mark Mack make the rotated plan appear to occupy a space forward of its attendant projection – the two orthographic views being fused together into a single image by multi-coloured particles of a sprayed pigment.

background, the contained figure will appear unstable. In fact, it will seem to be sliding down the format. To counteract this movement we have to reposition the black square slightly higher than halfway up the white field. The result is a compensatory 'visual ledge' of white space on which the black square appears to come to rest. All kinds of visual ledges occur in architectural graphics. For example, there is the conventional boldness of the groundline in elevations and sections which functions to root the image of the building to the paper. There is also the stabilizing use of bands of lettering, which are often located below the dynamic of a tilted axonometric or isometric in order to create a ledge.

Lettering

When conceived as a design component, lettering can perform several functions in a display. One of the most important is its use as a transitional element between other graphic elements. However, lettering should find its own scale in a layout without appearing either too mean, or assuming an over-sized proportion that might negate the impact of an attendant drawing. A direct means of selecting size is simply to test a chosen face over the predicted viewing distance. Also, the selection of a simple and efficient style of lettering, used in a consistent fashion, will aid clarity of communication. As in a newspaper page, there can be up to three or more sizes of letterforms in a presentation, with the largest functioning as a title and the smallest operating within the format of an individual drawing. Beyond size, this hierarchical use of lettering is achieved by variations in boldness, placement in the layout and colour.

Lettering Drawings

An efficient method of annotating drawings is to stack written information into blocks positioned either above, below, or to one side of the drawn image. Labels can

then be clearly keyed into their graphic counterparts without confusing the drawing. Another method annotates drawings with numbers — the numbers referring the viewer to a legend which, within the overall sheet layout, is located clearly in relation to the drawing. When annotating an element in a drawing, you should aim to create compact blocks of lettering. In this way, the block becomes a manageable design component. Also, when labelling room spaces in plans, select a lettering size that sits comfortably within the space. And when lettering irregular-shaped spaces, position labels at their visual centre of gravity. When using stencil and pressure transfer lettering two forms of letter spacing are in common use: mechanical and optical. Mechanical spacing refers to those sheets of instant lettering (and some stencils) that incorporate registration marks which regulate the distance between letters. On the other hand, optical spacing involves the arrangement of letters by eye. This is a positive-negative exercise that aims to create visually unified elements. A good tip for beginners is to practise optical spacing by initially spacing letters as close as possible without their actually touching.

Traditional Layouts

Traditionally, design drawings are arranged on sheets following a serial system in which the elevation is directly extruded from the plan, and the section extruded from the plan and the elevation. In reflecting the principles of third angle projection, orthographic elements are all drawn to the same scale for ease of drafting and visual cross-referencing. The direct working relationship between the plan and the elevation is a traditional graphic that is often fused to avoid the two images apparently floating around on the sheet. For example, this fusion is a recurrent theme in the distinctive work of Mark Mack, who will colour render the ground plane slice below the elevation. This vertical plane then functions as a field on which the plan, together with surrounding details, will be recorded. Another feature of his personalized modification is that the plan is tilted in response to an elevation drawing that presents two facade planes within a three-quarter view of the building design. Many designers develop a personal version of the traditional orthographic configuration. This preference in layout will often subordinate in scale repetitive drawings while promoting in size a favourite drawing type that the designer feels best conveys the design concept.

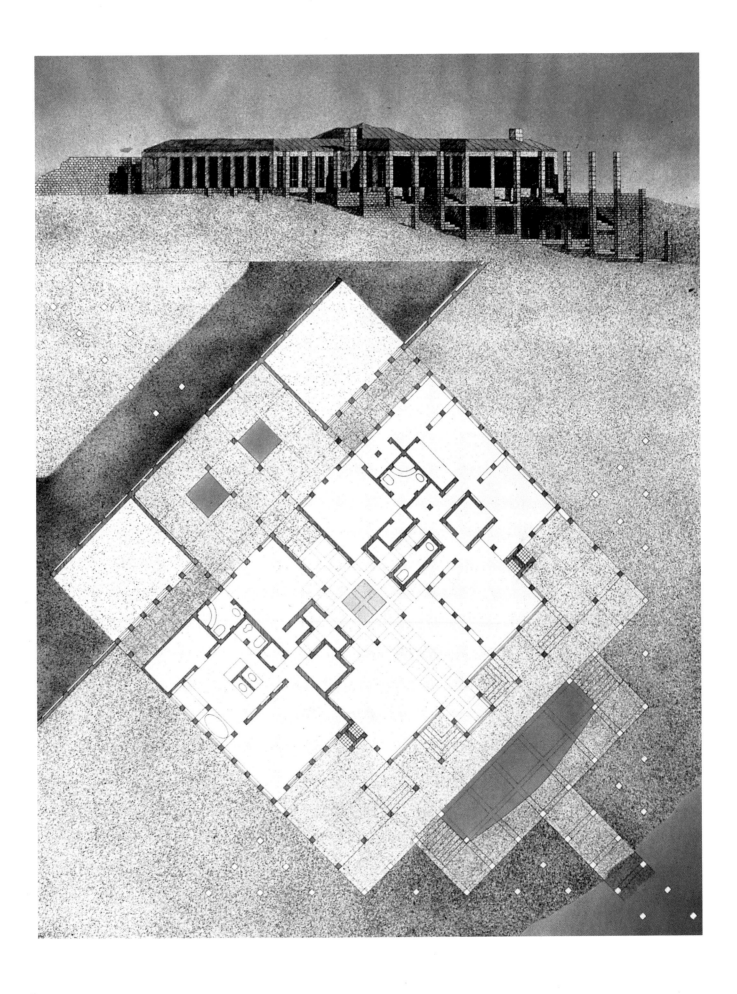

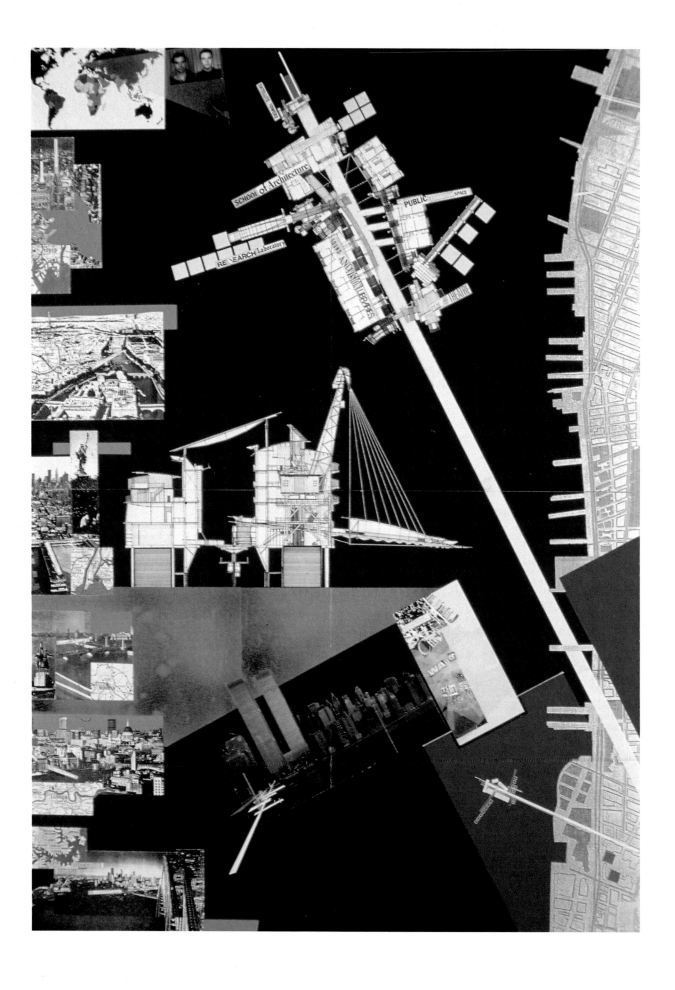

Experimental Layouts

Presentation layouts now comprise a wide range of traditional, modified and hybrid graphic arrangements. A major influence on this experimentation has been the growth of the international design competition and the subsequent publication of prizewinners in design journals. As a result of the competition restriction on size and the number of sheets, and the designer's need to catch the judge's eye in preliminary rounds of selection, this more dynamic and adventurous approach to layout design has evolved. The competition layout is characterized by considerable variation in the scale of drawings and the squeezing together, overlapping and layering of graphic information within the format. Such layouts are carefully orchestrated, being reminiscent of how an artist might plan an abstract composition. Indeed, the assembly of a series of multi-view fragments into the frozen dynamic of a large and complex layout has obvious roots in Cubism and Constructivism.

Structuring Layouts

Architectural layouts often comprise a range of graphic material that can include various types and sizes of drawings, prints, photographic images and text, etc. — a diversity that necessitates the creation of a collage presentation. The best method of arranging constituent parts is to structure their layout against a lightly drawn grid. Usually, the shape of the site or the building design will determine the basis of the overall graphic structure. For example, if the shape fits within a square or rectangle the grid can be used to brace and co-ordinate the sequencing of images.

Meanwhile, the 'negative space' between each graphic element should be designed to help guide the viewer's eye on a pre-planned journey around the format. When images appear to float, simply tighten up the negative space between them. And as part of this sequencing, remember that lettering can function to support, anchor, and link the components of the layout. The grid can also be eroded by the layout while still retaining its underlying integrity. Furthermore, a parent grid can generate other grids in order to develop the dynamic of a counter-structure. This kind of structural interplay is exemplified in the diagonal dynamic of the prize-winning single-sheet submission by Ron Gibbons and Mark Newey (see facing page). However, even within the most dynamic of layouts, harmony, balance, hierarchy of size, desired sequence of information, together with contrast and focus are all qualities that should be investigated before the layout becomes permanent, and a rehearsal in the form of thumbnail sketches worked against a grid is a good way of proceeding.

Left: Competition Layout. Ron Gibbons and Mark Newey. This condensed prize-winning design communicates its ideas in a refreshing manner using a structure of static and dynamic graphic elements.
Right: Presentation Layout. Camden Theatre design. Nigel Dancey and Julian Gitsham. An unusual vertical layout that arranges its drawn, printed and photographic components against a diagonal grid.

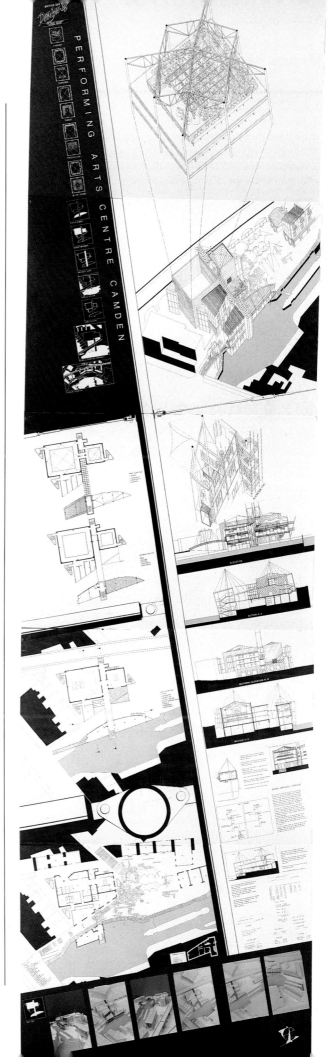

Presentation: Modified Drawing Types

Each layout design will adapt to the uniqueness of each design project and will be generated by the range of drawing types and images found necessary to adequately describe its complexity. Also, within the layout certain types of drawing may be modified in order to fulfil specific communication roles.

The emergence of the key drawing as the central communication vehicle in a presentation usually involves the recycling of a graphic type that has already proven its worth as a descriptive tool earlier in the design sequence. Having been identified as the best graphic model to represent the design, this graphic type can also become subject to a radical modification. Furthermore, this modification can also evolve the hybrid combination of two different types of drawing as a means of increasing their powers of communication beyond the level which they can achieve individually.

Split elevations provide one such example. Produced by cutting away part of the facade in the plane of the elevation, they simultaneously convey information about the inside and outside of a building.

Historically, split elevations were symmetrically arranged around a central, vertical dividing line that

separated the elevational view from the sectional view. Whereas modern versions of this hybrid drawing type tend to indulge in a deconstruction of the facade so that a direct working relationship between envelope and structural support is exposed.

In also allowing a simultaneous sectional and elevational view, the split or part-elevation results from a sectional slice being removed from a selected portion of a building design. Meanwhile, that part of the building not included in the slice — i.e., planes existing behind the line of the slice — remains intact to appear in elevation form.

Part Elevation of the Herman Miller Distribution Centre, Chippenham, Wiltshire. Nicholas Grimshaw. By allowing a view of its underlying structure, this part deconstruction of the facade is a modern relative of the split elevation – a drawing type much used in the past to convey simultaneous impressions of exterior and interior appearance. To produce this image a pen and ink drawing was photocopied for a rendering treatment involving a combination of markers and coloured pencils.

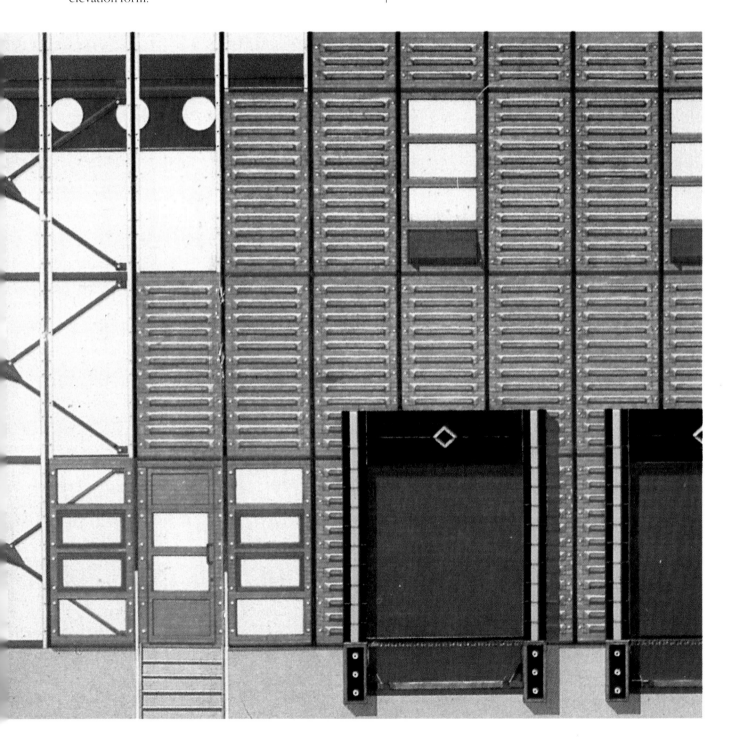

Cutaway graphics can also combine the section with the three dimensions of paraline projections and even perspectives. In these hybrid drawings, portions of wall and roof are removed to give an aerial visual access to interior spaces and their details.

In contrast to the removal of the roof (as in a 'lidless' axonometric), or the facing wall (as in a sectional perspective), the section — when applied to axonometrics — can travel in three dimensions in response to the kind of view that is required to be exposed.

In such drawings the graphic begins as an exterior view of architectural form, before it is cut into to expose the selected area of the interior space. Whenever such a cut is made, however, it is important to ensure that its trajectory is both deliberate and obvious. Also, any potential confusion between the exterior and interior will be avoided when the abstraction of the slice — usually indicated in black poché work to reveal the thickness of sliced wall, etc. — is clearly shown.

Exploded drawings are a drawing type that is borrowed occasionally from the techniques of the graphic designer. In stretching the space between architectural components, they attempt to explain the working relationship between them. This graphic represents the disassembly or fragmentation of elements along vertical and horizontal or radial directional paths — the 'explosion' being frozen graphically at the point that best explains the interdependence of the elements.

Expanded drawings are simply a variation of the exploded graphic. In stretching the space between planes in a single direction, this drawing type is exemplified when a roof structure is raised above an axonometric to create a view of internal space.

More complicated versions can stretch a whole sequence of architectural elements, such as the commonly employed expansion of a vertical stack of related floor plans in a multi-level building. This graphic technique is particularly useful for the unimpeded view of individual but related isometric floor planes.

Serial drawings have their roots in the comic strip frame and the movie storyboard. They are employed when the designer wishes to take the viewer on a conceptual journey around, towards or through a building design. Usually shown as perspectives, serial drawings can also incorporate a whole variety of drawing types in a frame-by-frame account of movement through the space of a design (see pages 150-51).

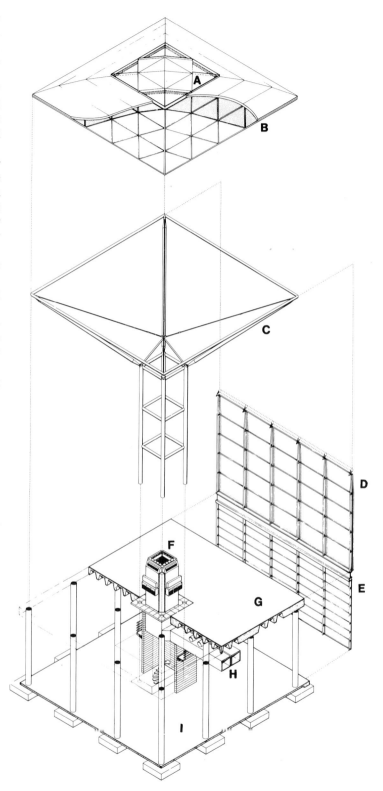

Expanded Axonometric of Support Structure, Stansted Airport Terminal. Foster Associates. Expanded and exploded graphics have many functions in architectural design. For example, they can be used to stretch a stack of floor plans when dealing with multi-level building designs or, as here, be employed to explain the assembly of components.

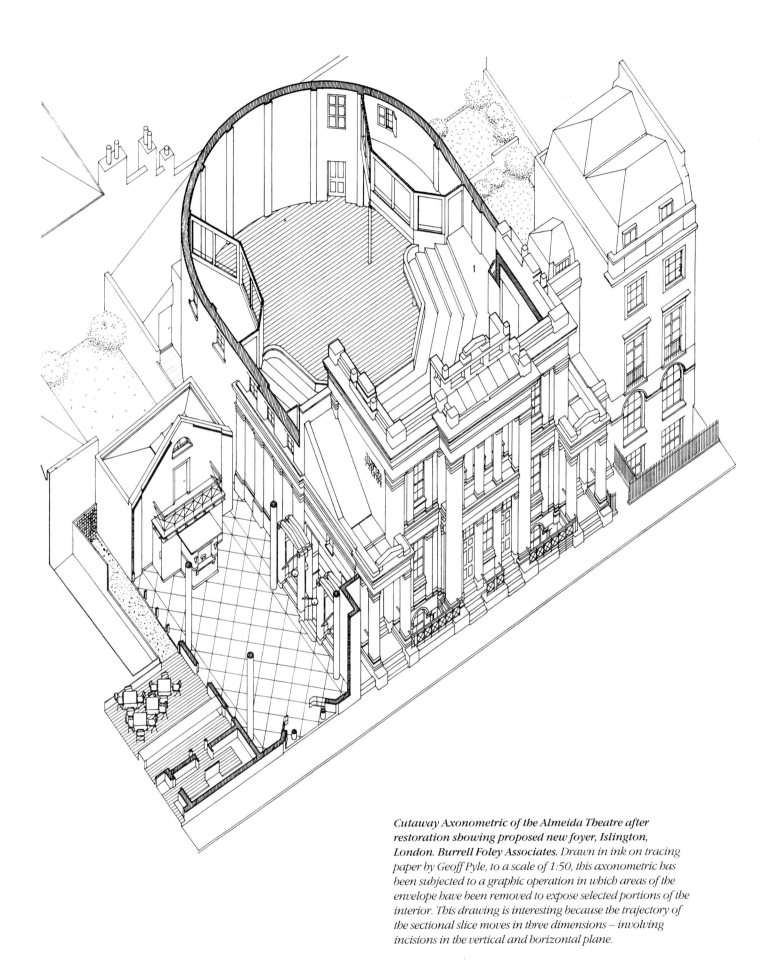

Cutaway Axonometric of the Almeida Theatre after restoration showing proposed new foyer, Islington, London. Burrell Foley Associates. Drawn in ink on tracing paper by Geoff Pyle, to a scale of 1:50, this axonometric has been subjected to a graphic operation in which areas of the envelope have been removed to expose selected portions of the interior. This drawing is interesting because the trajectory of the sectional slice moves in three dimensions – involving incisions in the vertical and horizontal plane.

Reproducing Drawings · Same-Size Reproduction

Copies of architectural drawings are made for many purposes. These include their use in presentation layouts and brochures, for publicity and publication, and for communicating design proposals to other designers and, of course, to clients and builders.

As some reprographic processes offer full colour reproduction and the facility to make reductions and enlargements, while others are limited to making monochrome and same-size prints, the selection of a reproduction process will be linked both to the nature of the original print and its intended function. However, as architectural graphics tend to be large in format and traditionally worked on transparent papers, the dyeline print process, in relying upon transparency for its method of reproduction, has become central to the day-to-day proliferation of architectural drawings.

Dyeline Printing

Developed in the 1920s from the earlier ferro-prussiate 'blueprint' process, dyeline printing enabled the rapid copying of architectural drawings to become universally practicable. Hitherto, copies of drawings had to be laboriously hand-traced or, before the advent of tracing paper, duplicated by the 'pouncing' technique — that is, pricking lines and their intersections through a master drawing and onto a backing-sheet, before redrawing them using the pin holes as guide marks. Also known as 'diazo' or 'white-printing', dyeline printing has, today, become the most common means of reproducing architectural drawings. It is a fast and comparatively cheap method capable of printing only one-to-one, or same-size, copies of large-scale drawings made on transparent drawing materials, such as tracing paper or film. Prints can only be produced as monochrome impressions — their hue being governed by the type of print paper and the kind of dyeline process in use. But the main drawback of dyeline printing is that its prints are not entirely lightfast; their extended exposure to a strong sunlight causing the image to quickly fade and the paper to deteriorate. Although commonly associated with the duplication of working drawings for the transmittal of construction details to the builder, the process is also widely used for printing presentation drawings in line and tone. The resulting prints are then used directly in presentation, but often receive a second-stage rendering in order to introduce colour — the techniques used being restricted by the unique qualities of different print papers (see below).

Another important aspect of dyeline presentation printing occurs when copies are made at an intermediate drawing stage. This technique involves making copies of a basic line drawing in order to use its prints as the basis of a development in two quite different graphic directions — such as a design drawing and a working drawing. The technique is employed as a time-saver especially when working against pressing deadlines.

The Dyeline Process

To make a dyeline print from a drawing, the original is placed face-up over a sheet of print paper which is large

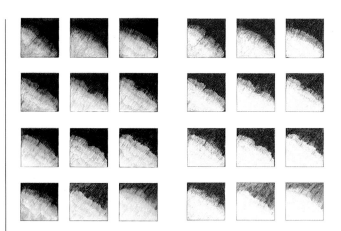

Dyeline Reproduction of Graphite Grades. Compare the range of hard to soft graphite grades on tracing paper, with their dyeline printed version (right). Graphite allows softer and more sensitive looking dyeline prints to be reproduced, which explains why many architects use pencils throughout the entire design process.

enough to carry the image, and with its sensitized face uppermost. This assembly is then offered into the machine for the first stage of printing. This involves the exposure and activation of diazonium salts carried in the print paper as it rotates around a glass cylinder emitting a high intensity ultra-violet light.

The second stage of the operation depends upon which dyeline process is being used. For example, in the ammonia process — and after the manual or automatic separation of the original from the print — the exposed print is developed in ammonia vapours. In the alternative process — the semi-dry process — the print passes through rollers carrying a developing solution.

The ammonia process reproduces superior quality prints, their potential for colour being inherent in the type of print paper selected. For example, there is black-line, blue-line, sepia-line and red-line. Whilst the semi-dry process developers offer black, blue, red and yellow monochrome prints — the print paper used in this process being more receptive to subsequent colour renderings. The degrees of contrast between the printed original and its background are regulated by the exposure setting on the machine: the faster the exposure the less time the coating is exposed and burned off, and the darker the resulting print.

The original drawing is called a 'negative'. When making extended print runs, amended drawings and copies of negatives for the addition of various types of information, the negative can be transposed onto coated tracing paper, sepia paper or the more durable polyester film. The subsequent print is known as an 'intermediate', or 'copy-negative'.

Print Papers

Most machines will accept paper up to 1000mm (40ins) wide and, if used in roll form, of virtually unlimited length.

The range of sheet print paper sizes extend up to A0, the most commonly used giving a dark blue copy on a white background. However, dyeline papers offer a range of qualities, such as textured, matt and gloss, in various weights up to 200 g.s.m.

Dyeline Drawing Techniques

Often associated with rigid and mechanical-looking drawing techniques, the dyeline print can be extremely sensitive to the more adventurous freehand line and shading techniques — even of the most spontaneous kind. In fact, the print — especially in its blue-line and sepia-line forms — can appear as a soft and delicate artwork, incorporating a mottled visual quality that becomes more distinct in darker prints. Many designers recognize and anticipate this quality, and develop their own touch and personal style when preparing originals for this print medium. As a consequence, they create highly evocative and atmospheric reproductions.

Line

Drawing for dyline means that originals must be worked on transparent papers. Generally speaking, the strongest line in the print will be represented by the darkest version of the colour associated with the print paper. For example, in a blue-line print the black ink lines of the

Sepia-line dyeline print. Jacqueline Yahn. The mottled quality of the (dark) print lends the design a sense of age and atmospheric charm.

original are printed as dark blue. This transformation has implications for pencil lines because, being a medium that can vary in line density and thickness, a reasonably firm pressure is needed to ensure a full and dense printed version. However, if too much pressure is applied to the tracing paper, indentations can remain — even after erasure — which may reappear as ghost lines in the resulting print. This articulation of line weight is most important for dyeline drawings — the exploitation of two or three technical pen stylo sizes creating an emphasis which leads to a more visually animated print. This hierarchy of line weight can be affected by the scale of the drawing. For instance, for drawings to a scale of 1:50 and less, a descending scale of line weight should be 0.2, 0.3 and 0.4. Whilst line weights suitable for drawings to a scale of 1:20 would be 0.3, 0.4 and 0.5. Exploitation of line emphasis is also seen in the dual use of graphite and ink lines, or technical pen and marker lines. This combination of fine and 'beefy' lines on tracing paper originals anticipates a differentiation in the print of the contrast between delineation and the abstraction of the sectional slice in plans and sections, or the base of groundlines in elevations.

Tones

As the dyeline process relies upon the passage of light through the negative, tonal mediums and techniques are employed for their varying capacities to filter or block the passage of light. For example, the different grades of graphite will reproduce as different tonal grades —

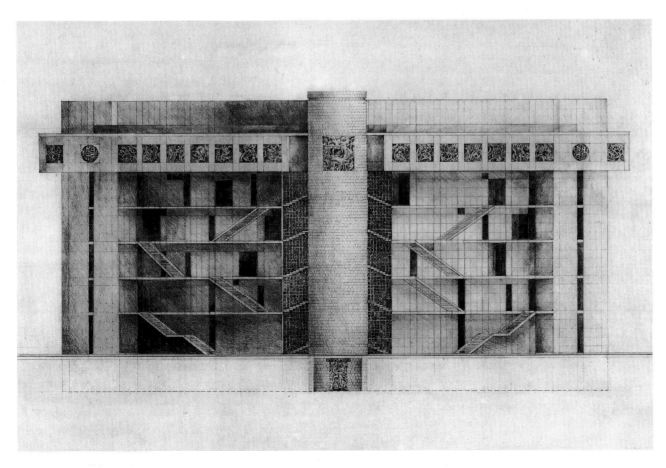

softer graphites printing as darker tones, and harder graphites printing as softer tones. Also, the lines and marks of different coloured pencils, inks and markers used on negatives will reproduce along a surprisingly wide scale of tonal value. Within an ascending scale of dyeline printed tones, yellow produces as darkest, followed by the increasing printed lightness of orange, green, turquoise, red, purple and, finally, blue and violet — which appear as a faint and almost invisible gray.

The use of hatching and cross-hatching in ink or pencil — either drawn freehand or against a straight-edge — is widely employed in the preparation of dyeline negatives. There is also the technique of bar-shading, which controls both line thickness and the intervals between lines to describe cylindrical and curving forms.

Various other combinations of mediums and techniques can also be used providing, of course, that their application does not distort the transparent support. For example, graduations of masked aerosol spray washes and splatter and stipple techniques are entirely conducive to the familiar grain of prints.

Dyeline Reproduction of Coloured Pencil and Marker Hues.
Before experimenting with the technique of using colour on tracing paper originals (left) in order to obtain tonal ranges in the subsequent dyeline print (right), you should be aware that blue-based colours filter the light and can fade into insignificance, whilst yellow-based colours block light, thus producing darker tones than are achievable with red-based colours.

There is also the potential of the ink-printed impressions of crumpled tissue paper and cotton wool wads — the degree of tonal contrast being regulated by the colour of the ink. And, traditionally, woodland trees in landscape plans have been quickly applied using simple potato cuts, or proprietary rubber stamps.

The graphite dust technique described in Chapter One is another tonal technique that produces delightfully delicate tones in dyeline prints. However, as with all the techniques, the scale of lightness can be extended into more subtle ranges by working mediums to both the front and the back of tracing paper negatives.

A quick and clean method of achieving large areas of an even tone involves attaching auxiliary and specially cut and shaped pieces of tracing paper (which match precisely the areas of the negative that are intended for tone in the subsequent print) to the negative, using the proprietary 'invisible tape'. During printing, this additional layer of film reduces the amount of light passing through the negative, thereby causing a tone to print — the density of which is regulated by the degree of transparency of the attached paper.

The ranges of pressure-transfer screens, such as those by Mecanorma and Letraset, can also be used on negatives, although great care should be taken to avoid cutting through the tracing paper support when trimming the lamination to size. To avoid this, pressure transfer tones can be applied to the back of the sheet. Moreover, their being on the side of the negative that comes into direct contact with the print paper results in a clear and

TRANSFERRING TEXTURES INTO NEGATIVES

Tracing paper negatives can be overlaid onto glass paper and the back of linoleum and hardboard. The surface textures of these materials are useful for incorporating large areas of textured tone into orthographics.

1. Place the tracing paper in position over the textured surface.

2. Using a soft pencil (such as a B) with a broad point, rub over the specific part of the drawing – eg. a roof or a wall – that you wish to render in a textured tone.

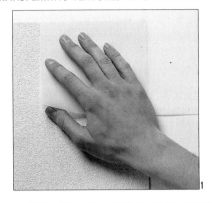
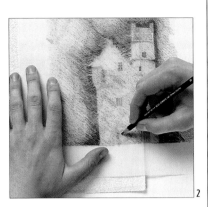

sharp reproduction. However, to avert the possibility of any face-mounted pressure transfer tone detaching in the heat of the print process, or sticking to the light roller, laminations must be well-burnished and, to be on the safe side, given a light spray of fixative.

Textured effects of different kinds can be easily transferred into selected areas of tracing paper originals, using the *frottage* technique. This costs nothing, and is achieved by placing the negative directly over the face of a textured surface and transferring its impression directly into the preselected area of the drawing using a soft grade pencil (see above). Depending upon the scale of the drawing, this technique can prove especially useful in plans and elevations for the simulation of different building materials.

An extension of *frottage* is the fabrication of specific textures (in various scales) by pencil-rubbing the modules of brickwork, blockwork, masonry, cladding and other finishes, including roofscapes, for elevations and plans. A template is made by scoring a sheet of thick card with a metal stylus. However, avoid producing the regularity of a 'toytown' effect and, when rubbing down these embossed impressions, vary the pressure on the pencil during transfer.

Yet, the beauty of tracing paper is most evident when it is used for the function that it was designed — that is, as a transparency that allows graphic information to be directly and accurately traced into a developing drawing. To do this, many students will avoid the high cost of pressure transfer equivalents by trace-copying from pressure transfer catalogues or magazine photographs. This practice brings the professionalism of seemingly well-drawn details to a presentation. And, for those who feel that this technique is somewhat uncreative, it does allow the personalizing or customizing of such details, while providing proportionally accurate source material.

Rendering Dyeline Prints

Traditionally, dyeline prints are often subjected to a second-stage rendering in order to add colour and atmosphere. However, the mediums employed are governed strictly by the weight of paper. As thinner papers tend to deform when subjected to liquid washes, the range of mediums is usually restricted to coloured pencils, markers and pressure transfer colour film. Of these, coloured pencils are the most widely used because a sensitive application can both harmonize with the line colour of the print, and also extend the suggested caste of tinted colour that is particularly associated with darker dyeline prints. A recognition of this distinctive mottling in, especially, blue-line prints can encourage the creation of highly subtle and spatially atmospheric drawings.

Thinner papers can receive a marker rendering — the softness and subtlety of the Magic Marker range making it possible to simulate the colour haze resulting from the apparent distance imposed by the scale of drawing in use! This effect is partly due to the paper surface, on which marker inks become muted — a visual quality particularly important when depicting space.

Furthermore, marker nibs can replicate the scaled appearance of a wide range of building materials. For example, by slightly overlapping the horizontal bands of appropriately coloured inks, the effect of masonry can be depicted. Also, the rendition of glazing (an habitual problem in elevations) is achieved using diagonal stripes of the more subtle blues and grays. Moreover, markers work well in conjunction with coloured pencils — common techniques being the coloured pencil modification of marker washes, and the insertion of highlights using a range of light-coloured pencils.

The thicker dyeline print papers are used for special presentation work. These represent high quality prints that transform negatives onto a range of tooth (from smooth to pebbled) and finish (from matt to gloss). Apart from the choice of line print hue, they are available in a range of whites, off-whites, tints and metallics.

If rendered, the gloss finish papers accept pressure transfer film and markers, but the latter can appear lurid and overbearing on their coated surface. Most successful for rendering are the matt finish art papers which, when textured, can substitute for watercolour paper and receive liquid washes. However, the smooth versions open up to a full-blooded colour rendition in any of the mediums and using most techniques.

Reproducing Drawings · Resized Reproduction

Judging from the size of originals submitted to print shops for reproduction, the vast majority of architectural presentation work is produced at A1 size. The ability to resize, however, provides the opportunity of reducing to smaller formats — either in monochrome or in full colour — for use in displays, exhibitions and insertion into reports.

Generally speaking, although the enlargement of drawings can improve their impact in presentations, it will not improve their inherent quality. Indeed, reproduction on a larger scale will amplify any imperfections in the original and erode lines and edges. However, it is commonly accepted that reductions of originals can assume a new and visually exciting life — the diminished image being improved by appearing denser and sharper, whilst any defects tend to disappear. When a drawing is reduced its format area becomes smaller while its dimensions, although diminished, remain proportionally the same. However, when designers talk of drafting originals 'half-up' and 'twice-up', they refer to linear rather than area scaling. In other words, a 'twice-up' or 2:1 reduction gives a reduced format area of one-quarter that of the original. Similarly, a 3:1 reduction is one-ninth that of the original format, and so on. As contrast and clarity are the main ingredients in reduction, it is important to structure original drawings using a discernible hierarchy of line weight. A basic hierarchy may comprise three or four line thicknesses. Being more susceptible to erosion by reduction, it is the thinner lines that are the most critical. For this reason their weight should be determined, at the outset, in relation to their intended reduction ratio. For example, a fine line weight can be selected by calculating backwards from its predicted reduction — ie., if a fine line is to exist in printed form 0.1mm, then the line, prior to a 2:1 reduction, should be drawn to a thickness of 0.2mm. The same reduced line thickness should be drawn at 0.3mm prior to a 3:1 reduction. From this fine line the other line weights can be determined. A further factor in reduction is the allowance made for intervals between lines. A common error, for example, is to draw a series of lines of hatching in close proximity which, when reduced, will tend to clog up and become solid. The basic rule of thumb is: the larger the reduction, the wider the spacing — and never draw lines with less than their own thickness as the interval between them. Also, always draw on a smooth hard surface, such as good quality art board, cartridge paper or tracing paper, if you intend to reduce.

Photocopy Print Process

After being fed face-up into the machine, the original is scanned by a high-intensity light. Depending upon the type of machine in use, the image is then transmitted via mirrors (when being resized) or via fibre optics (when being same-sized) onto a magnetic drum. After receiving its magnetized version of the image, the drum rotates through a chamber filled with an agitated haze of carbon dust or toner. As it passes, particles of toner are attracted to the magnetized image before being transferred from the drum to the recipient paper as it passes below. The newly deposited image is then subjected to a fusing stage in which the toner is electronically charged for its 'flash fusion' to the paper. This process instantly fixes a dense and slightly raised black print which, when issued from the machine, can be detected with the finger tips. An added bonus with the photocopying process is the ability to retrieve a print from the machine in an unfused state. The facility allows for any printed blemishes and unwanted lines in the original to be removed. This is done by carefully dusting away the toner using a putty eraser before the print is reintroduced into a separate fusing chamber.

Photocopying

The state of the art technology of electrostatic photocopying (xerography) has come a long way since the duplicator and the thermal process office copier together with their attendant need for specially coated print papers. Modern photocopy machines allow large, original drawings, made on both transparent and opaque materials, to be printed monochromatically at same size, or to be resized up to A0 or down to A4 formats.

Prints can be made on any kind of paper, including coloured papers up to 150 gms in weight, together with tracing paper and plastic drafting film. This freedom of choice allows designers to supply their own selection of print paper — providing it conforms to the weight acceptable — when delivering originals for reproduction. The result is an extremely sharp, black line print which, when made on clean white paper, releases a selection from the full range of colour mediums when a second-stage rendering is planned. Therefore, photocopying has come to rival the traditional dyline printing of architectural drawings and is now widely used to proliferate reductions, enlargements and same size prints from line drawn originals of up to the largest size in common use. Photocopying accepts and prints all kinds of linework and most tones — from the sharpness of technical pen lines to the more deliberate applications of graphite shading. However, print quality can vary with the type of machine that is used and the print shop operator will usually help you to achieve the best possible results from the original.

Photocopying Hints

One of the golden rules when preparing drawings on transparent materials for photocopying, is to avoid attaching pressure-transfer film to the back of originals. Although this technique is traditional in dyeline printing, the practice can cause problems in photocopy reproduction. This is because, in contrast to the dyeline process in which the light passes through the original and is printed from the *back* of the drawing, the photocopying process prints from the *front* of the original. If this rule is not followed, some loss of tonal clarity may be experienced in the final print. Also,

Cibachrome Print. Tim Janes and Richard Whittaker. An A3 Chromacopy produced from an A1 presentation board comprising a mixture of graphic elements.

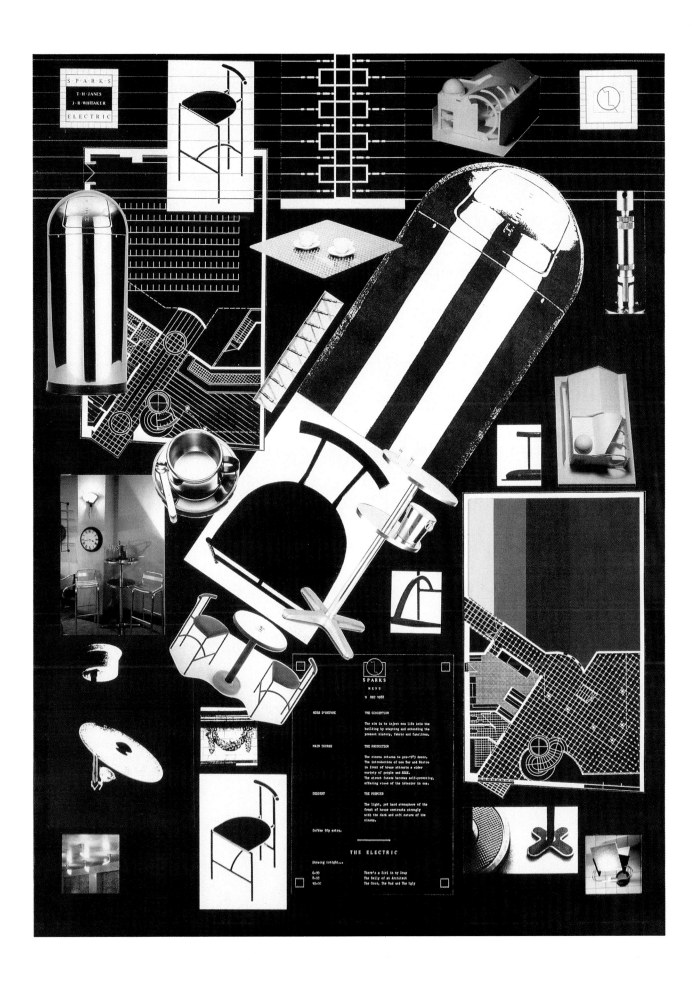

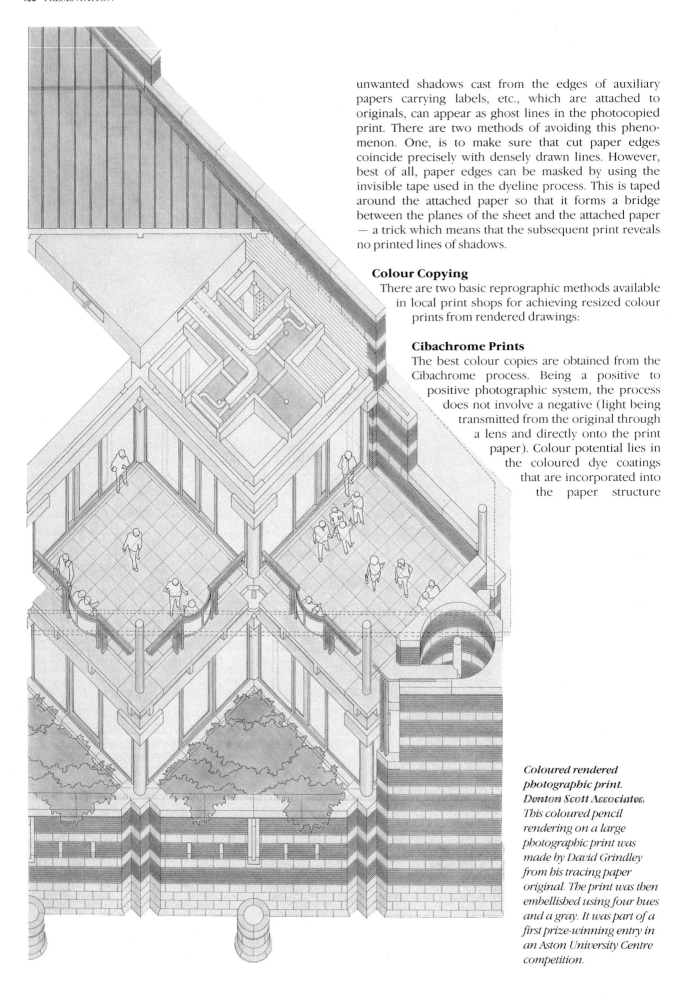

unwanted shadows cast from the edges of auxiliary papers carrying labels, etc., which are attached to originals, can appear as ghost lines in the photocopied print. There are two methods of avoiding this phenomenon. One, is to make sure that cut paper edges coincide precisely with densely drawn lines. However, best of all, paper edges can be masked by using the invisible tape used in the dyeline process. This is taped around the attached paper so that it forms a bridge between the planes of the sheet and the attached paper — a trick which means that the subsequent print reveals no printed lines of shadows.

Colour Copying

There are two basic reprographic methods available in local print shops for achieving resized colour prints from rendered drawings:

Cibachrome Prints

The best colour copies are obtained from the Cibachrome process. Being a positive to positive photographic system, the process does not involve a negative (light being transmitted from the original through a lens and directly onto the print paper). Colour potential lies in the coloured dye coatings that are incorporated into the paper structure

Coloured rendered photographic print. Denton Scott Associates. This coloured pencil rendering on a large photographic print was made by David Grindley from his tracing paper original. The print was then embellished using four hues and a gray. It was part of a first prize-winning entry in an Aston University Centre competition.

during manufacture. Cibachrome is a 'dye destruction' process in which, during printing and processing, unwanted areas of dye are selectively burned away by the light. Although not cheap by student standards, this process produces prints on a while-you-wait basis, some agencies claiming to produce colour copies in under ten minutes. Cibachrome prints achieve a very high quality reproduction on gloss or matt photographic paper or plastic film. Most machines accept A1 size originals for reduction only to A4 or A3, with some machines offering the A5 format. Obviously, same-size prints can be made from originals at these latter sizes but some main agencies can also offer the same service using 35mm transparencies as originals. Furthermore, the major city print shops can, at a price, produce extra-large prints and, using the new large format machines, also make reductions from A0 sized artwork. The clean white background achieved by Cibachrome colour prints makes it easy to mount them onto white backing sheets for presentation purposes. However, for exhibition work I have found that mounting prints under glass on black grounds brings a visual punch that compels attention. The Cibachrome print also offers the ability to transform originals comprising a montaged jumble of drawings, photographs, labelling and lettering etc., into the singular appearance of a second-stage reproduction.

Colour Photocopying

Modern colour photocopying is a much cheaper reproduction process than Cibachrome. The evolution of the new laser printers provide a state of the art photocopy technology that uses four colour toners instead of one. These include cyan, magenta, yellow and black. And the printers can be computer programmed to balance or bias the resulting colour impression. Originals can range from rendered artwork to 35mm transparencies which, after scanning by the laser, have their images transmitted in layers of coloured toner onto plain paper. The result is a facsimile with a more-than-reasonable quality that, when compared with Cibachrome reprography, may appear to suffer from some colour distortion.

The smaller, more common machines can reduce to A4, enlarge to A3 and produce same-size copy in both formats. The rapid development of these machines, however, has gradually increased the size of same-size printing and enlargement to A1 and beyond. Larger format prints can be achieved on the smaller machines using a system of composite printing. To do this, the original is placed on the platen and the machine is programmed to make copies in a precisely matching sequence of enlarged and segmented prints. These are then reassembled and mounted into overall formats that can exceed A1 size.

35mm Transparencies

Another means of transforming and ultimately resizing drawings is to photograph them using Ektachrome film. The use of Ektachrome is important because this enables an overnight, if not same-day, processing into 35mm slides. Once processed and mounted, slides can theoretically be projected up into enormous proportions. But their main function is within sequential projector presentations. For example, my students will often shoot the complete design sequence — from concept drawing to the definitive orthographics and perspectives. These are then projected in a darkened room — a presentation technique that not only allows total control over the timing and disclosure of graphic information but also focuses the viewer in a distraction-free manner. When preparing drawings for their camera-conversion into slides, it is important that the height-width proportion of original drawings should correspond to that of the slide mount aperture. A recognition of this proportion avoids the possibility of having to crop parts of the artwork or, conversely, having unrendered strips of the drawing surface appearing on the slide. For this reason, a clear frame of reference should be established before drawing, together with a use of fine grain papers. This is particularly crucial for perspectives, as the incidence of floating images on the projected slide, coupled with the amplified appearance of textural grain, will tend to countermand any intended illusion of pictorial depth. All kinds of drawings, mediums and techniques can be processed into transparencies. However, strong, simple ink line drawings, embodying coloured pencil, marker and watercolour wash renderings, project more visual punch than softer graphite drawings. Also, the fact that slides afford the opportunity for retransformation into photocopied colour prints and Cibachrome positives is a potential that should not be overlooked.

Photographic Prints

Ektachrome colour slides can also be quickly printed by local colour laboratories into the standard range of photographic print paper sizes. This process is comparatively cheap and the transformation of original colour-rendered drawings can, by a third-stage distancing and reduction, often bring a pleasantly surprising result. Many design practices will also make large black and white gloss or matt prints from photographs of drawings, to bring a professional touch to presentations. Being more popular, prints are sometimes colour-embellished with coloured pencil or the transparent type of pressure transfer film. Colour is often applied to prints to function as a schematic colour zoning of building elements or areas. But there are many superb examples of this medium — such as in the published work of Birkin Hayward and Robert Venturi — where the luminosity and transparency associated with a watercolour wash is beautifully simulated in perspective drawings. Finally, the ultimate form of reproduction occurs when architectural graphics are selected for publication in journals and books — for which printers will require high quality prints and slides. For colour plates, 35mm transparencies are acceptable but the 5 × 4 in format, or a larger one, is preferred. When printing in black and white, 10 × 8 in gloss prints should be submitted. However, as the publication format will usually demand a far greater reduction than that associated with traditional techniques of presentation, the need for a basic working knowledge of line weight and line interval (as described on page 136) becomes even more crucial.

Reprographic Special Effects

Any survey of architectural graphics will reveal an occasional experimentation with printed special effects. These range from various 'adaptations' of the different reproduction processes, to the hybrid combination of drawings and prints and the alternative forms of reprography that can radically alter the appearance of an original.

Reversed Prints
The recent revival of reversed printing, especially in architectural journals, is a recycling of a technique that was popular in design drawings in the sixties. The technique involves the transformation of black line drawings — either for presentation or publication — into white line drawings on a black ground. The

dramatic impact of this reversal is perceptually interesting because, in contrast to black and white, the intensity of a white delineation is visually increased. The result is an optical illusion in which the white parts of the image seem to appear whiter than they actually are. Reversed prints made from drawings can be made by local print shops and resized to a prescribed format. Of the two processes used for this conversion, photographic and photocopy, the former produces the more professional end product. There is also a simple do-it-yourself method for making reversed prints, much used by my students and effective and cheap to produce: the original drawing serves as a negative, and should be drawn, using deliberate line weights, on to thick tracing paper or plastic film that is both flat and immaculately clean. To

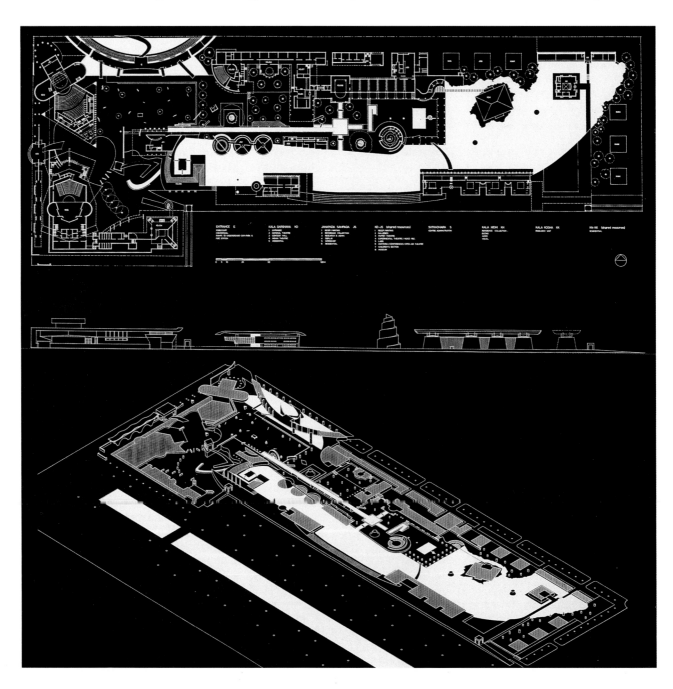

produce a blemish-free print, my students will often wear gloves during the drawing phase. The completed drawing is then moved to a photographic darkroom for the printing stage:

First, the original is placed right-way-up on a drawing board covered with a same-size sheet of grade 2, 4 or multigrade photographic paper, its light-sensitive side uppermost. Before exposure, and to keep the drawing completely flat, a sheet of clean, dust-free glass is placed over the original. Next, the glass-covered drawing board is set up under the enlarger, having ensured that the latter is set high enough so that the whole of the drawing format will be evenly exposed. Depending upon the grade of print paper, exposure can vary from one to five seconds. After exposure, simply develop the film in the normal way

Once developed this technique can produce excellent results. However, in order to avoid any disappointment, it is always wise to make a series of trial exposures using test strips of the selected print paper prior to reversing large drawings or extended series of prints. Also, when drawing for reversed printing make sure that the line techniques are kept fairly simple. And, avoid tight cross-hatchings and very fine lines, as these can burn out and fade during exposure. However, once achieved, a full reversed print can serve as a high contrast graphic in a presentation that will undoubtedly help to grab the attention of viewers.

Hints for Dyeline Prints
A simply achieved dyeline special effect can simulate a graduated sky wash above printed elevations. Usually accomplished with the aid of the operator, this technique relies upon the negative being fed bottom-first into the dyeline machine. Immediately after the elevation drawing of the building design has been exposed normally, the exposure setting is speeded up to cause the area of the print above the elevation to be printed in a progressively darkening tone. This trick produces a print with a 'dyeline wash' sky — the effect not only framing the drawing but also bringing additional atmosphere and apparent depth to the resulting image.

Another common dyeline special effect employs a negative drawing that is run three or four times through the machine. Every print is made at different exposure speeds to obtain a set of prints each in a different tone. Then a composite print is made by trace-cutting selected parts from each print for their reassembly, by glue-mounting, to a backing sheet. The resulting image can be designed to reinforce a chosen message. For instance, by ordering different arrangements of the various tones, the spatial qualities or areas of interest in a plan can be highlighted or emphasized. Furthermore, when presented in tandem with a tonal legend, the composite print can be used as an analytical diagram to communicate

Left: Reversed print. Proposal for Indira Ghandi Memorial Arts Centre. Tas Ahmad. An ink on tracing paper original was photographically reversed into a white on black print. Notice the apparent intensity of the white image – an optical illusion generated by the figure-ground interaction.

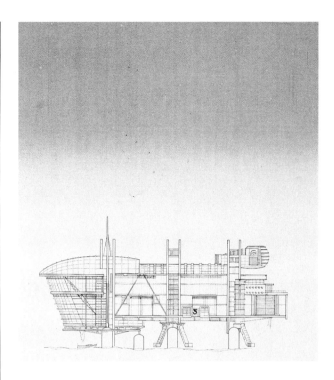

Dyeline 'wash' sky. Design for technological museum. Simon Reed. To introduce the sky 'wash' the original sketch was fed into the machine bottom-first. Immediately after the elevation had been exposed, the machine was speeded-up to cause an increasing under-exposure – resulting in a progressively darkening printed tone.

an instant picture of, say, relationships between public and private zones.

Yet another dyeline technique is used occasionally by designers for producing enlarged prints from 35mm transparencies. This technique is generally employed for making A1 size prints from photographs taken of the site for a proposed building design. Once developed, the print can then become the basis for a drawing that inserts and superimposes a perspective view of the proposed architecture as it might appear on the site. The procedure could not be more simple: Pin a sheet of unexposed dyeline print paper on to the wall of a darkroom or blacked out studio. The paper functions as a screen on to which the slide is projected and focused at the required size. Exposure time can take up to forty minutes, but its progress can be checked intermittently by momentarily switching on and off the darkroom or studio light. When exposed the chemically-coated surface of the print paper should be protected from any light source, before being developed in the dyeline machine in the usual manner.

Photo-Drawing Montage
Another excellent method of communicating a highly convincing perspective of a building design in the context of its proposed setting, is to introduce a drawing into a photographic print of the site. The technique begins by photographing the site from vantage points that predict the best possible view of the building design

within the context of its surrounding. It is wise to take a series of shots that frame plenty of foreground information such as people, trees and vehicles, as, in the later integration of the two graphic elements, these will increase the sense of function — especially if allowed to overlap the edge of the drawing when it becomes part of the print. The best shot is then selected as a 'parent' image and processed into the largest print size possible. The print is then covered with a sheet of tracing paper so that the scale and basic perspective form of the design can be plotted. This is done by responding to cues in the photograph, such as any rectangular planes that are coincident with those in the building design. By projecting lines back from the edges of these planes, the eye level (horizon line) and respective vanishing points can be determined. Based on these co-ordinates, a preliminary outline sketch of the basic architectural form should be made in light graphite.

After making a plain paper photocopy from the tracing paper co-ordinates, the drawing and shading stage can commence. However, at this point two strategies should be considered. The first involves developing the drawing

Above: Composite drawing-photograph for the Building Design and Stone Firms competition. Robert Voticky and Robert Maxwell.
Right: Composite drawing-photograph for a proposed building in Times Square, New York. George Ranalli.

into an ink hardline rendition in which little attention is paid to any pictorial fusion. In other words, the drawing of the design remains as an abstract contrast to the photographic quality of the site print. Alternatively, you can extend the photograph into the drawing. In this case, a sharp and contrasting print quality will be mirrored by an incisive shading technique, while a diffuse or grainy print will indicate an equivalent graphite softness. As part of this second strategy, the direction of photographed light and shadow will be extended into the drawing and, to increase the illusion, objects in the photograph will cast their shadows onto the planes of the drawing.

When the drawing stage is finished, the contour of the building is cut out and carefully mounted into position on the site photograph. If an increased realism is

Embossed print. Design for the Holocaust Memorial Museum in the Mall, Washington DC. David Statman. The designer photocopied his tracing paper line drawing from behind to produce a back-to-front print. This became the basis for the mould. After embossing, the print received two watercolour washes, applied with an airbrush. Prior to the rendering stage, the embossed surface was selectively masked – the exposed areas receiving an angled wash that exploited the raised portion of the section.

required, the montage can be re-photographed or printed, using the Cibachrome process, into the ultimate fusion of a second-stage print.

This drawing-photograph combination has an obvious and striking function when used for communicating design ideas and is a method often used in competition entries when architects attempt to convey the impact of their designs on major public spaces.

Embossed Drawings

One technique that my students have imported from the United States is that of embossing drawings. This particular special effect — although not strictly reproduction — has gained in popularity ever since it was used by Charles Moore. He employed it as a means of communicating design drawings of a private house to the partially-sighted client. By 'printing' a raised surface in his orthographics, Moore provided a braille drawing that was read via the finger tips.

To produce an embossed print of a plan, section or elevation, a basic line drawing is first worked on tracing paper — the transparency of which is essential as a photocopy print on plain paper is then made from the back of the tracing paper original to achieve a handed, or back-to-front, image. Next a laminated paper block that will act as a mould is made by spray mounting successive layers of thin paper onto a thick cardboard base. The lamination should be 5mm (⅒in) thick and cover an area greater than the format of the drawing. The stage is completed when the photocopy print — with its obverse printed image uppermost — is laminated as the top layer of the paper 'sandwich'.

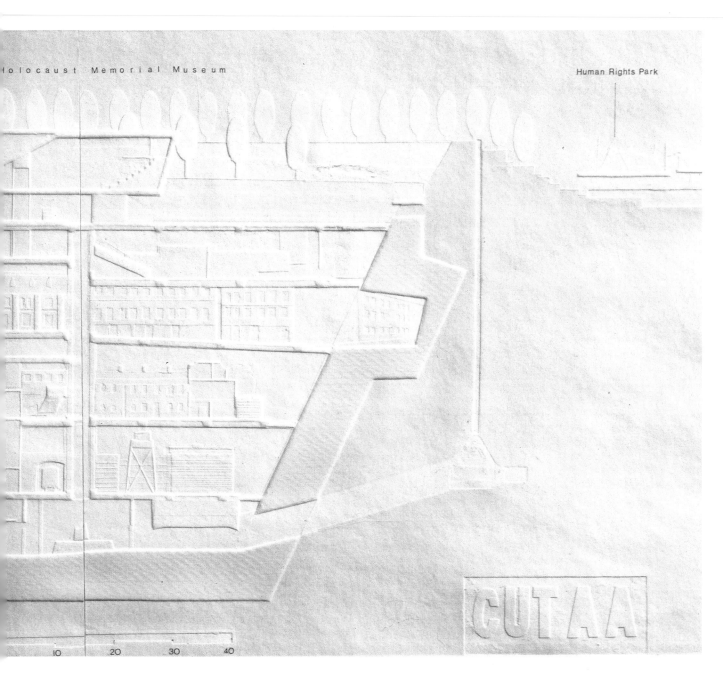

Holocaust Memorial Museum

Human Rights Park

embossing can be used: positive or negative. For instance, in plans and sections the choice is whether to emboss the sectional slice or the contained and surrounding spaces. The same consideration applies to elevations — to which this technique affords the opportunity of raising prominent features in the facade.

Once the laminated mould is finished, and using a scalpel and the back-to-front print as a guide, vertically slice into the face of the block — cutting around and removing all the negative shapes. Depending upon the desired effect various depths of incision may be made, providing that penetration stops short of the cardboard base layer.

After coating the surface of the paper mould with a waterproofing agent, such as glue size or pvc glue, which is allowed to dry completely, a sheet of heavy-duty watercolour paper is used to take the impression. This is first soaked in water and, after removing excess moisture, placed over the top of the mould. Finally, several layers of felt or a sheet of foam rubber is placed over the top of the sandwich, before the complete assembly is placed into a heavy-duty book press. After extreme pressure has been applied, causing the wet watercolour paper to deform against the mould, the paper is left in the press to dry completely into its new shape.

When the embossed image is removed from the press it can then be subjected to a range of rendering mediums, including the singular or combined use of watercolour wash, graphite or pastel dust applied on a wad of cotton wool, and, notably, aerosol or airbrush spray, the application of which will exploit the three-dimensional quality of the surface of the image.

9
DRAWING COMPARISONS

The significance of architectural drawing is indisputable. In fact, the international reputations of many famous designers have been founded primarily on their drawings, rather than on their buildings. Furthermore, our knowledge and mental picture of significant buildings is often not of the actual architecture, but of a well-published graphic version of it. But what exactly is the relationship between drawing types and mediums and the way that we design; and how well do drawings stand up when compared with the three-dimensional reality of the actual forms and spaces they predict?

Many architects have established their names and reputations well before they have produced any buildings of note. For example, it was a series of five charcoal drawings exhibited throughout post World War One Germany that established Ludwig Mies van der Rohe in the public's mind as a leader of the Modern Movement. Drafted between 1921 and 1923, these extremely large and powerful perspectives not only projected his vision of a new architecture, but also promoted his virtuosity and graphic skill. Similarly, the rapidographed cross-hatching of Paul Rudolph, widely published during the fifties, launched him as a designer, and consolidated his standing in America long before the construction of any of his more important works.

There are also examples of notable designers whose major contribution to the architectural debate has been almost exclusively graphic. Familiar icons range from the austere geometrical forms of C. N. Ledoux and Boullee, to Vladimir Tatlin's famous elevation of the 1920 Moscow Monument to the Third International. Today, this use of drawing as a flagship for alternative design philosophies remains the medium of the avant-garde — experimental forms and new architectural ideas proliferating as an unbuilt architecture in the highly influential drawings and renderings of, amongst others, Laura Thermes and Franco Purini in Italy and Christine Hawley and Peter Cook in England.

Moreover, our attitude to many existing buildings is shaped more by the associated and published drawings than a visit to the site. In fact, the drawings of many well-known edifices are more widely known than their physical counterparts — one keynote drawing, such as an elevation or perspective often capturing the essence of an architectural intent and becoming a mental icon 'visited' and 'revisited' in the mind's eye. What's more, the very *type* of drawing used in the design may influence the outcome of the form. For example, it is accepted that the targeting of a static and central vanishing point in perspective drawing can induce the unwitting architect towards a straightness of line and a formal symmetry — an effect first experienced by Renaissance painters when they experimented with linear perspective.

Monument to the Third International in Moscow, Project. Vladimir Tatlin (1920). The precision of this Constructivist drawing underlines Tatlin's promotion of the fusion of fine art and, particularly, sculpture with architecture. The exacting lines and hatched tones meticulously etch the spiral character of a sculptural steel construction – the enormous scale of which is indicated by the minimal depiction of the city skyline.

Einstein Tower, Potsdam. Erich Mendelsohn (1920).
Immediacy and fluidity of line are hallmarks of Mendelsohn's
Expressionist and influential architectural graphics. The
calligraphic nature of this ink sketch reflects his philosophy
that a building should have a character similar to a natural
organism, and that the natural contours of the site should
control the formal appearance of the built form.

Another side-effect is induced by the box-like nature of paraline projection, which appears to discourage the containment of anything other than cubic forms; one has only to attempt to draw spheres in isometrics in order to experience this. Moreover, as opposed to perspective, which encourages looking at, through and up at a graphic architecture, the axonometric and the isometric cause the viewer to assume an overhead, hovering and almost godlike viewpoint.

Quite apart from its 'encouragement' toward a square-ness of form, the need for the designer's elevated eye to penetrate its cubic interior has led to the speculation that the first modern use of the paraline drawing system influenced a fashion in the 1920s for the erosion of the corners of buildings. In other words, the graphic surgery required to be able to see the insides of para-line drawings resulted in the subsequent insertion of windows at these points. This was a feature innovated in Walter Gropius' design for the Fagus Factory in Germany — a design derived primarily from an axono-metric. Moreover, the adoption of the axonometric by leaders of the Modern Movement appears to parallel the advent of a new technology of transparency, which came to express itself in the glazed curtain walls of an ensuing International Style.

Strong links can also be detected between the drawings and drawing mediums in the architecture of several well-known designers. We can see this if we compare the Expressionist freedom of Erich Mendelsohn's perspec-tive for the Einstein Tower project in Potsdam with the stabbing lines of Antonio Saint Elia's Futurist vision. However, it is the influence of the isometric's co-ordinates on the work of many architects, such as Herbert Beyer, that is quite extraordinary — their architectural adulation of the right-angle appearing inextricably knitted into the mechanics of this projection drawing. Similarly, the pencilled planes of Frank Lloyd Wright designs for prairie houses seem to derive from the horizontal dynamic of the elevation drawing.

A further connection between the use of mediums and the appearance of the resulting architecture has been touched on by Peter Cook, who explored a speculative architectural machine aesthetic in the sixties. He employed coloured Pantone film not to simulate the intended colours of his buildings, but to zone and differentiate functional areas in the design. However, he suggests that this practice of schematically clarifying with colour took over and became an end in itself. As a result, the ensuing 'high-tech' buildings of the seventies came to be associated with a vibrant colour coding. Moreover, the colours appear to have been directly influenced by the then limited range of raw primary and secondary hues available in pressure transfer film!

However, when we turn to making graphic simulations of the predicted building design, these still appear in the form of 'handmade photographs'. Even though they attempt to reconstruct a picture of their future reality, they cannot simulate a real-time experience of form in space because the view they provide is fixed in space and frozen in time. Quite apart from their static points of view they are rarely shown under snow, or in windy, wet or night-time settings.

An additional factor in this context is that our interpretation of an architectural design will be partly determined by how much of the picture the architect

Citta Nuova Project. Antonio Sant'Elia (1914). The piercing
clarity of this ink line perspective drawing portrays Sant'Elia's
Futurist vision of an ideal urban architecture – though it
never progressed beyond the drawing board. Notice that its
symmetrical composition is sketched around a central,
vertical guideline, and that the speed and incisiveness of the
line, together with variations in its weight, betrays the rapid
movements of a steel pen nib subjected to a range of pressures.

Above and left: Elevation drawing and photograph of LBDC/TWA stormwater pumping station, Isle of Dogs, London. John Outram. Note the predictive quality of, and the striking similarlity between, Outram's presentation elevation and the completed building.

Right and below: Perspective drawing and photograph of Fenchurch Street building, London. Terry Farrell. The remarkable likeness between the architectural proposal (a perspective rendered in coloured pencil) and the finished building chiefly stems from a keenness of vision on the part of the delineator in predicting the spatial effect of the building's pink and brown coloured granite.

wants us to see. The technique of selectively cropping images can involve leaving out relevant information. Indeed, a tradition has evolved for an almost exclusive focusing on the building design. This means that in orthographics, paralines and, especially, perspectives immediate settings can be ignored and the architecture presented in a state of glorious isolation. In so doing, this practice not only blinkers the designer to problems of environmental suitability but also distorts the understanding of the viewer and further distances the resulting graphic from any simulation of the actual experience.

Finally, a direct comparison between some perspective renderings and photographs of the same, and subsequently built forms, makes an interesting study. On the one hand, subjective graphic predictions can come very close to providing a precise and almost photographic record of the future architectural event. On the other hand, drawings can describe surprisingly different conditions. Moreover, while perspective renderings seek to create an artist's impression of the building-to-be, the actual building invites us to consider its graphic as a work of art in its own right.

10
CAD AND COMPUTER GRAPHICS

Many of a new breed of architects have replaced their Rotring pen, clutch pencil and drawing board with keyboard, mouse and VDU screen. Those in offices where drawing boards are seen as a thing of the past claim that computers offer an increased scope in design. Spatial ideas can be tried and tested (and discarded) at a rate hitherto impossible. The new technology means the design process can be one of continuous experimentation.

Without doubt, the graphic presentation method which has grown and gained most attention in the last few years is that which involves the computer and its ancillary equipment. Strictly speaking, CAD and computer graphics are different disciplines using a common tool. However, elements of one are to be found increasingly in the other, and each offers a powerful facility for the architect. The acronym CAD means different things to different people. To some it means 'Computer Aided Drafting' — i.e., the exercise of electronics on the drawing board. To others it stands for 'Computer Aided Design', a wonderfully wide-ranging term potentially encompassing every aspect of the design process, from working drawings, through schedules and lists of quantities, to orthographics and perspectival visualization.

The Benefits of CAD

Whichever definition one chooses, the computer offers a number of ways of manipulating the myriad inputs of the design process. For example, as any graphic need only be drawn once, CAD offers economy of effort. Having been drawn, the graphic — or part of it — may be enlarged or reduced in scale, handed, mirrored, inverted and duplicated. Therefore, components and details created for one project may be saved and used in later projects. And a library of commonly used elements may be assembled. Also, the same drawing (or parts of it) may be quickly adapted for different purposes by the various specialists within the design team — such as structural engineer, electrical engineer and heating and ventilation engineer. As architectural graphic elements represent input with reference to their real (rather than scaled) dimensions, great precision is maintained. Furthermore, because these dimensions are not being constantly re-calculated and re-drawn by different people for different purposes, dimensional reliability is improved. A further advantage is that amendments to drawings are far more easily undertaken than with conventional graphic mediums. This facility can lead to more polished projects, primarily because the designer is less concerned about making changes — whether major or minor. There is widespread belief that increased drawing productivity forms the kingpin of CAD benefits. Certainly it is the main area in which it is possible to carry out accurate cost-benefit analysis, and thereby demonstrate a saving to offset the relatively high capital cost of a system! Indeed, it is generally claimed that a productivity

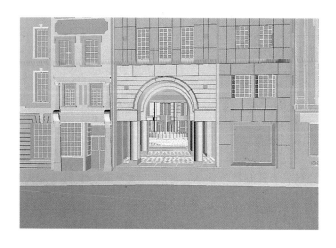

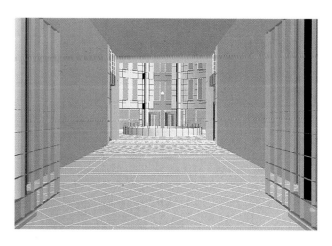

factor of between two and three is obtainable. However, it is only possible to generalize because productivity factors depend on so many issues — such as the project size, its degree of repetition and complexity, the experience and skill of the operator and the amount of information already stored in data libraries. The advantages listed so far are available by using CAD at its simplest level — that is, as a two-dimensional drafting machine. However, by using the computer to construct a three-dimensional model of a building design or environment, a new range of facilities are now open to the architect.

Three-Dimensional Modelling

By including the third dimension, the possibility of ambiguity or the misplacing of elements is much reduced. It is also possible to employ programmes which are capable of clash detection — that is, the ability to identify a conflict of elements within the space of the design. As conventional and computer-aided drawings are assembled as separate plans, elevations or sections, any modification to one part of the drawing requires a conscious decision to update other views. However, with a complete three-dimensional model, orthographic drawings may be produced as a reduction of that model, with the additional advantage that any change to the model will appear automatically in any other appropriate view. But, perhaps, the most immediately appreciable and 'magical', advantage of the computer's powers is its ability to generate highly accurate perspective views of the three-dimensional computer model from specified vantage points and from specific viewing angles. On the one hand, these can be used at any time during the design process. For instance, they may be employed initially to gain an impression of the mass and modelling of the proposed object or environment. On the other hand, they may be employed later on in the design process to examine links and sightlines through elements and, perhaps, finally to explore the effects of colour and lighting. Because computing a perspective view can be an enormously complex task, the time taken means that it is rarely possible to do other than provide key views made from appropriate points. Ideally, it should be possible to provide a flow of images representing, for

instance, a walk through and about the space of a building. However, when it is realized that conventional video requires the production of twenty-five pictures a second to create the illusion of smooth movement on a television screen, it will be seen that the realization of this ideal is no slight undertaking. Essentially, CAD uses representational devices to describe a particular reality. Although computer graphics are still limited at present to a two-dimensional rendering of that reality, it may, depending on the needs of the moment, operator skill and the limitations of the system in use to be presented in a more or less realistic fashion.

The 'Paintbox'

The basic tool of computer graphics is the 'Paintbox'. This is a trade name that, like 'Fibreglass' and 'Hoover', has become generic. Essentially, the Paintbox is a device combining software and hardware which can hold one or more frames of a video image facilitating manipulation of that image either in part or in its entirety. The original image can, at any time, be modified either by the incorporation of some other image or by the direct image intervention of the graphic artist. This is achieved by using a stylus and digitizing tablet, which can 'paint' directly onto the screen. The stylus can be switched to replicate any form of line-drawing implement — from pen through chalk to airbrush. Perhaps most impressive is the palette of colour available to the designer. This depends on the particular equipment in use, but a choice from 16 million colours would not be unusual. It is quite clear, therefore, that the designer has a tool of tremendous power at his or her disposal and one that can be employed in any design field where the manipulation of two-dimensional imagery is a necessity. For example, in an architectural context it is easy to see the advantage of being able to inlay a building into a townscape or landscape, or of being able to re-scale or

Below and opposite: Whitefriars Building, London. Designed for Kumagi Jumi by York Rosenburg Mardell. These three serial perspectives – studying movement towards and through an archway and into a courtyard – plus an aerial view of the proposed building design were generated from a 3-D computer model, using the Intergraph system.

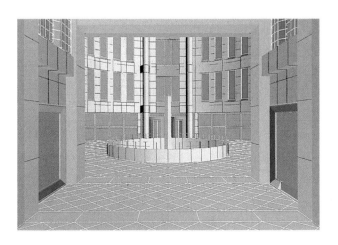
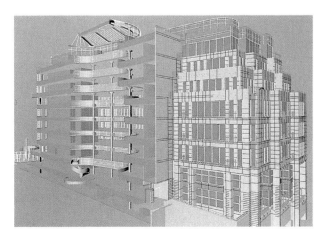

remove all or part of the building; or simply to change the colours of a facade.

Having created a satisfactory image, there remains the problem of demonstrating this image to others. It may be possible to store the image on a hard or floppy disk or, by enlisting a stop-frame video recorder, on video tape. Both these options require the availability of appropriate pieces of compatible hardware wherever the image is to be displayed. Photographic film overcomes this drawback, but it is not a cheap option, particularly where multiple copies of an image may be required. Where a highly detailed and subtly coloured image is concerned there is really no option but to use one of these methods. However, for everday design work it may be quite satisfactory to transfer the image to paper. Indeed, there are a number of plotter and printer types that will produce highly acceptable monochrome line drawings. However, when colour, and particularly block colour, is introduced they all display shortcomings of one sort or another. Therefore, in many cases, the monochrome print is employed as a structural underlay, the drawing being worked up in colour using one of the many conventional rendering techniques described throughout the earlier sections of this book.

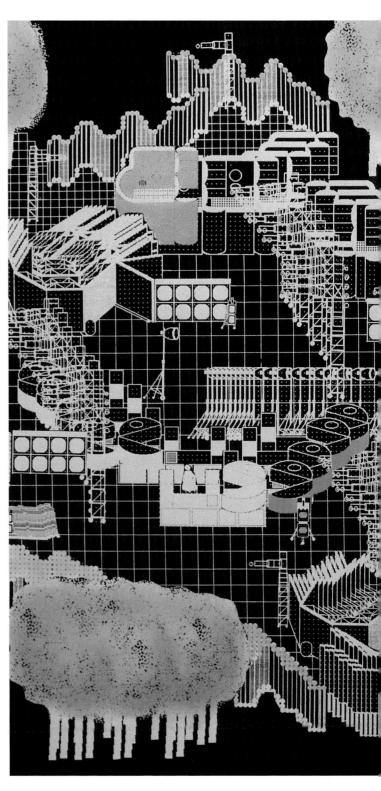

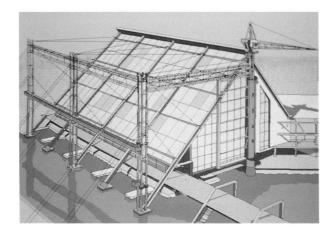

Below Left: Special Projects Gallery. Herron Associates.
This interior perspective of a gallery space for the Imagination Building, London, was generated on an IBM personal computer using Picture Maker (Cubicomp).

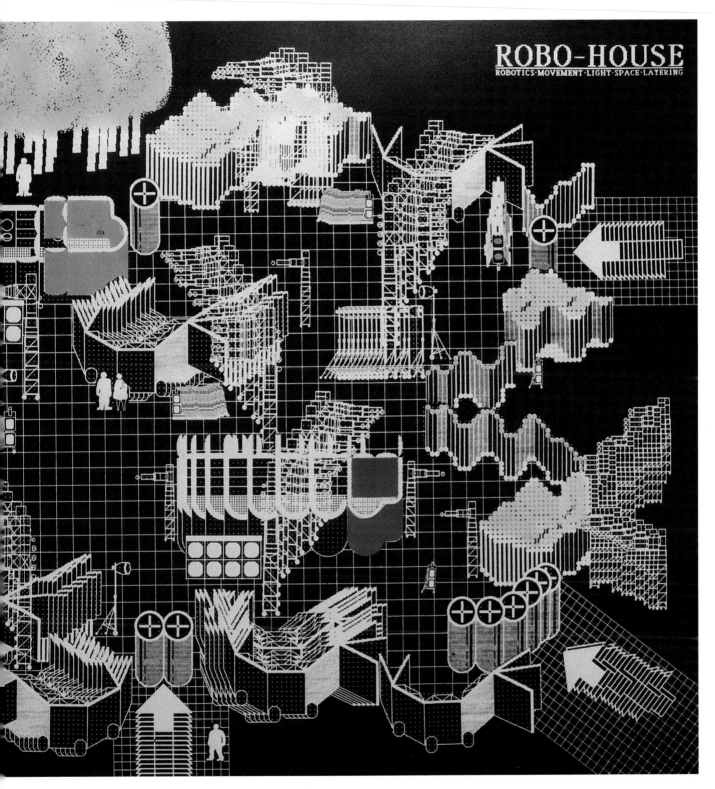

ROBO-HOUSE
ROBOTICS·MOVEMENT·LIGHT·SPACE·LAYERING

Above Left: Docklands Museum. Design and computer model by Amin Junid (using the Capitol Modelling and Painting System). Creating a 3-D computer model of a building enables it to be examined from an infinite variety of viewpoints. In this example a view of the wire-frame image has been edited and coloured using the electronic paint system to convey the illusion of depth.

Above: Robo-House. Herron Associates. The Robo-House was Herron's entry for the Shinkenchiku competition. It was generated on a 512 Apple Mackintosh computer by dragging elements across the screen, thereby leaving after-images and building up a collage.

Still taken from 'London Flyover CAD Sequence'. YRM (York Rosenburg Mardell).
YRM's venture into the world of computer animation enlisted the highly sophisticated 3-dimensional modelling and rendering capabilities offered by Modelview software linked to the Intergraph 360 workstation. The system allows still frames to be loaded into the computer's memory and rapidly recycled to create a 'flicker book' animation. This type of movement simulation was first used by YRM for a Channel Four television program to illustrate the impact of the building boom on the City of London as seen from a flight over the capital. Differences between proposed buildings, those under construction and those completed during the last five years, were colour coded, and the story board design stage for the flyover sequence suggested two flight paths: one going from Trafalgar Square to St. Paul's cathedral; the other flying under Tower Bridge and on toward Canary Wharf – from which this still is taken.

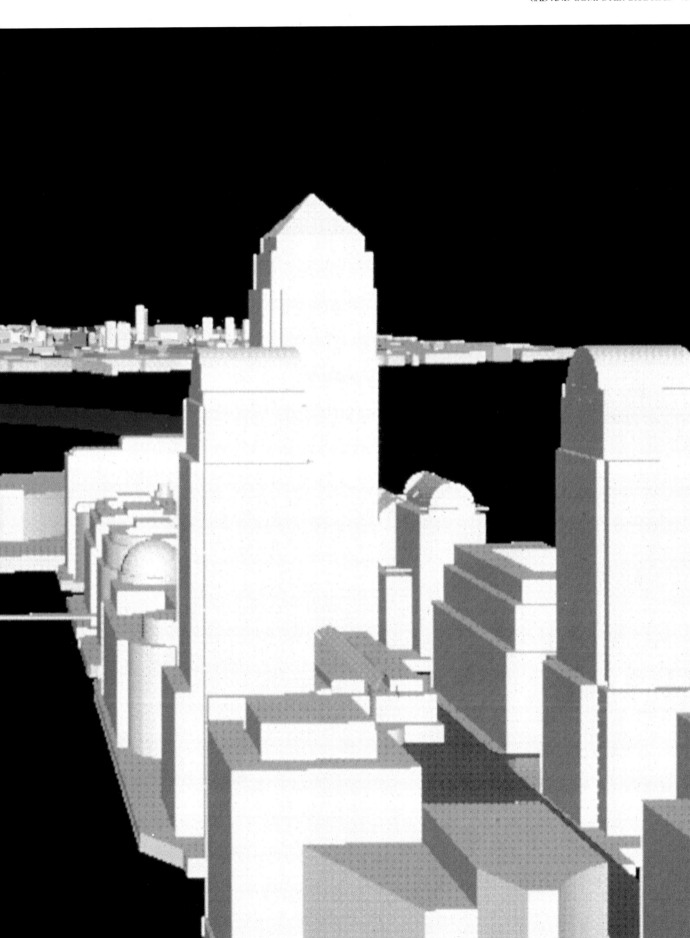

CONCLUSION

At the beginning of the book I referred to architectural drawings as alluding to an art form. However, according to Martin Lazenby in an article entitled 'Contemporary Architectural Drawings', essential differences exist between architectural graphics and fine art.

Lazenby believes these differences exist primarily because architectural graphics, in order to communicate their meaning, are bound to a visual language involving specific symbols and conventions; whilst fine art enjoys a complete freedom of creative expression. Moreover, a further distinction lies in the fact that, since the Renaissance art has existed for its own sake, while an architectural drawing, no matter how beautiful its execution, remains as a means to an end – that is, as part of a process leading to the realization of a building.

However, although the majority of drawings and their formulative techniques are portrayed in this book as functioning to fashion and predict habitable form and space prior to its physical presence, some drawings fulfill quite a different purpose. Being detached from the business of making real buildings, the images they portray function to question the very nature of accepted architectural thinking and push back the frontiers of understanding. Such drawings represent architecture in its purest, most essential form. They often make direct reference to movements in art and, within the confines of the drawing board, exist as ideas for their own sake. In so doing these drawings not only hold the potential for provocation and/or inspiration, they also form a bridge between the disciplines of architecture and art.

It is for these reasons that I can derive as much pleasure from the abstraction of a scintillating cross-hatch seen at close hand as I can from the essential meaning of a drawing; and why I can enjoy the lines of a Purini as much as those of a Piranesi, or the colours of a Cook as much as those of a Le Corbusier. This is because, for me, their works all belong to the world of architecture and art.

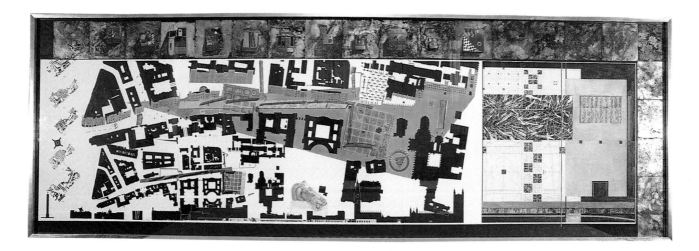

Above: Parliament Square Ideas Competition. Prize Winner. Kevin Rhowbotham and John Serjeant. Moving away from the reduced simplicity and excessive precision associated with architectural graphics, this design ('a magnificent work of art', according to the judges) employs a multitude of mediums, scales and drawing modes on an eight foot panel.
Right: Music Room for Hermannstrasse. Alsop and Lyall. This large, acrylic on Mylar painting by Alsop and Lyall is typically innovative of their work and part of a submission of ideas for the upgrading of the eastern sector of Hamburg.

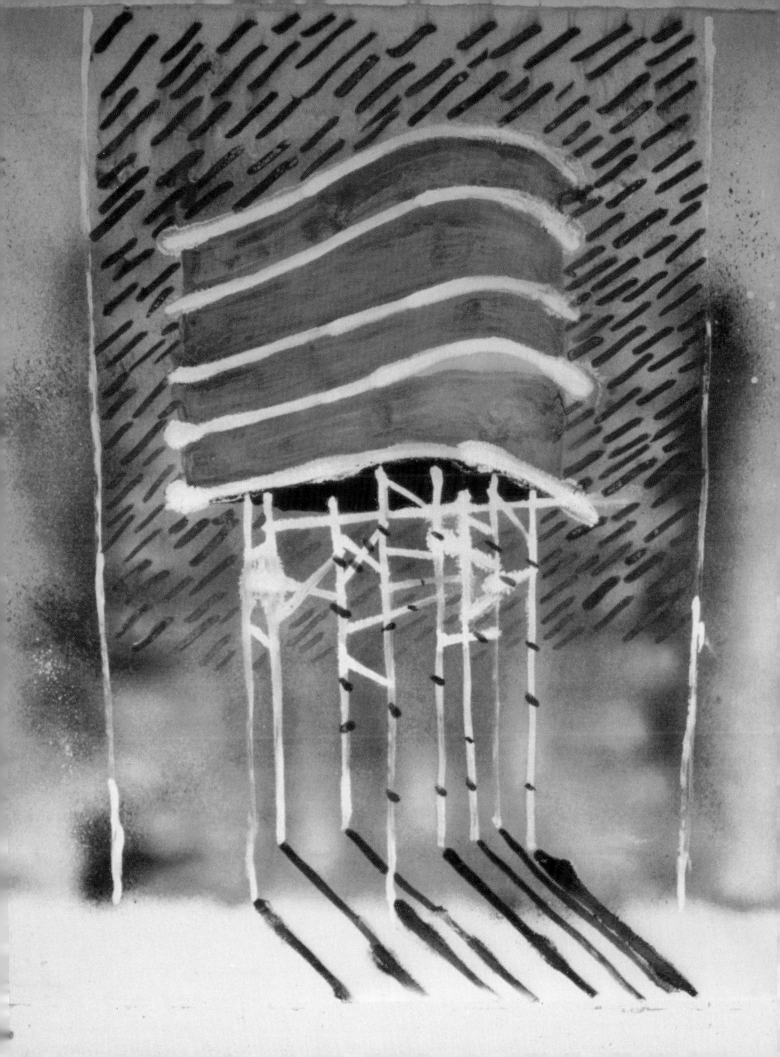

INDEX

ACKNOWLEDGEMENTS

FOR ANDRÉE AND HOLLY

I would like to offer special thanks to John Stewart Coles, Senior Lecturer at the Middlesex Polytechnic, for his expert contribution to the chapter on CAD and Computer Graphics; to David Cripps, Director of the Thames Print Room, Reading, for advice on reprography; to Simon Reed for working on the step-by-step artwork, and to Richard Whitaker for producing the line drawings.

I would also like to thank Sarah Snape, Judith More, Clive Hayball, Cathy Lockley and John Wainwright for their hard work in helping to produce this book.

And finally, I wish to thank the following for their unstinting help and encouragement: Richard L. Adams; Juan Carlos Calderon; Martin Cook; Rodney Cooper; Ian Deans; George Dombek; Sue Farrell; Jack Forman; Julian Gitsham; John Grimes; Ron Herron; Ron Hess; Ian Latham; Mike Leech; John Letherland; Sue Manley; Ed Potter; Ray Semple; David Statman; Doug Streeter; Mick Timpson; Catherine Tranmner, and Hugh Whitbread.

TOM PORTER

In addition to those individuals and companies whose work appears in this book, the publishers would also like to thank the following for their kind permission to reproduce photographs:
(Key: A-above; B-below; C-centre; L-left; R-right, and T-top)
Arcaid 119B; Bulloz 11; *Fondation Le Corbusier* 12-13; Devonshire Collection, Chatsworth, Reproduced by permission of the Chatsworth Settlement Trustees/ Photo: Courtauld Institute of Art 10L, *Civico Museo Storico G. Garibaldi*, Como 147; Dennis Gilbert 148BR; Donna Grossman Gallery, Los Angeles 7; R.I.B.A. Drawings Collection 22, 53; R.I.B.A. Library 146; Sir John Soane Museum, London 8B; *Museo Egizo*, Turin 6; Uffizi Gallery *(Cabinetto Fotografico)*, Florence 8-9; By courtesy of the Board of Trustees of the Victoria & Albert Museum 15.